Food and Drink and
Travelling Accessories

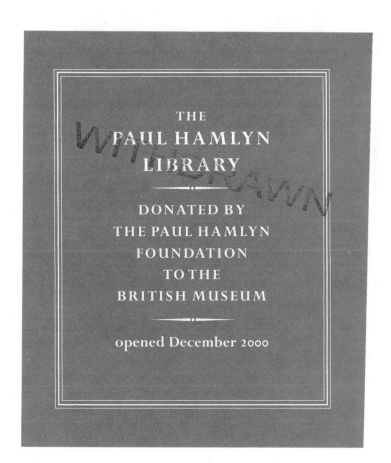

Professor Gösta Berg joined Nordiska Museet in 1924. He gained his doctorate, published as *Sledges and Wheeled Vehicles*, in 1936. From 1935-55 he was the Director of Ethnological Research in Nordiska Museet, from 1956-63 Director of Nordiska Museet and Skansen, and from 1964-69, Director of Skansen. He was given the title of Professor in 1959.

He has been Chairman of The Royal Patriotic Society of Sweden since 1973. From 1969-74, he was President of the Royal Gustav Adolf Academy.

Food and Drink and Travelling Accessories

Essays in Honour of Gösta Berg

Edited by
ALEXANDER FENTON
and
JANKEN MYRDAL

Published by
JOHN DONALD PUBLISHERS LTD
in association with
THE NATIONAL MUSEUMS OF SCOTLAND
SKANSEN AND NORDISKA MUSEET
1988

ISBN 0 85976 209 2

Distributed in the United States of America and Canada
by Humanities Press Inc., Atlantic Highlands, NJ 07716,
USA

Typeset by Print Origination (NW) Ltd., Formby, Merseyside, L37 8EG
Printed in Great Britain by Bell & Bain Ltd., Glasgow.

FOREWORD

In August 1985, Nordiska Museet, Stockholm, organised a discussion meeting on agricultural museums and on the future development of the Swedish Agricultural Museum at the estate of Julita, in Central Sweden's richest agricultural county. The estate was gifted to Nordiska Museet in the will of its owner, Lieutenant Arthur Bäckström, who, moved by the national-romantic spirit of the early 1900s, began to collect household and farm equipment, turned an old smithy into a museum, and in 1926 set up a special museum building. In his dedication to collecting and preserving material for the cause of Swedish folk culture, he was reminiscent of Professor Gösta Berg, to whom this book is dedicated, though he did not have Gösta Berg's great range in scholarly research.

It was a privilege to attend that meeting of experts from Sweden, Norway and Denmark, and to take part in the eager discussions about how an agricultural museum should be shaped to take into account the needs of modern times. It was also a pleasure to stay with my co-editor, Dr Janken Myrdal, in his Stockholm flat, before and after the meeting. In the context of these discussions, we touched on the topic of people who had made great contributions to agricultural and folk museums in Sweden. The name of Gösta Berg stood very high on our list. We resolved then to contact a number of colleagues in various countries to see if we could put together a volume in his honour, as a mark of our deep respect for his work and abilities and of the friendship in which we hold him. We made a list of colleagues, very long but, even so, far from complete. If all had contributed, there would be not one book, but twenty. We had to restrict the subject matter in order to bring to birth a book that had internal thematic consistency, and in so doing had to restrict the number of contributors. We apologise now to the many who had to be left out, but we consider that the dedication of this present volume to Gösta is in the name of all ethnologists who know him personally or who have been influenced and helped by him and his writings. International collaboration in research into the cultures of nations has never had as great a degree of importance as at the present time, and we offer this volume also as a contribution to international work and understanding. 'Interest begets interest', says Janken Myrdal in his personal appreciation of Gösta Berg. Let international collaboration beget international collaboration also, in the way that Gösta Berg would wish.

We are greatly indebted to the bodies that have supported us financially in the publication of this volume. They are:

The Royal Patriotic Society of Sweden
Skansen
Nordiska Museet
The National Museums of Scotland
The Russell Trust.

Alexander Fenton
Janken Myrdal

Contributors

Dr Iván Balassa, Batthyány u. 3, III/13, H-1015 Budapest, Hungary. Formerly Scientific Director of the Hungarian Agricultural Museum. Foreign Member of the Royal Gustav Adolf Academy in Sweden.

Professor Nils-Arvid Bringéus, Head of the Ethnological Institute, University of Lund, Sweden. Member of the Royal Gustav Adolf Academy in Sweden.

Hugh Cheape, National Museums of Scotland.

George Dalgleish, National Museums of Scotland.

Godfrey Evans, National Museums of Scotland.

Edith Fél, H-1056 Budapest, Belgrád rkp. 27, Hungary. Formerly of the Textile Department, Hungarian Ethnographic Museum.

Dr Alexander Fenton, National Museums of Scotland. Foreign Member of the Royal Gustav Adolf Academy in Sweden.

Dr Tamás Hofer, Institute of Ethnology, Hungarian Academy of Sciences.

Dr Eszter Kisbán, Institute of Ethnology, Hungarian Academy of Sciences.

Grith Lerche, International Secretariat for Research on the History of Agricultural Implements, National Museum of Denmark.

Dr Janken Myrdal, Nordiska Museet, Stockholm.

Professor Arnold Niederer, Hofwiesenstrasse 63, CH-8057, Zürich, Switzerland. Until 1980 Professor for European Ethnology, University of Zürich.

Dr Holger Rasmussen, Fuglsangvei 30, DK-2830, Virum, Denmark. Former Director of the Danish Folk Museum. Foreign Member of the Royal Gustav Adolf Academy in Sweden.

Professor Nils Storå Head of the Ethnological Institute, Åbo Academy, Finland. Foreign Member of the Royal Gustav Adolf Academy in Sweden.

CONTENTS

		Page
Foreword		*v*
List of Contributors		*vii*
Janken Myrdal	Gösta Berg: a Personal Comment	1
Hugh Cheape	Food and Liquid Containers in the Hebrides: A Window on the Iron Age	6
Edith Fél and Tamás Hofer	Pots and Tastes at Átány in Hungary	28
Alexander Fenton	Pigs and Mugs	38
Eszter Kisbán	Bread and Bread Bowls	50
Holger Rasmussen	The Collecting of Seagulls' and Lapwings' Eggs	61
Grith Lerche	The Woodcock and Royal Game	68
Nils Storå	Barrels and Bundles of Herring	76
Nils-Arvid Bringéus	Swedish Butter Firkins	91
Janken Myrdal	The Plunge Churn from Ireland to Tibet	111
Arnold Niederer	Wooden Milk Vessels in the Swiss Alps	138
Iván Balassa	Tokay Wines: Types and Production	152
George Dalgleish	The Silver Travelling Canteen of Prince Charles Edward Stuart	168
Godfrey Evans	The *Nécessaire de Voyage* of the Princess Pauline Borghese	185

GÖSTA BERG: A PERSONAL COMMENT

Janken Myrdal

In an attic in a town in the middle of Sweden a thirteen-year-old boy was building up a folk-life museum. It was at the beginning of 1917. In summer he collected objects in the villages around the farm where his grandparents lived, and where he was sent during the holidays. He also organised his school-mates and persuaded others to add their contribution to the collections. A boy who was rather good at drawing had to make pictures of old farm-houses, another boy whose father was a musician wrote down folksongs. Everything was incorporated with numbers and signs in the archive of the museum in the attic of Gösta Berg's parents. A main catalogue was made in August 1918.

Gösta Berg also, with his closest friend, built a camera out of a cardboard box (factory-made cameras were rare at that time) and made a photographic documentation of the collection (Fig. 1).

1. A photo of the museum in the attic, taken with the camera built by Gösta Berg and Ingemar Gustavsson, about 1917-1918.

Later, when Gösta Berg had become a member of the staff of Nordiska Museet, he presented most of the objects to this institution, where it still forms one of the most representative collections from a single area, i.e. the parish of Frändefors in the province of Dalsland in West Sweden (Fig. 2).

2. Gösta Berg shows objects from his museum to other members of the board of The Royal Patriotic Society, in spring 1986. He has been for many years Chairman of The Royal Patriotic Society in Sweden.

What stimulated this thirteen- to fifteen-year-old boy to make these efforts? Of course part of the answer lies in the simple joy that young boys feel in collecting items, whether stamps or butterflies. The intellectual aspect of Gösta's collection can also be explained in part by the milieu in which he was growing up. His father was a schoolteacher, and the father of Gösta's best friend and collaborator in the museum, Ingemar Gustavsson, was also a teacher. Furthermore, the area where they lived was a newly-built part of the thriving city of Örebro, and the town council had used it to entice good teachers to the town. Schoolteachers at that time in Sweden were renowned for their enthusiasm in spreading culture and knowledge to their pupils and to the rest of the common people. Many of them regarded the work they were doing as a mission.

A boy in his lower teens can intellectually be a grown-up (which clearly was the case with Gösta Berg, whose wide reading even included encyclopedias), but emotionally he is still, in a good sense, much like a child, and can thus be very sensitive to the intellectual tides of the time. Therefore, we have to look beyond Gösta Berg and his Museum to understand it.

Following the first enthusiastic appearance in the late nineteenth century of an interest in the older forms of folk-life, with Arthur Hazelius as the foremost pioneer, the subject had a popular breakthrough in Sweden in the decade before World War I. Several local museums were founded, and big outdoor meetings were held. It was a national movement. Politically it was a broad movement, one of the foremost figures being Karl-Erik Forsslund, who later was to become a famous teacher at the 'people's high school' of the Social-Democrats. (Besides this, Forsslund's sister was one of the most prominent members in the local committee for antiquities in Örebro; Gösta Berg became the youngest member in 1919.)

This movement in Sweden may have been stronger and broader than in any other country in Europe, and certainly more so than in most other countries; but also in general, in large parts of Northern and Eastern Europe and in some parts of Western Europe, the first part of the twentieth century was a high point for folk-life research. A large amount of knowledge was collected about ordinary life in former times. I see this as one of the big achievements of science in modern times, a great leap forward in our understanding of ourselves.

As a student in the upper-school I had little idea of what ethnology, folk-life research, was. I thought it was something to do with fairy-tales and gnomes, which interested me less then than now. I was a young Marxist (the year was 1968), and wanted to study the material culture of the people in former times. When I went to the university I found that this was exactly what ethnology was, or rather had been, doing. In Sweden, and especially in Stockholm, the new ethnology, which bordered on sociology, or, to put it in other words, which was taking over a part of sociological research, had at that time been introduced and was having its day.

Economic history, therefore, became my subject, but I realised that I had to speak with and learn from the older generation of ethnologists: Ragnar Jirlow, John Granlund and last but not least Gösta Berg. Interest begets interest and I went deeper and deeper into the subject of ploughs and harrows. In this research Gösta Berg has been one of my main teachers.

It is not necessary to be an adherent of historical materialism to realise the importance of material culture (actually most researchers in the field are not). One of the main reasons for the importance of this subject is that material life literally is the base for the existence of man. But it is more than that; it can also be a mirror for most sectors of life.

In a way this volume in homage to Gösta Berg and his life's work is not just a book about food and accessories but also provides concrete examples of what can be achieved by studying material culture. Perhaps it can have some influence on modern ethnology, strengthening the links with the best parts of the 'old ethnology', in whose study Gösta Berg is one of the most important scientific practitioners in Europe.

The articles that follow exemplify the changing premises for living, and give insights into what life really was like when food storage, bread baking and the like were household duties. We begin to realise how comfortable our own life really is. We can see, too, how relatively comfortable the better-off were in earlier days.

We can see how growing efficiency in handling food and other items leads to a loss of knowledge, and I do not hesitate to say art and beauty also, when old handicrafts, such as coopering and pottery, are wiped out.

The study of material culture also reveals other facts. Food-producing, and production as a whole, interacted with economic and social contexts, as the interchange between butter-making and the butter-trade or the use of certain aspects of the hunting-catch as a royal prerogative show. Objects given an artistic or personal touch tell us much about the thoughts and ideals of the people using them, including the splendid services that are a mark of conspicuous consumption.

Gösta Berg has written many articles on many different subjects. He is a poly-historian. But it is not my intention here to give a survey of his life and work, since this has already been done .[1]

However, I wish to mention a less well-known side of his activities. Besides being active in research himself he has been the adviser and helper of many others. Everyone, not only scientists but also young students, can go to Gösta Berg and they will get much valuable help on the subject asked about. A more generous scientist than Gösta Berg can hardly be found.

And this generosity has a firm base. Gösta Berg did not stop collecting when he left his little museum and went to the University of Uppsala. In the twenties he started to collect excerpts about the different subjects that interested him, and he still continues to do so, always with pieces of paper specially cut for the purpose in his pocket, and spending enormous amounts of time in different libraries. During more than sixty years he has built up a huge collection of quotations about ethnology, covering nearly a hundred thousand excerpts.

There must be hundreds of scientists from all over Europe who have been provided with information from this collection of knowledge. To give a personal example: when I was working in the library of Nordiska Museet on the article which appears later in this volume, Gösta came by and asked what I was doing. I had to confess that I was studying butter-churns. A few weeks later he came with a pack of excerpts about churns, that were put to good use in the writing of the article.

NOTES

1. *Gösta Berg's tryckta skrifter 1919-1973*, Stockholm 1973; *Gösta Berg's tryckta skrifter 1973-1983*, Stockholm 1983; N.-A. Bringéus, Inledning, Gösta Berg's tryckta skrifter 1919-1983. In *Saga och Sed*, 1983.

FOOD AND LIQUID CONTAINERS IN THE HEBRIDES: A WINDOW ON THE IRON AGE

Hugh Cheape

Crogain or 'craggans' are general terms, the first Gaelic and the second an English rendering of a dialect version of the same word, used to describe storage jars for food and liquid of hand-thrown, low-fired pottery, locally manufactured in parts of the Hebrides or Western Isles of Scotland. *Crogan* (plural *crogain*) is a word in Scottish Gaelic still applied to almost any form of jar or pot, often in some areas some generations after the original forms of *crogain* have disappeared. Though cognate with the English 'crock', the source is Old and Middle Irish *croccan*, often defined and qualified in early Gaelic written sources as *croccan chriadh*, 'a pot of clay'. A dialect version, *cragan*, common in the Island of Lewis where this pottery was first described as a phenomenon of material culture, was adopted by archaeologists and collectors in the late nineteenth century as a generic term for Hebridean pottery (Fig. 1).[1]

1. Hand-thrown storage jar or *crogan*, late nineteenth century, from the Island of Lewis. (Photo: National Museums of Scotland)

6

Ceramics is not an art in which Scotland has distinguished itself, lacking the necessary abundance of suitable high-quality clays, yet the country has made some significant contributions to the history of world ceramics. One or two examples will suffice. Beakers, food vessels and cinerary urns helped Scottish archaeologists in the nineteenth century to define early chronologies by inhumation rituals in British and European prehistory. The Delftfield Pottery in Glasgow developed a significant export trade to North America in the seventeenth and eighteenth centuries, imitating the prized porcelains of China, and another Glasgow pottery, J. and M.P. Bell, imitated oriental decorative patterns to build up an export trade in earthenware to South-East Asia itself, returning the artistic motifs to their countries of origin. Less prominent in terms of quantities and artistry, but no less significant in historical and archaeological terms, are the *crogan* pottery food and liquid containers of the Hebrides.

The survival of handmade pottery techniques in parts of the Inner and Outer Hebrides and adjacent mainland, long after the general adoption of the potter's wheel elsewhere, has created considerable interest for archaeologists, antiquaries and collectors of the past hundred years. Similar traditions have been recorded in Brittany, in Nordic countries and in eastern Europe. [2] These remarkable prehistoric-looking pots were then found not only in use in the Hebrides but still actually being made by some local families. The same families continued to make them until the 1930s and the techniques were closely observed and recorded. The focus of archaeological interest has been generally on techniques of manufacture, but if interpretation and extrapolation from observed evidence can be used to illuminate a remote past in this context, the evidence of recent historical sources and oral tradition in which the National Museums' archives are rich throws light equally on the function and uses of such pottery and should tempt us in the twentieth century to lift briefly and look behind the curtain on a window on the Iron Age.

Pottery, even in fragments, is customarily imbued with great importance to the extent that it is used as a label and an indicator of cultural variation, change and development; it is archaeological artefact evidence *par excellence*. Dating is generally the first or most important question that the archaeologist asks of his material evidence. It is almost impossible, with the exception of classes of pottery such as Roman Samian ware, for the scholar to assign precise dates to surviving ancient pottery. It is one of the demonstrable paradoxes of Hebridean pottery that precise dates can be given to *crogain* which have been made to order in the Hebrides during the last hundred years or whose precise origins have, almost by chance, been recalled and recorded. The paradox which is an exciting one lies in the form, style and method of manufacture which may be presumed to be of Iron Age character and early, and certainly prehistoric, origin.

Both quantitative and qualitative analysis of Hebridean pottery is difficult because few good complete examples survive, say between fifty and one hundred, nearly all in national and local museums, and their find location or origin is poorly recorded in the records of these institutions. The collection of Hebridean pottery in the National Museums, for example, the foundations of which had been laid in 1860 and the details of which were published at the time in the *Proceedings of the Society of Antiquaries of Scotland* and elsewhere subsequently, were classified in a group of thirty-five items in the Museum's published *Catalogue* of 1892 as 'homemade pottery . . . from Harris'. This error and misconception, locating the pottery in a different and geologically distinct area of the Hebrides, has, until recently, gone unquestioned.

The early distribution and therefore the use, widespread or otherwise, of *crogain* is by no means clear. Archaeological evidence in the form of coarse, low-fired, pottery sherds in profusion suggests a wider distribution than the historical evidence of a surviving *crogan* tradition. Without closer analysis and comparison, archaeology suggests that *crogan* ware was widely distributed throughout all the Hebrides while the historical evidence limits its distribution to Lewis, Skye, Coll and Tiree.

It may be assumed that this type of coarse pottery was once made in many locations by a great number of potters and was the standard food and liquid storage jar and container throughout the Hebrides, approximating perhaps almost to the areas of survival of the Gaelic language, the *Gaidhealtachd*, and amounting, *inter alia*, to a cultural indicator and also an indicator of relict culture. This is the inference to be drawn from the early commentators of the nineteenth century and has perhaps been allowed to go unquestioned with the result that easy assumptions and consequent misunderstandings have been allowed to develop. Other assumptions have significance for social and economic description, analysis and evaluation, that the many potters declined from many to a few, that the areas of manufacture, distribution and use contracted, and that modern imported commodities supplanted the native wares for reasons of demand, function and prestige. All these assumptions are testable although the evidence is scattered and scanty, and often confused because of a lack of clarity and understanding over terminology between English and Gaelic and between scholarly and popular reference.

Beginnings have been made in the petrological analysis of the pottery fabric of *crogan* ware to identify and classify its mineralogical composition and to relate it to its geological environment of origin. The results of this research have not yet been far-reaching and conclusions few beyond the confirmation of facts known from historical sources, for example that surviving *crogain* originated in 'potteries' adjacent to known clay deposits on the west coast of Lewis, in the north of Skye and on the south-west end of the island of Tiree, in each of which the local geological conditions were comparable and particularly distinctive.

In general terms, the broad similarity of *crogan* pottery may be taken as a good indication of function and, more specifically, of function as a storage jar for food and liquids. In fact, *crogain* can be broadly characterised and categorised as food and liquid storage jars or vessels. There are specific variations and exceptions to this categorisation which emerge from oral and literary sources. Minor stylistic variations, though prominent in the eye of the scholar-researcher, may be regarded as idiosyncratic and an indication of specific origin and, less certainly, of date.

When we come to consider more carefully the historical functions of surviving Hebridean pottery, interpretation may be risky. Relatively little explanation and interpretation have in fact been offered in archaeology for pottery as a functional artefact. Now the field of debate is being widened and the processes of analysis themselves developed to include questions of function of pottery, and the materials and techniques of pottery-making.

The consistency of style of round, narrow-necked, everted rim jars (cf Fig.1) informs us more about the pottery-making tradition than about their function. The diameters of necks and rims, for instance, do not seem to vary noticeably in proportion to overall diameter or height. No recorded analysis of organic deposits in *crogan* pottery has yet taken place although considerable possibility for such analysis exists. This might help to explain varieties in shape and, most commonly, in style in terms of distinctive and specific function. Explanation along these lines would have considerable implications for Scottish social and economic history and even prehistory in terms, for example, of diet and factors of local economy. The examination of Hebridean pottery has been limited in extent, perhaps superficial, and of most significance in the recent (that is nineteenth and twentieth-century) periods from which ethnological parallels have been drawn.

The experience of other countries lends emphasis to the importance of Hebridean pottery of *crogan* type. For Ireland, it is assumed that a significant pottery-making tradition did not survive the Neolithic period, that in later prehistoric and early historic times fine wares were imported in small quantities from the Continent to be bought by the wealthy, and that the greatest proportion of the population did without pottery. A Dutchman, quoted by Professor Estyn Evans, writing of Ireland in the early seventeenth century, said that ' . . . the use of earthen vessels hath been very rare among them, and to the most part unknown even until these very last times, although a great number of English potters have set up their trade'. The significance of the English potters, if indeed this account is strictly accurate to the letter, is that exotic but relatively cheap, wheel-turned pottery became more widely available in Ireland c.1650. The English potters too would probably have become Irish within a generation or so and would also have been joined by Irishmen, probably as their apprentices. Professor Evans draws directly on the example of Hebridean *crogan* ware in order to make a point by comparison:

No tradition of handmade pottery survived in Ireland as it did in the Barvas ware of Lewis in the Hebrides. [3]

When a young Edinburgh doctor visited the Island of Lewis in the Outer Hebrides in 1863, he expressed amazement at finding a woman in the Atlantic coastal township of Barvas still making by hand just such pottery as was made by the early prehistoric inhabitants of Scotland. [4] This was the inspiration which ultimately led to the first of the Rhind Lectures in the National Museum in 1876 and Dr (later Sir) Arthur Mitchell's notable book *The Past in the Present: What is Civilisation?* As the title suggests, Mitchell's work was a product of the far-reaching mid-nineteenth century debate on evolution and progress. He may have been aware of the limitations of nineteenth-century archaeology when he formulated his thesis of the survival of the past in the present. The style and decoration alone of pottery was studied for the identification of place of origin and date of manufacture, and Mitchell was interested in the possibilities of extending the field of inquiry to the interpretation of methods and the art of manufacture and technological solutions and accomplishments. He was cautious with his conclusions, nowhere claiming explicitly an unbroken continuity for primitive surviving traits from the early settlers in the Highlands and Islands.

Previous publications based on Hebridean travels had concerned themselves mainly with historical and literary feataures, ruins and topography. Apart from the exceptional and distinctive pioneer accounts of Martin Martin, the university-educated Skyeman, of 1703, and Edward Burt, a London civil servant, of 1754, the initial stimulus to such topographical literature had been provided in the 1760s by 'Ossian', the largely fictional poetry of a third-century Gaelic bard, as well as by changing attitudes to landscape. The tours of the naturalist writer, Thomas Pennant, and of Dr Samuel Johnson and James Boswell established a fashion which led to a growing flood of tourists especially after the introduction of steam navigation in the nineteenth century.

After 1851, the formation of the MacBrayne steamship company made the furthest Hebrides more readily accessible from the Clyde and, as the railway network expanded, steamer services linked up the railhead ports of Oban, Mallaig and Kyle of Lochalsh with all the islands. Among the tourists of the new moneyed classes, scholars and antiquaries mingled with the sportsmen and the curious. Some were under the influence, consciously or unconsciously, of such developing disciplines as anthropology and folklore studies. Abroad, the new breed of travellers and scholars in the field studied and collected the material culture of indigenous and aboriginal peoples whose tools and techniques seemed to differ little from those used by Stone Age man. Then, just a century after 'Ossian', the new and very different scientific controversies initiated by Charles Darwin's *Origin of Species* (1859) stirred the educated world, Arthur Mitchell, the young doctor, clearly amongst the rest. He later wrote of his discoveries in the Island of Lewis:

In driving from Uig to the village of Barvas on the west coast, we passed a stone-breaker sitting at the roadside eating his dinner out of a vessel which struck us as remarkable. We found it, on closer examination, to be even a stranger thing than it seemed to us, as we first caught sight of it. We waited till the stone-breaker had eaten its contents, and then we carried it off; but we had acquired little information regarding its history, because the stone-breaker and we had no language in common.

Before reaching Barvas we had a detour to make and some business to transact. When we got there, we found that our acquaintance of the roadside had preceded us. He had hurried home to tell of the profitable sale he had made, and while our horse was feeding, we were visited by many people carrying vessels like the one we had bought, and offering them for sale.

They are called 'Craggans', and we learned that, at a period by no means remote, they had been made in many of the villages of the [Island of] Lewis, though at the time of our visit their manufacture was chiefly, if not entirely, confined to Barvas. [5]

Increased communications between the Hebrides and the Scottish mainland began the transformation of the social and economic structure of the islands in the second half of the nineteenth century, concluding the effects of several generations of economic decline. It opened up the islands to the curious gaze of this new breed of person, the tourist, and it brought scholars and archaeologists to explore what was perceived to be an ancient world peopled by a society that the new Victorian moneyed classes might consider primitive. The fact that the inhabitants spoke another language widened the gulf between Victorians and Gaelic islanders. [6]

Steamship navigation brought a new range of commodities to the Hebrides, especially ceramics and glassware. [7] Most of the crockery and earthenware to be found in the islands, now for the most part in broken and sherd form, can be identified as 'spongeware' bowls, porringers and plates from Glasgow and Kirkcaldy, teapots and jam jars from East Lothian, and storage jars from Port Dundas, the latter generally always acquiring the adopted name of *crogain* in Gaelic. Shops and stores began to be established in the straggling island townships and travelling merchants acquired a new stock in trade. Within living memory, for example, a shop in Laxdale, Lewis, was known as *Buth a'Chragain*, the 'Craggan Shop', an indication of the availability of dried and preserved foodstuffs in jars of earthenware and glass.

2. Teapot purchased by Dr Arthur Mitchell in Barvas, Island of Lewis, c.1860, with a casual attribution to Staffordshire.
(Ref Arthur Mitchell, *The Past in the Present*, Edinburgh 1880, 30)

3. 'Barvas Ware' teaset from the Island of Lewis, c.1900.
(Photo: National Museums of Scotland, by courtesy of Mrs Thelma Aitken, Lanark)

4. Milk jug from a 'Barvas Ware' teaset from the Island of Lewis, c.1900, showing impurities and gritty intrusions in the clay.
(Photo: National Museums of Scotland, by courtesy of Mrs Thelma Aitken, Lanark)

What Mitchell also discovered and described was that the Lewis potters made cups, saucers, milk jugs, sugar basins and teapots in imitation of nineteenth-century tea services too, which they would readily sell to tourists (Figs. 2-4). This type of pottery is now generally referred to as 'Barvas Ware', after the township of Barvas on the west coast of Lewis. It has always aroused considerable curiosity in museum collections, but for our purposes it offers analytical potential only, but no similar window on the Iron Age as *crogan* pottery. Mitchell was of course deeply impressed by what he saw in Lewis and described so eloquently. In the contemporary atmosphere of scholarship and of the developing discipline of anthropology, Mitchell was outlining the archaeological relevance of the study of contemporary pottery-making, a message implicit in his catchphrase 'The Past in the Present'.

He may have been disappointed that his lectures and book did not inspire the sort of initiative which he advocated. Clearly a diffusionist as regards the westward spread of bronze and iron manufacture and wheel-thrown pottery, he probably thought of his 'neo-archaic' (to use his own term) objects such as *crogain*, distaff and spindles, beehive dwellings and primitive types of cultivating implements, as modern survivals scarcely modified from very remote times. Though perhaps wisely, even necessarily, vague as to remoter origins, he demonstrated that their late survival was due to their suitability to the special circumstances of their generally disadvantaged, though far from unintelligent, users. But, in Mitchell's own day, scholarship tended to focus on Roman archaeology, and the study of pottery itself concentrated on artistic detail and aesthetic value. Excavation and often random digging took place to procure objects for sale to museums and private collectors, and *crogain* were eagerly ordered and bought in the Hebrides for the same purpose.

An indication of late nineteenth-century interests can be gleaned from the encyclopaedic *Ceramic Art of Great Britain* of 1878 by Llewellynn Jewitt, the antiquarian, tourist guide writer and editor. He included a section on Hebridean pottery which undoubtedly stimulated demand for it. Jewitt introduced his description of pottery available for sale in Lewis in terms designed to excite the serious collector: 'Hand-made pottery is still made and used in all its primitive simplicity'. He quoted the words of a friend in the House of Commons who had ordered a Barvas pottery tea-service from the factor of Sir James Matheson's estate. Walter Morrison MP had written in 1868:

The remarkable thing is that the pottery is distinctly copied, rudely enough, from modern pottery. The forms are ordinary Tottenham Court

Road forms, and their continued use in an Island with a regular steamboat service from Glasgow strikes me as very curious. [8]

The interest generated by the scholarly reflections of Mitchell and his contemporaries and the popular appeal generated by writers such as Llewellynn Jewitt in turn generated a demand for Hebridean pottery, the fruitfulness of which may be reflected in the fact that the pottery of Barvas was advertised in the national press. Prices obtaining were as follows: cups 6d., saucers 6d., egg cups 6d., cream jugs 6d., sugar bowls 6d., teapots 2s., craggans 1s., vases 1s.6d. The *Scottish Leader* ran an article on 5 August 1893 under the title 'An Interesting Highland Industry' in which it described the state of the art, concluding colourfully that:

> . . . a tea set of Barvas Ware is not the sort of thing one would set down on a table in the house of a grandee. It is not suited for afternoon tea. It does not seem to be meant for very extensive use, though perhaps it might do for a few cailleachs [old women] in the wilds of the Highlands. It is out of keeping with modern times. Its home is in that wild island village that looks out on the angry Atlantic and seeks to thrive on an uncongenial soil.

'Barvas Ware' teasets were produced in considerable quantities in the nineteenth and twentieth centuries while tea was still not an established element of diet. This exotic tradition seemed to have been entirely a response to market demand. Although tea-drinking was by the 1870s a well-established trait of fashion and diet in the British Isles, it was not yet by any means a staple item in Hebridean diet. It was probably only as late as the 1870s and 1880s that tea-drinking became a widespread dietary habit in the Island of Lewis. At the turn of the century, for example, when it was an almost unknown item of diet in the Outer Hebrides and in the 1870s, a native of Stornoway in Lewis told the President of the Inverness Scientific Society: 'The teapots are not used, but are made for ornament and sale'. [9] Between the 1870s and the First World War, Hebridean pottery in the form of tea-sets was manufactured in considerable quantities on the west coast of Lewis and was almost exclusively made for sale in the growing tourist trade. [10] It is therefore no indication of dietary change or development. Reporting the depositions taken from crofters in Lewis by the Napier Commission in 1883, the radically-inclined *North British Daily Mail* quoted in its edition for 7 June 1883 the words of a sixty-eight-year-old Barvas crofter, John Matheson:

There was in the district a scarcity of milk and butter—the latter they had lost entirely of late. They were obliged to give the children tea for the want of milk. He was the father of a family before he could distinguish between tea and coffee, and nowadays the children could tell the difference before they were four years of age. They were not at all as innocent in that respect as he was.

Since *crogan* pottery had played such an important part in the handling and storage of milk, it may have been no wonder that its manufacture and use declined in the contemporary nineteenth-century atmosphere of economic decline and collapse.

The earliest historical references to *crogain* are in the compilation by the seventeenth-century Skye tacksman, Martin Martin, in his *Description of the Western Islands of Scotland* of about 1695. He made a qualitative distinction with reference to *crogain* in his description of the island of Lewis:

The soil is generally sandy, excepting the heaths, which in some places are black, and in others a fine red clay; as appears by the many vessels made of it by their women, some for boiling meat and others for preserving their ale, for which they are much better than barrels of wood. [11]

The same containers and their function, ' . . . for boiling water and dressing victuals', were referred to a century later by Rev. John Buchanan, a Church of Scotland missionary minister in the Hebrides.

There is little or no amplification of the point made about the use of *crogain* for preparing meat in later historical sources. This may be a reflection of dietary change in so far as meat began to play a proportionately smaller part in everyday diet as the eighteenth century progressed; or it may be a reflection of the material changes introduced by the mass-production of ironwork, in that in the same period a variety of iron cooking pots took the place of *crogain* in food preparation. Earthenware is widely recognised, of course, as a good medium for cooking because heat is distributed evenly through the walls of the vessel while on the fire; it is for example, as is well known, favoured in French cuisine. The latter influence may be the most significant in the possible displacement of *crogain* in cooking and food preparation. We have to look more closely at the balance of evidence in order to provide more indicators for research and ceramic analysis. This is most plentiful in the subject areas of techniques of manufacture and the processing and storage of milk and dairy products.

We are fortunate that the methods of making *crogain* have been preserved in several eye-witness accounts which all agree in broad terms. The earliest available description is by the botanist, geologist, and parish minister, Rev. Dr John Walker, who also held the Chair of Natural History in the University of Edinburgh. In an official report on the Hebrides, he described the making of *crogain* in the Island of Coll in 1764:

In some parts of the Island, there are pits of reddish clay, which the Inhabitants manufacture into different kinds of Earthen Vessels which they call crockans. This sort of Ware, the most rude and simple that can be anywhere made, they frame in the following manner. The Clay without any mixture, they form by the hands, into the shape of the Vessel required, and then place them in the Sun, till they are thoroughly dry. After this, they are filled with Milk and set upon a strong fire, where they are kept until the Milk be entirely boiled away which finishes the operation. This sort of Ware, though rough and unshapely, is a close firm Substance and very durable on the Fire. [12]

The significant technical detail in the sequence of production is the nature of the clay, in its raw state without any admixture or temper, the drying out of the pots outside in the sun, and the creation of a milk glaze upon which all later sources agree, describing it as a device against porosity or permeability and a form of decorative finish. The treatment of *crogain* with milk in the 'finishing' process is a technique which may be prehistoric, and it might be considered a valuable exercise to compare analyses of organic deposits on early pottery with the 'milk glaze' on *crogain* in order to throw more light on early pottery production sequences and technology.

The manufacture of the pottery was exclusively the preserve of women according to all oral information and historical data referring to the period from the seventeenth to the twentieth centuries, but this carries little or no connotation of inferior status; it is a specific illustration of the subtle allocation of roles and division of labour in Gaelic society. Women, in common with men, had specific tasks allotted to them such as the handling of stock in the annual seasonal migrations to summer grazings, and certain other tasks as their exclusive province. Pottery making was always carried out by women, a fact given specific mention in 1695 and just as true when a woman made the last of the *crogain* to order in 1935 (Fig. 5).

That this was not a despised art or sign and symbol of a decayed society is evident from consistent oral and literary evidence within the Gaidhealtachd. Clearly there was a sustained demand for *crogan* ware on

5. *Crogan* pottery made by and bought from Mrs Catherine MacLean, Brue, Barvas, in 1935. It was commissioned by Mr A.D. Lacaille for the collections of the Wellcome Institute.
(Photo: National Museums of Scotland)

functional grounds alone, but its presence in a site of well-defined social standing, Breachacha Castle in the Inner Hebridean island of Coll, stratified with technically superior, glazed, imported continental wares must be of great significance. [13]

The production of *crogain* was not supplanted by the availability of wheel-turned and glazed pottery growing out of the technological and industrial revolution in ceramics in England and Scotland in the eighteenth century. Production continued at a rate which is difficult to determine but which seemed to have remained consistent until the early twentieth century. The tradition was a conservative one and innovation of style and technique unknown. Inferences to be drawn from this may be that the demands of function and diet remained unchanged, that the number of manufacturers remained few and dispersed, that the art remained in the hands of the same few families for generation after generation, and that sources of clay, pockets of glacial till in the glacial moraine of the Hebridean island chain, were never extensively exploited or explored.

The survival of pottery in profusion may obscure facts for which no comparable mass of evidence survives, for example that at different times and in differing proportions, other types of containers and storage vessels for food and liquid were more commonly employed. Its very exclusiveness and the failure of other material to survive may also be distorting our view of this aspect of material culture. Recent excavations and sophisticated conservation techniques for example have revealed more information about lathe-turned wooden vessels and staved wooden containers. [14]

It is instructive to look in this context at the processing of dairy products. Various containers might be used in the past for churning butter, depending on what was convenient and to hand. Cylindrical staved plunge churns, though they have a long history of use in Scotland, were certainly unknown in the Hebrides, especially the Outer Hebrides, until a relatively recent date or even the twentieth century in some parts. [15] Like so many features of material culture, innovations would not necessarily supplant or obliterate their precursors; they would co-exist, finding their respective functional or economic slots.

The earlier methods of churning would have used skin bags and earthenware vessels of *crogan* type. A landowner of Moidart in west Inverness-shire who lived from 1896 to 1957 described how old people had told him that butter was made by shaking in a leather bag. [16] An account from a different area but approximately the same date of making butter in Melness, Sutherland, about 1870, shows how the simple technology or drudgery of making butter was turned to good account by committing the chore to the social and convivial gathering in the *ceilidh* house:

'Bha iad 'cur a's cracainn uan no cracainn carora 's bha iad 'ga thilgeil bhon darna fear gus an fhear eil' . . . . (They put [the butter] in the skin of a lamb or the skin of a sheep and they threw it from one to the other . . . When the housewife put the cream in the skin, they were throwing it from one to the other. By the time it had gone fourteen or fifteen times round the company, you had the butter). [17]

A description of two women making butter in Skye in 1768 by tipping the container back and forth between them, perhaps for several hours, is complemented by the survival of large *crogain* described as churns in one or two museum collections. A good example from the Island of Coll in the Inner Hebrides is 35cm high and approximately 35cm in diameter, with the usual style of rim to allow a covering to be stretched over and tied on, and with the added feature of a perforation in the area of the top of the shoulder which was said to be necessary to let gases escape that were generated in the process of churning. [18] Churning using a *crogan* was observed in Braes, Skye, about 1920.

We may be in error to be categorical about the comparatively recent introduction of staved vessels. Wooden staved vessels were used for churning and other domestic uses in the early middle ages, and archaeo-logical evidence suggests continuous use and growing sophistication from prehistory to modern usage. [19] The technique of using such a container for making butter in the same way as the *crogan* might be used, was de-scribed by Alexander Carmichael as he probably observed the practice in the Uists in the latter half of the nineteenth century:

The cream having been put in, the mouth of the vessel was covered with the dressed skin of lamb, sheep, kid, goat or calf, and tightly bound with a cord of linen or leather . . . . The *cuinneag* [stoup] thus secured was placed on a bench, bed, table or other suitable place, and the process of churning consisted in agitating it rapidly to and fro. [20]

By implication, local pottery was considered inadequate or undesirable for the dairy work of a big house in Gairloch in the early nineteenth century. Here, on an improved farm, sixty cows and followers were kept and then sent to the shielings during the mid-summer months:

No finery of china or glass or even coarse earthenware was ever seen in those days; instead of these, there were very many flat, shallow, wooden dishes, and a multitude of churns and casks and kegs . . . [21]

This was an area of the West Highlands comparatively well-endowed with trees, and wooden vessels were undoubtedly more common than in

6. Two small lidded *crogain* from the Islands of Tiree and Coll in the Inner Hebrides. These small vessels are associated with a medicinal usage in connection with respiratory illnesses.　(Photo: National Museums of Scotland)

the islands. Nevertheless, it was probably a matter of some pride and prestige at this date that the dairy should be equipped with staved wooden vessels bound with metal bands or withies.

Descriptions of *crogain* as milk-carrying and processing containers are inseparable from references to the annual migration of livestock to the shielings and also to the traditional method of sealing the containers in use in these tasks. For most purposes, the mouth of the *crogan* was covered over when in use as a storage container (Fig. 6). The method of closing the container with a patch or scrap of dressed sheepskin which was then tied securely with a thong or cord round the neck of the vessel is a detail which remains strongly fixed in the communal memory in the Hebrides. The need to close the *crogan* in this way also helps to explain the distinctive traditional shape of the narrow mouth and upstanding, everted rim of the vessel. The type of skin covering has been variously called *immideal* (with the vbariant spellings *iomaideil* and *iombhuideal*),

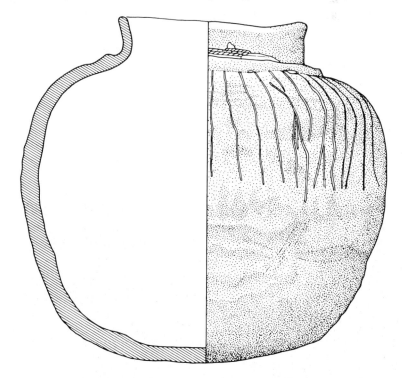

7. *Crogan*, described as a 'potato pot', from Callanish, Isle of Lewis, early nineteenth century, showing bulbous profile, shoulder with simple scratch decoration, everted rim and fragments of cord binding on the neck.
(Drawing by Helen Jackson, National Museums of Scotland)

craicionn, *fuileach*, *buileach* and *builich*. The covering was tied on with *iall*, a thong, implying a tie of leather, and *snathan imideil* has been recorded in Lewis for a tie of modern string (Fig. 7).

The importance of keeping the *imideal* clean is implicit in the proverb recorded in North Uist in the late nineteenth century: *cho glan ri imideal* ('as clean as a covering skin'), it was said, and the process of cleansing the *imideal* described to the collector:

> It was scrubbed thoroughly in cold water; thereafter it was scraped on a flat, smooth stone, with a blunt knife to remove from it all particles of milk or anything else; and, in order to keep its pliability, was then placed in cold water with some salt. [22]

Arthur Mitchell introduced the subject of organic residues in pottery and the tainting of the material stored. The careful and fastidious treatment of the skin covers of *crogain* may amount to a fallacy in that no amount of cleaning could avoid contamination of the contents. Mitchell derived his information from the Island of Lewis and pointed out a characteristic of *crogan* pottery that would be, to modern taste, unpalatable:

> The craggans, in consequence of their porousness, generally contain organic matter in a state of putrescence. And I have been told that, as the result of this, when fresh milk is put into a craggan, it soon becomes tainted—so soon that there arises a practical difficulty, where craggans are much used, in obtaining sweet milk, the taste of which is thus unfamiliar to the people, who come to like best what they know best and to prefer what is unpalatable to us. [23]

The Gaelic phrase, *blas a'chrogain*, 'the taste of the crogan', is still common in colloquial speech, and is undoubtedly derived from the experience of the contents such as milk or butter at the bottom of the *crogan* acquiring a sour taste from the earthenware and going sour or rancid. *Ghabh e blas a'chrogain dheth*, for example, implies that the subject has tired of the object or has even taken a dislike to it. Such a phrase may be an innovation of recent generations as the use of *crogan* pottery has been declining. Changes of diet and refinement of taste might have led people to begin to dislike the tainting of food induced by *crogan*.

The author of an account of customs in Skye published in 1879 drew on his memory of the locality of Kilmuir in the 1820s. He described in detail a specific function of *crogain* that has a bearing on the porosity of low-fired pottery and the contamination or fermentation of the contents through the agency of organic deposits. In referring to the use of the early form of open oil lamp or *cruisgeann*, he continued:

> The oil was dark, like port wine, but thin and good. It was procured from
> the livers of the different kinds of fish which they caught for family use. On
> coming home from the sea-beach with creels of fish of all descriptions, the
> females commenced immediately to gut them, and to throw the livers into
> an old pot or into a craggan, until they melted them down into a partially
> liquid state; they then set the decayed livers on a slow fire to dissolve them
> completely. In this state, they poured off the pure liquid oil, put it into a
> craggan and threw away the refuse. [24]

The tainting of food might not have been so readily accepted as might be
imagined. There are several descriptions from the neighbouring islands
of Coll and Tiree in the Inner Hebrides, in the late nineteenth and twentieth centuries, which specify a medicinal use for small *crogain* as a
means of giving hot milk to people with respiratory complaints. The doctor in Tiree, Dr Alexander Buchanan, described this island tradition in a
letter in the 1870s:

> The only Craggans now made in Tiree are small globular vessels, in which
> milk drawn directly into them from the cow, is warmed and given to per-
> sons showing a tendency to consumption. Milk so treated is said to be
> "milk without wind", and is supposed by the people to have special cura-
> tive effects. [25]

There are several accounts from Tiree in recent years of the practice of
administering 'milk without wind', *bainne gun ghaoth*, in the Sound Archives of the School of Scottish Studies in the University of Edinburgh. A
description of pottery making in Coll specified a slightly different version
of this practice in that a certain *Mairi Alasdair* or Mary MacKinnon
(1860-1939) made beakers or tumblers of grey clay, locally called 'blue
clay', which were here also regarded as good for respiratory complaints;
the first milking after a cow had calved known as 'beest' or 'beestin', was
taken directly into them, the milk was then brought to the boil and given
to the patient. [26]

The same principle of using a *crogan* in which to warm or boil a drink
of milk or water and to administer the drink was recommended as a dietary specific and a prophylactic in a Gaelic medical manuscript of the late
fifteenth or early sixteenth century. The *Regimen Sanitatis* or 'Rule of
Health' compiled by the hereditary family of physicians, the Beatons, and
drawing on the best of European medical knowledge derived from the
teachings of Arab, Greek and Roman philosophers, includes a chapter on

B

dietary advice for the preservation of good health. The author refers to the *crogan* in this context as 'a boiling vessel', *croccan fhiuchach*. [27]

A circumstantial account of the rescue of a young Lewisman, *Iain Ruadh MacAmhlaidh*, who had been tied up and left in the snow to die of exposure turns on the same virtues of *crogain* as containers for hot milk. The account is one episode of internecine warfare, relating possibly to the late fifteenth century or c.1500, in a large manuscript compilation of 'Tales and Traditions of the Western Isles' by Donald Morison of Lewis (1787-1834), known familiarly as *An Sgoilear Ban*. The foster-father of the victim, *Iain Ruadh*, was warned in a dream of his foster-son's plight:

> Finlay Ciar now got up and made his wife milk the cows which were in the house into a crogan, and boil it on the fire; when it was boiling hot, he wrapped the crogan in a skin, and on a frosty moonlight night, set off for Tobhta Choinnich. There he found Iain Ruadh bound hand and foot, and almost dead from cold and hunger; but he soon revived the boy by a great draught of the warm milk, and wrapping him in his big coat, he took him on his back and returned to Mealista before daylight. [28]

Whether this is true in every detail or reflects accurately the historical situation in fifteenth-century Lewis may be difficult to corroborate satisfactorily; what may be as significant in such an account is the fact that the story in its early nineteenth-century telling contained elements which the contemporary islander would immediately recognise in his own day and which would help to convey the truth of such a story of events three hundred years previously.

In the parish of Diurinish in Skye the *crogan* has been immortalised in the folk memory in *Bliadhna nan Crogan*, 'the Year of the Crogans', which recalls an event which shook the parish during the darkness and hardship of the Second World War. A large merchant ship, the *Iurlana* from Montevideo in a convoy bound for the Clyde, was wrecked in a storm and remained on a reef for some weeks before finally disappearing below the waves. Among the cargo of military materials in the hold were a hundred tons of corned beef packed in six-pound cans, likened by the author to manna from Heaven. Within days every house in the parish was full of *crogain* and every family full of corned beef, and the evidence was hidden away from the authorities. The story has been vividly told in a Gaelic biography *Cunnartan Cuain* ('Sea Perils') by a native of Diurinish, Angus MacPhee, who has described the way of life of a crofting and fishing community of the Hebrides in the last hundred years through the lives of three generations of his own family. [29]

Although *crogain* are no longer made or used in the Hebrides or elsewhere, the term *crogan* is still in active use in Gaelic. It is used to describe any container or jar of earthenware, and its use has been extended to some other forms of containers of different materials such as glass and also of modern, mass-produced type. Thus today we have *crogan silidh*, a jelly or jam jar, *crogan meala*, a jar of honey, *crogan sioraip*, a jar or tin of syrup, and *crogan treicil*, a jar or tin of treacle. Other more remarkable modern attributions for the term *crogan* are *crogan feoil*, a tin of meat, as in the Skye story quoted above, and *crogan leanna*, a 'jar of ale', a can of beer, or more specifically, a can of lager, recalling the earliest references to *crogain* in the late seventeenth century by Martin Martin. Apart from the implicit similar function of preserving food, the other noteworthy characteristic of the modern *crogan* is a narrow neck and everted rim precisely as in the *crogan* of prehistory (Fig. 8).

8. 'Barvas Ware' teapots in a newly-fired state in peat on a central hearth in Barvas, Lewis, 1907. On the dresser behind the figure, two more teapots can be seen together with factory-made pottery.
(Photo: Mrs E.C.Quiggin, by courtesy of Edinburgh Central Library, I.F.Grant Collection)

NOTES

1. Rev. J. Cameron, Parish of Stornoway. In *New Statistical Account* 14 (1845), 117; W.A. Smith, *Lewisiana, or Life in the Outer Hebrides*, London 1875, 206; A. Mitchell, *The Past in the Present*, Edinburgh 1880, 25-28; E. Beveridge, *Coll and Tiree, Their Prehistoric Forts and Ecclesiastical Antiquities*, Edinburgh 1903, 70, 93, 96, 123.

2. For example, A. Steensberg, Primitive Black Pottery in Jutland. In *Folk-Liv* III (1939), 113-146; J. Miln, *Excavations at Carnac*, Edinburgh 1877, 20-21, 41.

3. E.E. Evans, *Irish Folk Ways*, London 1957, 73-74.

4. A. Mitchell, *ut supra*, 29.

5. *Ibid.*, 25-26.

6. E.C. Curwen, The Hebrides: A Cultural Backwater. In *Antiquity* (1938) 281-282.

7. Rev. A. MacGregor, Notes on Some Old Customs in the Island of Skye. In *Proceedings of the Society of Antiquaries of Scotland* 14 (1879-1880), 146-147.

8. Ll. Jewitt, *The Ceramic Art of Great Britain, From Prehistoric Times down to the Present Day*, London 1878, Vol 2, 522-523.

9. Capt. F.W.L. Thomas, Papers and Correspondence, 1886, *Society of Antiquaries of Scotland Manuscripts* 28, fol 3; A. Ross, Presidential Address to the Inverness Scientific Society, 13 November 1877. In *Transactions of the Inverness Scientific Society*, 1 (1875-1880), 92.

10. *Report to the Secretary of State for Scotland by the Crofters' Commission on the Social Condition of the People of Lewis in 1901 as Compared with Twenty Years Ago*, Glasgow 1902, LXXXI; Descriptive List of Loan Collection Illustrative of the Highlands and Islands of Scotland. In *Scottish National Exhibition Edinburgh 1908*, Edinburgh 1908, 16.

11. D. MacLeod, ed., *A Description of the Western Islands of Scotland by Martin Martin*, Stirling 1934, 85-86.

12. M. McKay, ed., *The Rev. Dr John Walker's Report on the Hebrides of 1764 and 1771*, Edinburgh 1980, 171.

13. Capt. F.W.L. Thomas, Papers and Correspondence, *ut supra*, fol 3; D.J. Turner and J.G. Dunbar, Breachacha Castle, Coll: Excavations and Field Survey, 1965-8. In *Proceedings of the Society of Antiquaries of Scotland* 102 (1969-1970), 182-185.

14. J. Barber, Medieval Wooden Bowls. In D. Breeze, ed., *Studies in Scottish Antiquity presented to Stewart Cruden*, Edinburgh 1984, 125-147.

15. A. Carmichael, *Carmina Gadelica*, Edinburgh 1941, Vol 4, 82.

16. I.F. Grant, *Highland Folk Ways*, London 1961, 215.

17. G. Gow, Making Butter in the Ceilidh-House. In *Tocher* 36 (1981), 385.

18. A. Mitchell, James Robertson's Tour Through Some of the Western Islands Etc of Scotland 1768. In *Proceedings of the Society of Antiquaries of Scotland* 32 (1897-1898), 15-16; L. McLellan Mann, Notices of a Pottery Churn from the Island of Coll, With Remarks on Hebridean Pottery. In *Proceedings of the Society of Antiquaries of Scotland* 42 (1907-1908), 326-327.

19. J. Barber, Excavations on Iona 1979. In *Proceedings of the Society of Antiquaries of Scotland* 111 (1981), 282-380.

20. A. Carmichael, *ut supra*, 82-83.

21. O. MacKenzie, *A Hundred Years in the Highlands*, London 1922, 14.

22. Rev. D. Campbell, Gaelic Proverbs. In *Transactions of the Gaelic Society of Inverness* 45 (1967-1968), 7-9.

23. A. Mitchell, *The Past in the Present, ut supra*, 45.

24. Rev. A. MacGregor, *ut supra*, 145-146.

25. A. Mitchell, *The Past in the Present, ut supra*, 28.

26. For example, D. Sinclair, Bainne gun Gaoth. In *Tocher* 1 (1971), 28.

27. H.C. Gillies, ed., *Regimen Sanitatis: The Rule of Health*, Glasgow 1911, 20,

28. N. Macdonald, *The Morrison Manuscript*, Stornoway 1975.

29. A. Mac-a-Phi, *Cunnartan Cuain*, MacDonald Loanhead 1981, 49-87.

POTS AND TASTES AT ÁTÁNY IN HUNGARY

Edit Fél and Tamás Hofer

For centuries, a great deal of the food consumed in Central and Eastern Europe by noblemen or peasants or burghers, was cooked in earthen pots, on open fireplaces. The potter's trade gave a living to whole villages and even to groups of villages and produced an enormous mass of small and big pots. The sherds of these pots have been excavated by archaeologists, and more recently-used specimens fill shelves in ethnographic collections. With changes in kitchen equipment, however, the art and skills of cooking in earthen pots fell into oblivion.

How many earthen pots were needed in the past by a peasant household? What categories were distinguished by the housewives among their cooking pots?

In the early 1950s, it proved still possible to provide accurate, precise answers to these questions in the village of Átány on the northern edge of the Hungarian Plain.[1] In the vast majority of the households there were already economy stoves, upon which cooking was done in smaller or bigger enamelled and iron pots and pans. But in the houses, the ovens in the shape of a truncated cone plastered with clay were still standing, the living rooms were heated by them, and bread was baked in them (Figs. 1-3). In winter, when heating was necessary anyhow, the big pots for warming water and cooking soup were set in the oven. The new iron pots usually replaced the smaller earthen ones. The bigger pots continued to serve. At the time of wedding-feasts a fireplace was built in the courtyard (usually a platform of wooden planks was put on a sledge and covered with adobe bricks), the huge pots of 20 to 30-litre capacity were put on this and the fire flamed around them. On the occasion of pig killing, a fire was frequently lit in the courtyard, surrounded by 8 to 10-litre pots. According to old people's opinion, food had a better taste if it was cooked in an earthen pot, than in an iron one. Women knew well the tricks and niceties of cooking in earthen pots, though the gradual decline in use of the vessels had been going on for about thirty years (i.e. since World War I). The earthen pots preserved and used on occasions formed imposing groups in the loft.

The following description is based on observations made in the 1950s and on the reminiscences noted down at that time.

1. Oven in the living room. C19071.

2. The arch separating the kitchen and its foreroom. C19076.

3. The mouth of the oven, opening into the kitchen and the fireplace in front of it. C19075.

Cooking in earthen pots

The earthen pots used at Átány were lead-glazed inside and without glaze on the outside. They had one handle, or two in the case of the particularly big pots. There were significant differences in size among them, ranging from 0.3 to 30 litres; almost all gradations of half and whole litres were represented. Clay suitable for fireproof pottery was not available in the Hungarian Plain, and therefore the potters there used to make vessels for serving and storing food as a rule. Refractory wares suitable for cooking and baking were supplied by the potters from the mountainous areas surrounding the Plain.[2] Potters' villages in Gömör county supplied Átány with their wares, and the itinerant potters, selling from their carts and coming from Rimaszombat (Rimavska Sobota, Czechoslovakia) were mentioned. After 1921 the overwhelming majority of the potters' villages of Gömör became part of Czechoslovakia, and the potters could not cross the new state border to come to the Plain to sell their wares. This fact also contributed to the replacement of the earthen cooking vessels by iron ones.

The housewives of Átány used to cook either in the dome-shaped oven, or on the fireplace in front of the oven, on a 40 to 55 cm wide bench built of adobe bricks.[3] The mouth of the oven which stood in the room opened into the kitchen, which was usually the central unit of the three-unit Átány houses. An arch divided the kitchen into two, a front and a back position, of which the latter was the actual kitchen, with an arched ceiling that directed the smoke towards the chimney.

There is very little wood in the Hungarian Plain. Straw, corn-stalks, the leaves of which were eaten by the animals, corn-cobs and dried dung served as heating materials. When the oven was lit, all of it was hot, so food to be cooked or baked was simply put inside, perhaps turned over once, and taken out. Only extremely skilful housewives could boil noodles in the oven without burning their hands. Baking in the oven is much easier than cooking. In winter when the oven was heated every day, mostly baked meals were prepared, and cooking was less frequent. The glowing embers were pulled together into the centre of the oven and the pots were placed around.

The housewife had an easier time on the fireplace in front of the mouth of the oven. She put the pots beside the constantly glowing, slow-burning fire and turned them around from time to time so that they could be heated evenly. The tall shape of the pots also indicates the idea of absorbing heat from the side (unlike casseroles with broad bottoms which are meant for the economy stoves, and therefore heated from below).

In addition, there were improvised fireplaces set up temporarily, for special occasions, as already mentioned.

Tastes, Smells and Sizes

In using the various earthen pots, two general characteristics of such vessels played a decisive role. One was that the cooking pots could be put to the fire only if filled to the rim, otherwise there was a danger of splitting. The other characteristic was that they readily absorbed the taste and smell of the food cooked in them.

Since the pot had to be filled up before cooking, its size had to suit the number of people to be fed. On the other hand, the housewife had to know exactly the portions: for instance, half a litre of soup might be enough for one person, but some voracious eaters would consume even more. Thus the lonely widow had a half-litre pot for soup and a family of six had a four-litre one, as there might be some among the six who would want more than half a litre. When buying a pot, the housewife first of all observed the size. 'The way the pots were put (the vendors put their wares on display on the ground), we could see that this would be sufficient for the two of us for soup. We could see it with our own eyes, but also asked the potter, how many litres could it take.'

At Átány usually 'two kinds', i.e. two courses, were served at a meal, the first always a soup, and the 'second kind' a thick food, such as noodles, mush, vegetables, etc. The amount of the second course was half that of the first, and so yet another series of pots was required for this, with half the capacity of the series for soup.

The household had to rely upon outside help for performing certain tasks. These extra mouths had also to be fed. Thus enough pots were needed to cater for the first and second courses of meals for 'increased numbers'. Pig killing was an annual event with a greater number of helpers and guests. The occasion had special kinds of dishes. Thus a separate group was constituted by the cooking and serving of pots of the 'pig killing'. The largest number of people were fed on the occasion of weddings. In the 1950s as many as thirty households could be invited for a wedding. However, except for the wealthiest families, most did not strive to acquire a complete set of cooking and serving vessels for such a wedding feast; instead, they were able to solve the problem by co-operating with two or three related families.

As the cooking pot absorbs the taste and smell of the food put into it, separate pots are needed for food of different tastes. There were separate pots for fat and salted stews, for sweetfruit soups, for the boiling of kneaded (dry) noodles in water, for cabbage, and also for heating water. There was yet another pot (though not in every house) for boiling maize consumed as a delicacy in winter.

Classes of Earthen Pots, the Pot Population of Households

The set of pots in each household was composed according to the above principles, reflecting not only the permanent membership of the household, but also its work organisation, the number of auxiliary hands and wage labourers at various seasonal tasks, and the number of relatives and neighbours eating together on festive occasions. Affluence and the status provided by wealth were reflected in the degree to which they could realise or approach the required norms of totality, how far they could differentiate among the various kinds of food and taste, and whether they had their own wine and vineyard or not, so as to make it worth having vessels for warming wine. The kitchen utensils reflected also the personal ambition of the housewife, which was manifested in two important fields: linen and a fine and orderly set of kitchen equipment. In the case of the latter the manifestation of ambition had greater possibilities through the use of glazed serving and storing vessels and milk jugs, decorated with floral pattern, rather than the plain, unglazed pots.

The following list gives a survey of the earthen pots of five households of different numbers and social standing. We describe the classes and categories of cooking pots on the basis of the concepts used by the Átány people (Fig. 4).

Pots for soup. This is the most important class, having the greatest variety, of which one or two spares are also needed, since they break relatively often.

1. Pot for soup made of beans, peas, crushed barley, etc., counting half a litre for each family member.
2. Pot for meat soup: usually of one or half a litre bigger capacity than the former ones, since the meat takes up some additional volume.
3. Bigger pot for soup, used for the above kinds of soup when labourers and auxiliary hands are also fed. One litre is counted for each labourer, since the meat in the soup is also taken into consideration.
4. Pot for the soup at a pig killing, 8- to 10-litre capacity or even bigger, adjusted to the expected number of guests, each counted by one litre.
5. Wedding pot: 20- or 30-litre capacity. Bigger ones than that were not made. Two or three such pots were needed at a time. One litre of soup was counted for one person.

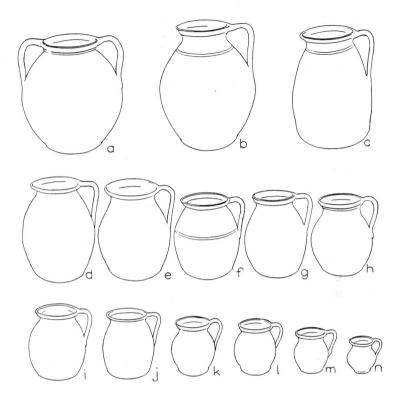

4. Earthen pots from Átány: a. Mush pot (capacity 11 litres); b. Pot for soup (10 litres); c. Cabbage pot (8 litres); d. Water heating pot (5 litres); e-f. Pots for boiling dried noodles (4 litres each); g-h-i. Pots for second dishes (2.5, 1.2 and 1.7 litres); j. Pot for boiling dried noodles (1.3 litre); k. Pot for second dishes (0.9 litre); l. Pot for meat soup for a single person (0.7 litre); m. Little pot for wine or tea (0.5 litre); n. Pot for roasted flour (thickening for a brown soup or for another dish, capacity 0.23 litre). C19072.

Pots for the second kind of dishes, or 'mush pots' in popular parlance. Their capacity is usually half that of the pots for soup.
1. Mush pot for the legumes seasoned with fat.
2. Pot for thick, fat gruels.
3. Pot for sour fruit and vegetable dishes.
4. Pot for boiling dried noodles, smaller than the others by a half or one litre.
5. Cabbage pot. More stuffed cabbage is made than is consumed at one meal, therefore the cabbage pots were at least of 6- to 8-litre size, but 10- to 20-litre ones were also frequent.

6. Meat-jelly pot. Meat-jelly was also not made for a single meal, thus the smallest pot was of 6- but mostly of 8- to 10-litre capacity.
7. Maize cooking pot. Grain of maize was cooked in it in large quantity. It was usually of 6- to 10-litre capacity.
8. The actual 'mush pot' for a wedding. It always had two handles. When sweet mush was also served, there were separate pots for cooking the sweet and the meaty mush. They were of 10- to 20-litre capacity. There was no bigger size in this category; two or three were used at a time, and half a litre was counted per person (Fig. 5).

Heating vessels. Their material and shape is identical with those above, only their function is different.
1. Pot for *curdling* milk for cheese. A 10-litre pot was needed for one cow, and none bigger than 20 litres was used. The skimmed, sour milk was heated in it to separate the curd from the buttermilk. Where there were more cows and more cheese was wanted, the procedure was either re-peated, or two similar pots were used.
2. Smaller water heating pot, 2- to 6-litre capacity. Water needed for the kneading of bread was made lukewarm in it.
3. Bigger water heating pot of 6- to 8-litre capacity. For answering the daily need for lukewarm water (for pigs' food, for washing up, etc.).
4. Wine heating pot from 0.3- to 3- to 4-litre. 0.3 to 0.5 litre was counted per person. In some households warmed wine was sweetened, and elsewhere paprika was added,
5. Heating pot for tea, 0.5 to one litre. There were two of equal size. In one water was heated, in the other the leaves were put to be warmed, before hot water was poured upon it. Camomile, lime-blossom and various other medicinal herbs for curing man and beast were used.
6. Pot for warming milk, from 0.5 to 2 to 4 litres, counting half a litre per person;

If we compare an Átány housewife's kitchen equipment in the 'earthen pot age' and later, in the age of the iron casseroles and pans, it is striking to see how much more elaborate and diversified the old equipment was. The versatile iron vessels could fulfil several functions one after the other, sweet mush could follow a fat, salted dish if the pot was washed in between. The functions of individual earthen pots were more limited and specialised, being tied to specific areas of taste and seasoning, and to specific quantities of food and liquids to be boiled or warmed up in them.

Thus, in earlier days, the range of cooking pots in a household revealed much information about the composition of the household and about the

5. Cooking pot populations of five households, representing different strata and levels of wealth. A. Samuel Kovács, well-to-do peasant, a family of 7 members. B. József Kakas, owner of one-half of a feudal *telek* (the legally fixed unit of ploughland, meadow etc. allotted to a serf), a family of 5 members. C. János Kolláth, owner of one-quarter of a *telek*, a family of 5 members. D. Gábor Gönczi, dwarf-holder earning his living as a share-cropper and wage earner. A family of 4 members, 2 of them little children. E. Erzsébet Papp, a solitary widow.— Categories of pots: 1. Pots for soup; 2. Pots for soup at a wedding; 3. Pots for second dishes; 4. Pots for second dishes at a wedding; 5. Pots for warming up water. C19073.

local food system. This short essay is limited to cooking pots. By considering other groups of vessels—for baking and frying, for storage, for carrying food etc.—the picture would be even more diversified (Figs. 6-7).

6. Cooking of cabbage in earthen pots in the courtyard, at a pigsticking, 1954. C19070.

7. Little pot for warming wine. C19074.

The size and use of cooking pots throws light upon a small segment of the system of portioning and rationing of the Átány peasants. By using these quantitative rules, measures and estimates, they could keep in evidence and ration the produce of a year, so that it should be enough for the subsequent year and if possible still leave some surplus, without having written accounts and calculations. They could portion the labour power of themselves and of their animals, and partly in accordance with levels of exhaustion at work they could portion 'dry' and 'cooked' meal, and fodder to the animals etc. In contrast with people living differently, like the town dwellers (who 'go to the shop for a paper bag of flour', buy their bread in the shop, 'do not eat bread made of grain in their own field') and with the poor people living on wages at Átány and in the neighbourhood, it was just this precisely elaborated system of rationing, order, the knowledge of what is much and what is too little, and what is enough and appropriate, that had given a sense of security and self-assurance to the Átány people (in the period of our fieldwork), and had made them proud of their peasant way of life. [4]

NOTES

1. In the village of Átány, Hungary, the authors carried out intensive fieldwork from the 1950s (Edit Fél from 1951, Tamás Hofer from 1954 on). As a result, three volumes were published on the social life of the village, on the concepts, measures and values utilised in farm and household management, and on the agricultural tools and equipment of the peasants. These monographs, especially the second, give background information to the data presented in this essay. They are Edit Fél and Tamás Hofer: *Proper Peasants. Traditional Life in a Hungarian Village*, Chicago, Aldine 1969; *Bäuerliche Denkweise in Wirtschaft und Haushalt. Eine ethnographische Untersuchung über das ungarische Dorf Átány*, Göttingen, Otto Schwartz & Co. 1972; *Geräte der Átányer Bauern*, Copenhagen-Budapest 1974.
2. Cf. Mária Kresz: Fazekas, korsós, tálas, (potter, jugmaker, dish-maker). In *Ethnographia* 71 (1960), 297-379.
3. Kitchen and oven in Átány: see E. Fél and T. Hofer, *op. cit.* (1972), 358-361, 365-369.
4. E. Fél and T. Hofer, *op.cit.* (1972), 455-474, (1969), 379-384. Cf. Fél: Hongrie: Un chercheur dans sa propre culture. In *Objets et Mondes*, 23, 3-4 (1983), 99-110; Hofer: Cognitive Aspects of Peasant Livelihood in Hungary. In J.P. Mencher, ed., *Social Anthropology of Peasantry*, Bombay—Madras—New Delhi, Somaiya Ltd. 1983, 191-203.

PIGS AND MUGS

Alexander Fenton

At the present time, life has many advantages. People who live in small flats and houses do not need a great deal of storage space for food, because the local shops have tinned and refrigerated foods in great plenty. These can be bought in small quantities as required. Household refrigerators take care of perishables for the time being, and can be readily stocked up again. The local shops act in lieu of the storage needs of earlier days.

It is difficult for us now to comprehend how much space was required for salt meat, fish and butter, for cheeses, oil and honey, and many other things, as well as the range of containers appropriate to specific substances and tasks. This essay concentrates on containers of crockery, those to which the names *mugs* and *pigs* were applied. It tries not only to identify what they were used for holding, but also what kinds of utensils the terms actually referred to. As often happens in lexicography, precise definition is not always possible, and statements made about meanings may have to be based on an informed judgement reflecting a balance of probability. Containers for food and drink are often uncertain creatures, because the sources that mention them regarded them as too commonplace to be in need of description. The notes that follow try to relate the words to the things in the case of two items only, leaving a host of other terms for interpretation elsewhere. *Mug* and *pig* have been chosen because they represent Scots usages, which in turn raises the question of whether the items so designated had particularly Scottish characteristics also.

Pigs

The word *pig* in the sense of a jar, pot or pitcher, made of *lame* or earthenware, has a long history, even if its origin is not clearly known. It is first recorded c.1440 in Early Middle English, as *pygg*, a container for wine,[1] and survives in Scots and in the Northumberland dialects of northern English to the present day. Though earthenware was the main material, other possibilities also existed. In 1488, there is a reference to a 'pyne pig of tyn'.[2] This, however, contained coins. The expression 'pyne pig' seems to mean a money-box, and this is confirmed by later nineteenth-century usage in Aberdeen, where it refers to a jar or other container for small coins laid past as savings.[3] In fact 'pig', qualified as 'pyne-pig', 'pint-pig' and, most commonly, 'pirlie-pig', became standard designations for money boxes, whatever the material they were made of, though pottery was most usual.

In 1588, an English will listed a 'litle wood pigge' along with other wooden dishes.[4] It is likely that in this case it was for holding food. However, the great majority of pigs for this purpose were of pottery.

Pigs usually took the form of open-topped containers, in a variety of sizes, for holding a variety of materials. Some must have had lids or stoppers for, as noted above, pigs could contain wine. There is a Scottish reference to wine in pigs in 1540,[5] and in 1551, the Elgin authorities prohibited the selling of ale with cogs, pigs or cups,[6] but even into the twentieth century, home-brewed ale was still being kept in pigs in Orkney.[7]

Water was taken in 1540 to the church in Ayr in a pig.[8] and the St Andrews Testaments for 1586 specifically mentioned 'ane watter pig'.[9] In nineteenth-century Shetland, a 'pig' would be used to carry drink to the hill for refreshment.[10]

Pigs were commonly used as containers for oil of various kinds. An 'wle pege' was specified in 1534-35, in connection with the painting of a decorative or heraldic lion,[11] and the Edinburgh hammermen had 'ane pig to put vlye in', in 1547.[12] One of the items in an Edinburgh testament was already an element of good cuisine: 'a pig with oley of sweit almondis vj unces price vj s'.[13] At 1/- an ounce, this was by no means cheap, but almonds were clearly liked in various forms, for one of the earliest Scottish cookery books, dating to 1736, includes recipes for making almond 'Bisket' and 'Squirts' (kinds of meringue), 'Cream', 'Pudding' and 'Tarts'. There were also instructions on how to 'preserve green Almonds', 'confect rough Almonds', and 'make fine blanch'd Almonds'.[14] On the other hand, the possibility cannot be excluded that in the testament reference, it was used, not in cookery, but as an emollient for medicinal purposes.

Olive oil kept in pigs was used in numerous contexts. In 1606, it was used to smooth the working of the clock in Dumfermline: 'to Harie bull for ane pigg oyle de olive to the knock'.[15] Edinburgh mills had 'oyldolie pigs' in 1615, 1632 and 1639,[16] in industrial contexts, and there are also references from farther north, from Brechin in 1625,[17] and Aberdeen in 1661-62.[18]

Other liquids or fluid substances mentioned as being kept in pigs were four ounces of turpentine in 1566,[19] tar *c*.1660,[20] poison in 1590,[21] 'devylische confectionis of sorcerie' in 1597,[22] ointment in 1681,[23] mustard in 1681,[24] 'one pynt honney in a earthen pigg' in 1717, [25] butter in 1818,[26] broth and beef in 1822 [27] and in 1875 an amount of whisky exceeding four gallons.[28] The 'whisky-pig', in fact, was by no means an uncommon phenomenon in Scottish farm-houses.

Pigs were also used for 'conserve', presumably preserved fruit, in 1697 [29] and for home-made table jelly, leading to the term, *jeelie-pig*. A North-East song rounds up a variety of such contents in the words: 'O there's eely pigs, an' jeely pigs, an' pigs for haudin butter.'[30]

In craft workshops, pigs were used to hold glue. 'Three piggs to melt glew in' were recorded in 1552-3,[31] which shows that they could be subjected to heat. In 1595, 'ane new pig with thre feit to put the glew in' was listed in an Edinburgh source.[32] Glue pots or pigs, therefore, were of a special form, with feet that could raise them above a source of heat. These might, of course, have been of metal, but there is no doubt that earthenware could be subjected to heat, for, amongst the 'lame' vessels listed in one Edinburgh household in 1641 were frying pigs,[33] so called at a time when the term frying pan, for a metal equivalent, was perfectly well known and had been long in use.

There is some evidence for dry contents, like a pig full of sheep bones found in a midden in 1636, [34] but it seems safe to assume that the great bulk of pigs, money-boxes apart, were used for liquid or semi-liquid contents.

Descriptions that can be used for purposes of interpretation are rare. The 'iij Flandrez piggis' mentioned in 1504 were no doubt imports,[35] but the bulk of those used were almost certainly made nearer home. Some were painted,[36] eight painted pigs being valued at 5/- each in Edinburgh in 1592.[37] It may be assumed that these were unglazed, since painting and glazing scarcely go together, and therefore more suitable for containing dry materials (if they were not, simply, ornamental).

Sizes could vary. As noted above, a pig held 4oz. of turpentine in 1566, though it may not have been full. Apothecaries used pigs for ointments and the like [38] and these were presumably of no great size. Two 'thre pund peegis' were estimated at 8/- for both in Edinburgh in 1653;[39] this value, 4/- each, can be compared with 24 earthenware pigs valued at 7/- in 1583, i.e. 3½d. each,[40] and likely to have been much smaller. The whisky pig holding about three gallons is the largest noted in the sources examined.

Pottery was made in quantity where suitable clay was available. In such cases, the professional potter might be called a 'pigmakar'. One called Moffat worked at Throsk in Stirlingshire in 1521.[41] The term survived in west Scots till the mid-eighteenth century.[42] Another name was 'pigger', as applied to 'Pollock James pigger in Throsk' in 1622. [43] In 1678, Dame Erskine's Account Book records 'Rec from James buchan piger, 12lb',[44] and a 'pigman' was mentioned in 1681.[45] The last-mentioned reference speaks of 'a pig-man's weed', indicating a special form of dress, perhaps a stout apron.

The place of work had various names. In the Gallowgate in Glasgow, there was a 'pig-house' for 'working of earthen pigs, pots and other earthen vessels', in the early eighteenth century. This was in the Blackfaulds district around the area of the Buttes. The Town Council records for 1722 relate that William Maxwell leased a plot of land in that year to make 'earthen pigs, potts, and other earthen vessels for the service of all the inhabitants'.[46] A pottery could also be a *piggery* [47] or a *pig-work*, as used in eighteenth-century Lanarkshire at a site where there was also a tile-works.[48]

The distribution of pigs, especially those of a fairly coarse, everyday character, was done very much through travelling folk. The nineteenth- and twentieth-century 'pig-an'-ragger' was a hawker who gave crockery in exchange for rags in Angus and the North-East,[49] carrying his wares in a heavy basket.[50] Itinerant crockery-dealers were 'pig-folk' in early nineteenth-century Ayrshire and elsewhere.[51]

'Pig-men' could be itinerant or might have shops. There was an 'Alexander Carr Piggman in Dunkeld' in 1808,[52] and a book of literary sketches from Fife spoke of a pigman's shop in 1926.[53] The term is fairly widely distributed in east Central and south Scotland. The *pig-merchant* was also an itinerant dealer.[54] Women played a role also, in the form of the *pig-wife* or *pig-woman*.[55] The late Lady Maitland noted in some reminiscences that 'the "pig wife" came round quite often. She had a flat cart and a pony. The cart was full of china, known as pig. The stone hot bottles for beds are pigs. She exchanged her bits of china for rabbit skins, feathers and rags'.[56] According to one source, 'Pigg-wives' were 'females who trudge the country with *trackpot ware, bowls, plates etc.*; they are only one remove from common beggars, and mostly more disliked'.[57] In Edinburgh, 'Robert Scott pigseller' presumably had a shop or booth in 1620.[58]

Some carried the goods in baskets, and some in carts. The *pig-ass* was the donkey that pulled the crockery-merchant's cart in a Banffshire source.[59] The *pig-cart* was known in West-mid Scots, and an unlocalised reference shows that the vendor rang a bell to let customers know when his cart was coming.[60]

Selling could be from door to door, in the case of those who exchanged crockery for rags, on specific stances on a street pavement, or in stalls or booths. A poem of 1821 told how:

> Already has the pig-wife's early care
> Marked out a station for her crockery ware [61]

and an Angus newspaper spoke of a 'pig-wife sittin on a stule an' a' 'er crockery spread out afore 'er on the street'. [62] The *pig-shop* or *pig-chop* was a stall or shop for cheap crockery, [63] the term being localised in Angus and Perthshire in the nineteenth century.

Mugs

The name *mug* goes back to 1400 in Middle English, and though itself of uncertain etymology, there are parallels in the Scandinavian languages, East Frisian, Low German and Dutch. The sense of an earthenware vessel or jar is a Scots usage, also found in the northern English dialects. It therefore closely parallels 'pig'.

Mugs are sometimes mentioned alongside pigs, which suggests that there were differences, though some of the functions overlapped. A 1586 reference speaks of 'certane muggis and piggis estimat to xs'.[64] They were used for carrying water.[65] Butter was commonly kept in them: 'ane mekill butter mug' was mentioned in 1616.[66] 'Mug butter' was commonly available in Lancashire in the second half of the nineteenth century.[67] Some, or even much, of this may have come from Ireland:

> For a number of years prior to the seventies a large quantity of Irish butter in red mugs was imported to England, but about 1875 was discontinued as the mugs got broken and claims were so frequently made against the various railway companies that they refused to carry it. It was much cooler and sweeter than in any other form.[68]

A mug costing 8d. was used for melting half a pound of glue in 1628.[69] A list of tolls in Glasgow in 1725 included:

> Every Carrdraught of Butter in Muggs, or Kits . . .0.2.0.
> Every Mugg of Honey, by Bridge or Water . . .0.0.8.[70]

In 1784, John Urquhart, merchant in Kirkwall in Orkney, placed an order for pottery with Watson's of Prestonpans, near Edinburgh, prominent in pottery-making. It is quoted here in full since it makes clear how sea-transport was organised, and also shows the company that mugs kept:

> In May last I had 3 Crates of your Stone Ware for which I paid your Clerk, and gave Content. I want some more of it by Note annexed, which I would be obliged to you if you'd send to care of Mr Thomas Gladstones, Leith, to be sent here by an Orkney Vessel, the William, Hugh Sclater Mar(iner) now on her passage, and if you send a Crate of earthen ware from G. Gordon, it will be obliging. I have advised my friend Mr David Balfour, James' Square, Edinr. to pay you the Contents of your Accot. on demand. Hoping you'll excuse this trouble, I am &c.
> The Brown Ware to be Pottingers, Mugs, and large Bowls
> 8 doz. deep, 8 doz. Shallow Supper Plates
> 12. 9 inch Oval dishes
> 4 doz. Butter flats
> 12. 9 inch Oval Soup do. 6. 12 In. do.
> 6. 16 In. do.
> 6. 10 Inch Covered do.
> 12. 12 do.
> 12. 14 do.
> 2 Sauce Tureens, Spoons & flats
> 2 large Tureens - 4/6
> 2 Smaller do. - 3/6
> 6 large decanters or 2 doz. 3 to the doz. 12 do.
> 6 to the dozen, large of the Kind
> 2 doz. Bowls 6 to the dozen
> 1 doz. Basons 4 to do.
> 10 or 12 of your dozens of egg cups, that can answer for dram glasses
> If there is any room left, make it up with Mugs, Plates or teapots, all of the plainest and best glazed kind.[71]

To judge by the comment at the end, mugs were high in the list of best-selling items.

As with pigs, there were also itinerant hawkers of earthenware mugs and similar vessels. These were called *muggers*, a word that has established itself in standard English in less savoury contexts, deriving from the bad reputation of such sellers, who were frequently associated with gipsies, for example in East Lothian and Roxburgh.[72] They assembled at fairs, and it is said that in the seventeenth century, at an annual fair held on 8-13 August at Netherwitton in Berwickshire, the squire had to entertain all the *muggers*.[73] They also came in numbers to St Boswell's Fair in Roxburghshire, with their tents,[74] though the men's main ploy there was not the selling of mugs, but dealing in horses. Originally the sense of the word did apply to the selling of earthenware items. According to a source of 1817, 'their common appellation is Muggers, or what pleases them better, Potters. They purchase, at a cheap rate, the cast or faulty articles at the different manufactories of earthen ware, which they carry for sale all over the country'.[75]

There was a 'Michell the Mogger' in Heddon-on-the-Wall in the North of England before 1743.[76] According to Sir Walter Scott in 1816, a white cooper's wares were being rejected in favour of the earthenware goods of muggers.[77] In 1884, Alnwick, also in the North of England, was a great resort of muggers or tramps who travelled around selling earthenware, as also was Whittingham in Northumberland about the same period.[78] Gradually, however, the sense of the word became increasingly pejorative and less associated with the selling of crockery. By the twentieth century an untidy house in Edinburgh could be described as a 'mugger's den'.[79] Association with tinkers is also perpetuated in the Roxburgh expression, 'a mugger's cup', for a cup of tea made by pouring boiling water on the tea-leaves in the way that tinkers do.[80]

At these levels of distribution, the items in question were of earthenware, but higher up the social scale, mugs of silver were to be found already in the late seventeenth century in England. There is a London reference of 1688 to 'A Mug, . . . a set of Casters, and an Orange-Strainer, all of Silver',[81] and there was a common custom of giving a silver mug as a christening present to a child. Some were also made in fine porcelain, at least from around the mid-eighteenth century,[82] porcelain being an excellent material for imitating the fine quality of silver.

The finer examples had some repute as gifts; those of coarser stuff were widely used, as in inns and taverns, where a measured type was needed for disbursing ale. Thomas Kennedy, Chirurgeon in Wigtown, had a 'quart mug' in 1750.[83] They are said to have been brought to great perfection between about 1760 and 1810, at a period when wine glasses and glass tumblers were not plentiful.[84] Several fine Scottish examples are known. Those that have been preserved survive because of fine decorations and interesting inscriptions as much as because of good style of manufacture, since the straight-sided form allowed for little variation, apart from being made taller or squatter. Many must have served as ornaments rather than objects of daily use. The masses of those in the latter category have simply vanished. A range of survivors, dating from *c*.1790 to the 1830s, and made by Scottish potteries in or near Edinburgh, Glasgow and Kirkcaldy in Fife, is illustrated in a recent volume on Scottish east coast potteries.[85] The tradition of inscribed and commemorative earthenware mugs continues, as gifts and for everyday use, as strongly at the present day as it has ever done.

What do the Names mean?

The notes above are based on analysis of a scatter of sources, many of them picked up from four major dictionaries: the *Oxford English Dictionary* (OED), the *Dictionary of the Older Scottish Tongue* (DOST), the *Scottish National Dictionary* (SND), and the *English Dialect Dictionary* (EDD). They constitute the beginnings of an attempt to assess the linguistic evidence. It is not enough to look at two terms; a number of others must also be examined in the future, such as 'greybeard', 'pitcher', 'stoup', 'wallie', 'delf' and others. Comparable containers of metal, wood and other materials, with a further range of names, must be studied also. As the essay by Hugh Cheape in this present volume shows, earthenware containers can have different names even when they appear to perform similar functions: the everted-rim 'croggans' of Highland Scotland are hardly likely to be all that different from the pigs of the Lowlands, especially those that contained oil and other liquids for which tie-on covers would have been desirable. In this context it is worth noting that the alleged derivation of pig from Gaelic *pigean* is erroneous.[86] It is true that Gaelic has *pige*, *pigeadh*, an earthenware jar, pitcher or pot, of which *pigean* is a diminutive form,[87] but these terms are, in fact, relatively rare in Gaelic and represent a somewhat weak penetration of the term from Scots into Gaelic.

What is also needed is a study of the shapes and forms of late medieval or early modern pottery, such as are represented by surface finds and recent excavations at sites like Throsk in Stirlingshire,[88] where, as we have seen, piggers were at work in the late sixteenth and seventeenth centuries.

Once these exercises have been developed, and once sources with specific senses for 'pig' and 'mug' (and other terms) have been isolated, if possible, from those with a more generalised sense of an item of earthenware, it will become possible to tie words and things more closely together.

Footnote: this study grew out of a visit to Throsk with my colleague Dr David Caldwell. My interest was roused in trying to clarify the linguistic background to the products of this site, as well as of others, as a means of getting closer to knowing what the generality of Scots held foods and liquids in, and what they drank from, on ordinary days, before the wide distribution of commercially produced containers began.

I am indebted to Miss Dorothy Slee for checking references.

NOTES

1. *Alphabet of Tales* (Early English Text Society 1904-5), 340.

2. *Accounts of the Lord High Treasurer of Scotland*, Edinburgh 1877, I, 79.

3. D.H. Edwards, *One Hundred Modern Scottish Poets* (c.1850), Brechin 1881, II, 45.

4. *Wills and Inventories, illustrative of the history, Manners, language etc., of the northern countries of England* (Surtees Society 1835), II, 312.

5. Sir W. Fraser, *Memoirs of the Maxwells of Pollok*, 2V., Edinburgh 1863, 409.

6. W. Cramond, ed., *The Records of Elgin, 1234-1800*, 2V. (New Spalding Club), Aberdeen 1903, I, 111.

7. *Old-Lore Miscellany of Orkney, Shetland, etc.* IV, I (1911), 22.

8. *Ayr Common Good Accounts, 1535-1603*, MS, quoted in DOST s.v. *Pig*.

9. *St Andrews Testaments, 1549-*, MS, II (1586), 68, quoted in DOST s.v. *Pig*.

10. *Shetland News* (13 May 1899), quoted in EDD s.v. *Pig*.

11. H.M. Paton *et al*, eds, *Master of Works Accounts, 1529-1679*, 2V., Edinburgh 1957, I, 128.

12. *Edinburgh Hammermen, 1494-*, MS, quoted in DOST s.v. *Pig*.

13. *Edinburgh Testaments, 1514-32, 1567-1700*, MS, III, 318, quoted in DOST s.v. *Pig*.

14. *Mrs McLintock's Receipts for Cookery and Pastry-Work* (Introduction by I. Macleod, reproduced from the first edition of 1736), Aberdeen 1986, 3, 4, 14, 19, 21, 28, 37-8, 38-9.

15. A. Shearer, ed., *Extracts from the Burgh Records of Dunfermline. In the 16th and 17th Centuries* (Dunfermline Carnegie Trust), Dunfermline 1951, II, 23.

16. *Edinburgh Testaments, 1514-32, 1567-1700*, MS, XLVIII, 271; LVI, 25; LIX, 212, quoted in DOST s.v. *Pig*.

17. *Brechin Testaments, 1575-1709*, MS, IV, 198b, quoted in DOST s.v. *Pig*.

18. L.B. Taylor, ed., *Aberdeen Shore Work Accounts 1596-1670*, Aberdeen 1972, 480.

19. *Accounts of the Lord High Treasurer of Scotland*, MS, XII (1566), 404, quoted in DOST s.v. *Pig*.

20. *Select Biographies*, I, Edinburgh 1845-47, 340.

21. R. Pitcairn, *Criminal Trials in Scotland, from A.D. 1488 to A.D. 1624*, 3V. (Bannatyne Club), Edinburgh 1833, I, II, 195.

22. *Miscellany of the Spalding Club*, 5V. (Spalding Club), Aberdeen 1841-52, I, 141.

23. S. Colvil, *Mock Poem, or Whiggs Supplication*, London 1681 (reprint, Glasgow 1751), 90.

24. *Account-book of coal and salt works at Fawside, East Lothian, 1677-85*, MS 70 quoted in DOST s.v. *Pig*.

25. H. Marwick, *Merchant Lairds of Long Ago*, 2V. Kirkwall 1936, I, 68.
26. S.E. Ferrier, *Marriage*, 3V., Edinburgh 1818, II, iii.
27. J. Galt, *The Provost*, Edinburgh 1822, xxxviii.
28. A. Hislop, *The Book of Scottish Anecdote*, Glasgow 1874 (1876), 275.
29. A.W.C. Hallen, ed., *The Account Book of Sir John Foulis of Ravelston, 1671-1707* (Scottish History Society), Edinburgh 1894, 212.
30. G. Greig, *Folk-Song of the North-East*, 2V., Peterhead 1909-12, cxxxvi, 1.
31. *Extracts from the Records of the Burgh of Edinburgh, 1403-1589*, 4V. (Burgh Record Society), Edinburgh 1869-82, II, 340.
32. *Edinburgh Dean of Guild Accounts*, MS, 622, quoted in DOST s.v. *Pig*.
33. *Edinburgh Testaments* MS, LIX (1641), 269, quoted in DOST s.v. *Pig*.
34. *Monteith Stewartry Court*, 19 Jan. 1636, quoted in DOST s.v. *Pig*.
35. *Accounts of the Lord High Treasurer of Scotland, 1473-1566*, Edinburgh 1877-, II, 439.
36. G. Douglas, *Virgil's Aeneid translated into Scottish Verse* (1513) (Scottish Text Society), Edinburgh 1957-64, VII, xiii, 25.
37. *Edinburgh Testaments* MS, XXV (1592), 26, quoted in DOST s.v. *Pig*.
38. M.P. Brown, *Supplement to the Dictionary of the Decisions of the Court of Session*, 5V., Edinburgh 1826, III, 182 (1677); R. Law, *Memorialls, or, The Memorable Things that fell out . . . from 1638 to 1684.* (ed. C.K. Sharpe), Edinburgh 1818, 232 (1684).
39. *Edinburgh Testaments* MS, LXVII (1653), 9b, quoted in DOST s.v. *Pig*.
40. *Ibid.*, XII (1583), 92.
41. *Extracts from the Records of the Royal Burgh of Stirling, 1519-1752*, 2V., Glasgow 1887-9, I, 10; R. Wodrow, *History of the Sufferings of the Church of Scotland from the Restoration to the Revolution*, 4V., Glasgow 1829-30, IV, 13.
42. A. McDonald, *A Galick Vocabulary*, Edinburgh 1741, 53.
43. *Stirling Commissariat Records*, MS, 1662, quoted in DOST s.v. *Pig(g)er*.
44. H. Andrews, Dame Erskine's Account-Book. In *Northern Notes and Queries, or The Scottish Antiquary* IX (1895), 107.
45. Colvil, *op.cit.*, II (1751), 24.
46. *Session Papers, Magistrates v. University of Glasgow* (10 Jan. 1722), 2; see also G. Quail, The Story of David Ramsay, Potter. In *Scottish Pottery Society, Archivist's Newsletter*, No. 3 (1978), 3-4.
47. J. Jamieson, *An Etymological Dictionary of the Scottish Language*, Edinburgh 1825, s.v.
48. *Caledonian Mercury* (26 July 1766), 353.
49. *Northern Notes and Queries, or The Scottish Antiquary* IX (1895), 187.
50. *Buchan Observer* (11 Oct. 1955).
51. A. Crawford, *Tales of My Grandmother*, 2V., Edinburgh, 1824, I, 277; J. Jamieson, *Etymological Dictionary MSS*, X (a.1838), 237.
52. Atholl MSS, 1808, quoted in SND s.v. *Pig*.
53. I. Farquhar, *Pickletillie Folk*, Edinburgh 1926, 156.
54. *Aberdeen Journal Notes & Queries* I (1908), 32.

55. Edinias (D. Tough), *Ramble of John Jorum and his Friends to Roslin,* Edinburgh 1813, 10.
56. *Reminiscences* by Lady Maitland, Reswallie, Angus, in Glamis Museum (copy, MS 1977/2 in Scottish Ethnological Archive, National Museums of Scotland).
57. J. Mactaggart, *The Scottish Gallovidian Encyclopedia* (1824), London, Glasgow 1876, s.v. *Piggs.*
58. *Index, Edinburgh Testaments,* MS, II (1620), 362, quoted in DOST s.v. *Pig.*
59. W. Taylor, *Scots Poems,* Edinburgh 1787, 79.
60. *Westminster Gazette* (25 Oct. 1898).
61. *Blackwood's Magazine* (Jan. 1821), 423.
62. *Brechin Advertiser* (20 May 1884), 3.
63. J. Jamieson, *An Etymological Dictionary of the Scottish Language,* Edinburgh 1880, s.v.
64. *Edinburgh Testaments,* MS, XV (1586), 100, quoted in DOST s.v. *Mug.*
65. H. Paton, ed., *Dundonald Parish Records. The Session Book of Dundonald, 1602-1731,* privately published for the 4th Marquis of Bute, 1936, 55.
66. *Edinburgh Testaments,* MS, XLIX (1616), 99, quoted in DOST s.v. *Mug.*
67. J.A. Ferguson, *Wot Aw seed ut th' Preston Eggsibishun,* Preston 1865, vi.
68. Quoted in EDD s.v. *Mug.*
69. *Master of Works Accounts, 1529-1679,* MS, XXII (1628), 4, quoted in DOST s.v. *Mug.*
70. *Table of Dues of the Bridge, etc., of Glasgow* (1 June 1725), quoted in SND s.v. *Mug.*
71. *Scottish Pottery Society, Archivist's Newsletter,* No. 1 (1976), 3.
72. Cf. J. Miller, *The Lamp of Lothian* (1844), Haddington 1900, 220; R. Davidson, *Leaves from a Peasant's Cottage Drawer,* Edinburgh 1848, 215.
73. *History of the Berwickshire Naturalists' Club 1892-1893* (1894), 241.
74. *Kelso Chronicle* (23 July 1920), 2.
75. *Edinburgh Magazine* (May 1817), 157.
76. *Heddon-on-the-Wall Parish Registers,* 1743, quoted in OED s.v. *Mugger.*
77. Sir W. Scott, *Old Mortality,* Edinburgh 1816, Introduction; cf. also *Blackwood's Magazine* (May 1817), 157.
78. *Manchester Examiner* (1 Sept. 1884), 5]1, quoted in OED s.v. *Mugger;* D.D. Dixon, *The Vale of Whingham, Northumberland,* Newcastle 1895, 184.
79. *Edinburgh Evening News* (12 Feb. 1958), quoted in SND s.v. *Mugger.*
80. Noted for 1963; quoted in SND s.v. *Mugger.*
81. *London Gazette* 1688, No. 2316)4, quoted in OED s.v. *Mug.*
82. H. Walpole, *Anecdotes of Painting in England, with some account of the principal artists; collected by G. Vertue 1762-71,* London 1786, V, 94.
83. Wigtown Commissariat Records, 1750.
84. Cf. J.A. Fleming, *Scottish Pottery,* Glasgow 1923 (reprinted 1973), 26.
85. P. McVeigh, *Scottish East Coast Potteries 1750-1840,* Edinburgh 1979, 115, 119, 120, 122, 132, 139, 163, 165, 189.

86. Cf. J.A. Fleming, *Scottish Pottery*, *op.cit.*, 21.

87. Cf. E. Dwelly, *The Illustrated Gaelic-English Dictionary*, Glasgow 1901-11, s.v.

88. For preliminary reports, see D.H. Caldwell and V.E. Dean, The post-Medieval Pottery Industry at Throsk, Stirlingshire. In *Scottish Pottery Historical Review* VI (1981), 21-27; Post-Medieval Pots and Potters at Throsk in Stirlingshire. In *Review of Scottish Culture*, 2 (1986), 105-112.

BREAD AND BREAD BOWLS

Eszter Kisbán

Bread bowls are containers of wood or of basketry used in the process of bread baking, mainly to hold individual pieces of dough for loaves to allow them to rise before the pieces are put into the oven. Their use generally marks a system of baking several big loaves at the same time, but the baking of numerous loaves on one occasion need not indicate that bread bowls are in use. Dough-raising bowls were used in home baking in a core area stretching from the Pyrenees to the Urals. They were not found in the Mediterranean or in northern Europe. They are still used by bakers, as well as in homes. In an eighteenth-century volume on French baking, wooden dough-raising bowls for smaller and bigger loaves were referred to as being used in the bakehouses.[1] At the present time in Hungary, loaves of over half a kilo in weight are all raised in bowls.

In the technology of baking, bowls are spoken of as facilitating the tipping out of the dough onto the peel, before placing it into the oven. At the same time, the bowls safeguard the light, loose quality of the dough, because in the final phase of preparation, the risen dough, if it is in a bowl, will not be handled any more. This allows the carbon dioxide generated during the raising process to stay in the dough.

The Hungarian practice can be followed to examine the use of bread bowls and see how far back in time they can be traced.

Home baking in the countryside came to an end in the 1950s-60s, and several urban households baked bread at home up till about 1920. Thus regional practices of recent centuries are quite well-known. The bread-baking oven, in which six to eight loaves were baked according to the size of the family, was an organic part of the dwelling-house. Bread was usually baked fortnightly, or at weekly or three-weekly intervals if required. The oven was always packed with loaves weighing 5 to 6kg each. According to the regional crops, bread was of wheat, rye or a mixture of the two. Solid, compressed yeast, a novelty of the mid-nineteenth century, never played an important role in home baking. In the rye-growing areas, the traditional raising agent was sour dough, dried and put aside from one baking to the next. In wheat-growing areas a home-made leaven was prepared in advance to serve for the whole year. This was bran-based, and mixed either with sour dough and the flowers of hops, or with must (grape-juice) before being dried. The bread-baking process, which took fifteen to sixteen hours, was timed so that the loaves could be taken out of the oven when the church bells rang at 7 o'clock in the morning. To achieve this, the leaven was soaked around 3 or 4 o'clock on the previous afternoon, the flour was sifted in the evening, the raising agent was added about 8 or 9 p.m., and then the housewife went to bed. She kneaded the dough at about 2 or 3 a.m. The loaves were put into the oven at 5 o'clock and the baking itself took two hours (Fig. 1).

1. Wheaten bread, Turkeve, Szolnok County, Hungary 1960 (Lajos Györffy).

The necessary ingredients were not formally weighed. The raising bowl was itself used as a measure, the fill of which made one loaf. The raising agent and salt were measured by the palms of the hands (Fig. 2). The flour was sifted into the long wooden trough, which was supported on legs. The preparation of dough was carried out in two stages. In the baking industry this was called 'indirect' preparation of dough. It ensured more perfect fermentation when large quantities were being handled. First, the raising agent was added to only a part of the flour, at most a third, and this was allowed to ferment, so that this dough would then act as a fermenting agent for the rest of the flour. After the fermenting mixture had been stirred, the housewife went to bed, leaving fermentation to take place for five to six hours. After that the remaining flour was kneaded together by hand with water, salt, and the already fermented dough. Kneading took 30 to 45 minutes for a mixture based on 25-30kg. of flour. After that the dough was left to ferment and ripen further in the trough for an hour to an hour and a half, whilst the oven was being fired. Finally the pieces of dough for the individual loaves were torn from the whole kneaded mass and rounded into shape by hand. The rounding was done on the emptied part of the trough, or on a table or plank. The lumps of dough were placed in cloths in the raising bowls and left to rise for 15 to 30 minutes. After that they were tipped straight onto the peel and put into the oven. The standard, average diameter of the baked loaves was 35-40cm. In the areas producing the best-quality wheat, wheaten loaves were 20-30cm. high, while if made of poorer quality wheat, or of rye, or of mixed wheat and rye, they were 10-12cm. high. An English natural scientist, Robert Townson, who travelled in the Great Plain in 1793, did not exaggerate when he spoke about the size of the loaves in the town of Debrecen:

> Lighter, whiter, and better flavoured bread than that made here I never ate; nor did I ever see elsewhere such large loaves. Were I not afraid of being accused of taking advantage of the privilege of travellers, I should say they were near half a yard cubed.[2]

The fresh bread was never cut before it had been allowed to cool. Every so often, however, the household stock of bread was completely used up by the time for baking. Therefore, along with the big loaves, a smaller one of 2-3kg. was also baked, because it cooled more quickly and could be cut sooner. Often there was a small dough-raising bowl for this small loaf.

In two small, widely-separated regions of present-day Hungary, Szigetköz and part of the Borsod-Abauj-Zemplén county, raising bowls made of wood were used into the twentieth century. Both areas were fairly archaic in their material culture. The bowl for big loaves was semi-cylindrical, with two handgrips, fairly deep. The one for the smaller loaf was less deep (Fig. 3). Everywhere else baskets of rye straw, rushes or reeds were used (Fig. 2). They had no handles. The height of the raising bowls was 20-25cm.[3]

In Middle Europe, such bowls were already described in South German households by W.H. von Hohberg in *Georgica curiosa aucta*, 1679. He said that lumps of dough were torn from the main mass of kneaded dough and 'put in raising bowls made of straw or wood, where they were left to rise a little' before being put into the oven. The two variants of raising bowl were known there, therefore, by that date. He illustrated small, shallow bowls along with baked loaves of about 20cm. in diameter. These took about an hour to bake.[4]

2. Bread bowl of straw, Kiskunmajsa, Bács-Kiskun County, Hungary (József Vorák, 1961).

3. Wooden raising bowl for normal-sized loaves (right) and for the smaller one (left), Ricse, Borsod-Abauj-Zemplén County, Hungary (Eszter Kisbán, 1963).

4. Wooden bowl for shaping loaves and four bread bowls of straw, Eisenberg/St. Martin a.d. Raab, Burgenland, Austria (Eszter Kisbán, 1979).

In Hungary, historical data go back to the sixteenth century. In 1585, in a dictionary by Calepinus, the wooden raising bowl first appeared ('artopta: szakasztó tekenö'). Another dictionary, the first edition of Albert Molnár, mentioned it in 1604. It appeared again in an inventory of 1635 from the city of Kassa (in the county of Abaúj, in present-day Slovakia): an urban household had two large troughs and twelve wooden bread bowls, i.e. probably two full baking kits.[5] This is the same region in which wooden raising bowls were in use until the 1960s.

A certain 'szakasztó cserény', documented in 1577 (*Oklevél Szótár*, dictionary of documents), definitely belongs to the category of bread-baking equipment, and the second element points to a basketry form. It can probably be interpreted as a dough-raising basket. Other references of early date are ambiguous because the attributive first element is used for the whole, and we cannot tell if a raising bowl of straw or of wood is in question. The first element, 'szakasztó' or 'szakajtó', refers to the 'tearing' of the pieces of dough for loaves from the whole mass. Definite evidence for the use of reeds in raising bowls comes from a dictionary of 1708 by Ferenc Páriz Pápai, in his definition of a 'kenyérszakasztó kosár' (bread-tearing basket). All of this evidence relates to domestic practices, and not to bakeries.

Leavened bread was not part of the diet of the Hungarians who settled in the Carpathian basin in 896AD. At this period, the word 'kenyér', which later indicates leavened bread, probably referred to a flat, unleavened bread. Leavened bread certainly became known in the eleventh century, but remained as a higher-class luxury item for a time. From medieval times, bakery items were included amongst payments in kind made by the common people to their superiors. It is often stated in twelfth-thirteenth century Latin records that small villages with only a few inhabitants had to pay very large numbers of bakery items, 'panis'. The obligation to pay in such large numbers was last recorded in the fourteenth century. At the same time, rarely in the thirteenth but frequently in the fourteenth century, the records mention payment by families of one, or two, pieces of 'panis'. This obligation continued unchanged into the fifteenth and sixteenth centuries, when it becomes clear from other circumstances that leavened bread was in question. There is a strong probability that the payments in large numbers were of flat, unleavened bread, whilst those in small numbers were of leavened bread. Sometimes in the fourteenth century and with increasing frequency in the fifteenth, there are references to one, or two, 'torta' or 'panis circulus' in the same tax payments. The use of the vernacular alongside the Latin name tells us beyond doubt that these were festival breads made of finer ingredients, in the shape of a round loaf, or of a twisted ring. This evidence indicates that common people had also begun to eat leavened bread, mainly in the course of the fourteenth century. In the sixteenth century the Hungarian legal expression, 'minden külön kenyeres' (every (family) with common bread) appeared. This referred to taxation of a single family unit, sharing the same bread. At this time bread was also playing an important role in provisioning the army. It was still regarded as such a precious commodity that the stealing of bread was recorded. In 1578 a magic practice by the common people is recorded in print: in order to ensure that the shape of the loaf should be round and high, it was advisable, when selecting a flour sieve for purchase, to look at it always from the outer side first.

When ordinary households began to bake bread, it is unlikely that the loaves were as large as in modern times. Not only was there a lack of experience in working with so much dough, but even in higher-level households only small loaves were baked. In the larger of such establishments where, in addition to the family, numerous noble and common officials and workers were fed, not even in the sixteenth and seventeenth centuries were large loaves baked, but small loaves of about a pound in weight. People were given a daily ration of whole loaves, in most cases two loaves. In most households two qualities were baked, finer for the gentlefolk and coarser for the workers. Students living in colleges got their daily portion each morning in the form of whole small loaves at that time. This practice continued in Transylvania up to the twentieth century. None of these small loaves was made with the help of a raising bowl.

The question of when big loaves appeared in Middle Europe has not been raised or systematically examined. However, in an early non-Hungarian sixteenth-century illustration of a monastic bakery, we can see big loaves being put into the oven.[6] Since Hungarian sources are poor, we can only say that the preparation of large quantities of flour following the two-stage fermentation system is recorded from 1470. The fireplaces of dwelling houses reveal, in connection with a fifteenth-century innovation, that in common homes then, not only was bread-baking regularly done, but large loaves were also being baked. At the period, in a central-Hungarian area, a smokeless living-room was added alongside the kitchen. An oven tiled with small pots was inserted into the living room. It was fired from the kitchen and served to warm the living-room in winter. This was the new fireplace of the house. In the kitchen, there remained for cooking the hearth with an open fire, and there stood there also a big clay oven which could only have served for bread-baking. A tiled oven cannot stand too hot firing, and was therefore suitable only for smaller items of baking. They would not last long if regularly used for bread-baking sessions of two hours at a stretch. These circumstances are in line with the fact that from the sixteenth century, dough-raising bowls are also recorded. This means that by the latest at the beginning of the early modern period, the system of baking large loaves two weeks beforehand was already fixed in the households.

Near Hungary, in Austria, a different use of bread bowls can be observed (Fig. 4). An individual household would have one wooden bowl and as many baskets as were required for the number of loaves to be baked. The bowl was used for shaping the individual loaves. Anni Gamerith [7] makes brief reference to this practice in her commentary on the map on bread in the Austrian Ethnological Atlas. The questionnaire only asked whether peasant households baked or bought their bread at the beginning of the twentieth century, but did not specify the use of bread bowls. Nevertheless Gamerith gives a short general description of bread-baking in Austria, pointing out that there are small regional differences in procedures and equipment used, which are not yet fully surveyed. Thereafter she describes the 'indirect' preparation of dough with the two-stage fermentation of flour, after which the dough for the individual loaves is torn off the main mass. These portions were again kneaded and placed in the wooden bowl. They were given a round shape by circular movements of the bowl that made the dough rotate, and at the same time by being tossed up. Then the shaped dough for each loaf was placed in a cloth-lined dough basket to rise. They were transferred from these straight onto the peel. Gamerith describes the bowl as a shallow two-handled wooden dish, and the baskets also as shallow dishes, mostly made of rye-straw or rarely of wicker or rushes. It could also happen, though infrequently, that the bowls for both purposes were of wood.

It seems that this practice refers primarily to Eastern Austria. In Tirol on the West, not rounded but disc-shaped loaves were shaped by hand and left to rise on a plank, without using a bowl. The ideal form of bread there was like a flat, cylindrical cheese. In Lower Austria and in Burgenland I came across the system of having in a household a wooden bowl for shaping the dough (including tossing up) and as many baskets as were needed for the separate loaves. Steiermark is the region best known to Gamerith, so the custom is likely to be general there. In contrast to the deep Hungarian bowls, the Austrian examples are shallow and flat, and the loaves smaller. The sharp division between the two forms of treatment of the dough at the language boundary is surprising. Burgenland, which is mainly German-speaking, borders on Hungary, and was even part of Hungary until 1920. In that area, the quite spectacular way of shaping the dough in a wooden bowl was an old practice, while on the Hungarian side bowls were only used for raising the dough, as elsewhere in Hungary. In West Hungary, the rye bread itself did not differ from that of Burgenland, and the differences in practice cannot readily be explained through the nature of the bread.

750km. east of the Austrian border, in Transylvania in Rumania, east of the city of Brasov, we again find in the Hungarian villages of the Hétfalu ('Seven Villages') area at the foot of the Carpathians the same specific use of wooden bread bowls. From the main mass of dough matured in a trough, the individual loaves were torn off, rounded by hand, then put into small wooden bowls and tossed up twice, falling into the bowl each time. There was a dialect word for this procedure: 'megvirkelik'. The dough was tipped out onto the peel and put into the oven at once, without leaving time for raising. Here, bread was made of a mixture of barley and rye about 1900, whilst in neighbouring parts of the Carpathians it was made of rye or if necessary of barley alone. Not only does barley not produce light bread, but the fermented dough can crumble during baking and the loaves can even fall apart. For this reason, people tried to knead barley-bread dough very well in such regions. However, this idea could scarcely have played a role in the Hétfalu area, where the custom had developed of tossing the rye-barley dough mixture in bowls.[8]

As a matter of fact, we again meet the process of shaping pieces of dough for loaves in wooden bowls farther to the east, in Eastern Europe. D. Zelenin, in his *Handbook of Eastern Slavonic Folklife*, says that in White Russia, the torn-off pieces of dough were rounded by hand, laid on the peel, and put straight into the oven without a rising period. 'Amongst the others (i.e. the Ukrainians and Russians), the dough was usually first placed in an oval bowl made of tree roots. The bread was rolled in this, and at the same time was tossed up and caught in the bowl again. The bread rose in the bowl, and was then tipped onto the peel to be put in the oven.' In the areas in question, the bread was made of wheat in the south and of rye in the north. Zelenin's description suggests that the number of bowls used in each household was equivalent to the number of loaves baked, the bowls being used for both shaping and raising the dough. We have no means of knowing how widespread this practice was in the enormous area being discussed.[9]

Lying between the bread-bowl using areas are others that do not use them. In the Hungarian language area, it appears that in Transylvania as a whole (except for the Hétfalu area which only used the wooden bowl for shaping) it was characteristic that the households did not use bowls of wood or basketry at all, though these were in general use in Hungary, in spite of the fact that Transylvania was part of Hungary until 1920. Dough-raising bowls were in general use up to the edge of the Hungarian Plain. The bread-baking practices in the 600-1800m. high mountain zone, which divides the Hungarian Plain from the Transylvanian Basin, are not known. However, in Hungarian villages known to me in the Basin, the home preparation of bread differed sharply in several points from the West Hungarian practices.

In Transylvania, the bread grain was mainly wheat, with rye in the South-West. In case of need, maize was added to the wheat, and barley to the rye. At the same time, it was the custom to bake five to eight loaves here. The raising agent was sour dough, but this was not kept in dried form from one baking to the next. Instead it was kept in one piece in earthenware pots, and sprinkled with salt to prevent it from being spoiled and growing mouldy. Though salt is good for this purpose, it reduces the fermenting power of the sour dough, and for this reason is avoided at this stage by professional bakers. The preparation of dough in Transylvania was also 'indirect', in two stages. The torn off and hand-rounded lumps of dough for loaves were not, however, left to rise, but put straight onto the peel and into the oven. There were neither wooden nor basketry raising bowls in the homes. The omission of the raising process prevents an open texture in the bread. Finally, the loaves were deliberately baked in such a way that the upper crust burned black. When removed from the oven, the crust was immediately knocked off when the bread was still hot. The loaf was set on its edge, held with the left hand, and the crust beaten off in fragments with a sickle, knife or rod. There is no explanation as yet for why the loaves were baked black and the crusts beaten off; this would have been unthinkable amongst the western Hungarians. The loaves in Transylvania were a bit smaller than in Hungary, with a diameter of 20-25cm. In this case the lack of bread bowls in the Hungarian language area of Transylvania goes together with a whole range of bread-making practices that differ from those in present-day Hungary.[10]

5. Bread bowl of reeds, bought at a Budapest market in 1985 and made in that year in the nearby village of Szigetszentmiklós. It has a cord for hanging it up. In the collections of the National Museums of Scotland. C/3021/11.

At present we do not know where or for what purpose the bread bowls were invented. Their use from the Pyrenees and Southern France through South Germany and the regions of Bohemia, Moravia and Austria as far as Hungary [11] provides a dense enough distribution for us to think of some connection between the practices of the units within this broad area. One possible link could be the working practices of medieval bakers, though we do not as yet know enough about their techniques. From the extensive Eastern European area, we do not at present have enough data about bread baking for us to be able to judge the density and modes of use of bread bowls. Zelenin, in his *Handbook*, depended on an extremely limited number of sources for this topic. My own accumulation of information on the subject has also been sporadic. A bread bowl of straw from the Rjazan district east of Moscow is on show in the National Museum of History in Moscow.[12] Farther to the East below the Ural Mountains, in the region demarcated by the cities of Kazan, Kirov, Perm and Sverdlovsk, the individual pieces of dough were put for raising into a wooden bowl or a container of a kind new in this story. This was of plaited birch bark, like other vessels from the region. [13] Its form, however, was not that of a bowl, but of a bottomless round frame.

NOTES

1. P.J. Malouin, D.G. Schreber *Ausführliche Beschreibung der Müller-, Nudelmacher- und Beckerkunst*. Die Beckerkunst 17-18, 296-297, table VII. (Leipzig 1769).

2. R. Townson, *Travels in Hungary* (London 1797), 242.

3. Hungarian data, if not stated otherwise, from Eszter Kisbán, *A magyar kenyér* (bread in Hungary) (Budapest 1966), Library of the Hungarian Academy of Sciences, Manuscript Collection D 3254.

4. W.H. von Hohberg, *Georgica curiosa aucta. Das ist: Umständlicher Bericht und klarer Unterricht von dem adelichen Land- und Feld-Leben*. Vol. 1. Nürnberg [1679], 294-296.

5. J. Mihalik, *Kassaváros ötvösségének története* (the history of the gold- and silversmiths of the city of Kassa). (Archaeologiai Közlemények 21) (Budapest 1899), 224.

6. In the household book of the monastery of the Mendelsche Zwölfbruderstiftung; from Stadtbibiothek Nürnberg, published in H. Meise, *So backt der Bauer sein Brot* (Bielefeld 1959), Fig. 65.

7. A. Gamerith, Herkunft und Herstellung des bäuerlichen Hausbrotes. In R. Wolfram, ed., *Österreichischer Volkskundeatlas. Kommentar* (2. Lieferung) (Wien 1965), 20.

8. E. Kisbán, A kenyér a táplálkozási strukturában (bread in the food system). In *Népi kultura-népi társadalom*, 4 (1970), 97-125.

9. D. Zelenin, *Russische (Ostslavische) Volkskunde* (Berlin-Leipzig 1927), 111-113.

10. As note 8.

11. F. Krüger, *Die Hochpyrenäen* (Hamburg 1939), Vol. A/2, 295; H. Heimberger: Die Strohkorbflechterei im Bauland. In *Mein Heimat* (Freiburg i.Br.), 26 (1939), 268-273; E. Kost, Strohkörbe als Urgefässe. In Württembergisches Jahrbuch für Volkskunde, 2 (1956), 54-63; Meise 1969 (as note 5); *Das Backen im Dorfbackhaus*. Ed. Hessische Abteilung im Institut für Volkskunde, Universität Frankfurt (Frankfurt a.M. 1955); F. Jilek, *Jihocesky clovek a jeho rec* (the South Bohemian and his vocabulary) (Ceské Budejovice 1961), 99; M. Ludviková, Ludové strava na Brnensku (the food of the people in the Brno area). In *Casopis moravského Musea*, 46 (1961), 95-98; A. Fenton, Bread Baking by the Herold Family, in Dunabogdány, Hungary. In *Petits Propos Culinaires*, 22 (1986), 75-76.

12. GIM 84107/94, K 5592 Novo Paskoe, Mihailovski uezd, Rjazanskaja gub.

13. G.S., Maslova, *Pishcha i hozyaistvenii utvar. Materialnaya kultura russkogo selskogo i zavodskogo naseleniya Priuralya. Materiali i issledovaniya po ethnografii russkogo naseleniya evropeiskoi chasti SSSR (Trudi Instituta Ethnografii NS 57) (Moskva 1960), 143-171.*

THE COLLECTING OF SEAGULLS'
AND LAPWINGS' EGGS

Holger Rasmussen

Gösta Berg has several times drawn attention to the collecting of wild fowls' eggs and their household use, most recently in the Cultural Historical Lexicon for the Nordic Middle Ages. [1] In his first article, as long ago as 1933, [2] he discussed the wide distribution of sea birds' egg collecting, above all in the areas around the Baltic. His point of departure was that domesticated poultry appeared relatively late on the scene as household creatures, at least in the northern parts of the area. 'It must be assumed that before that period, the eggs of wildfowl played a very great role', as he said.

The kind of collecting that took place was from the birds' natural resting places and was often unrestricted. Already in the sixteenth century, Olaus Magnus referred to the 'countless eggs which anyone who sails there can freely lay hands on'. [3] However, there was and remains a specialised form of egg collecting using artificially constructed nests which were set up along the coasts and river banks in the northern parts of Sweden and Finland. This phenomenon, however, was unknown in Denmark and will not be discussed farther here.

In Denmark and its most closely adjacent areas, the collecting of wild fowls' eggs took place wherever natural circumstances allowed (Fig. 1). The practice is undoubtedly as old as in North Scandinavia, but the earliest accounts scarcely go back to the eighteenth century. The *Danske Atlas* (1769) speaks of a little grass-grown island, Fuglholm, in the Limfjord, owned by the manor of Hindsel, which had 'no other inhabitants than birds, the eggs of which were taken once a year by the people of Hindsel. These birds were lapwings, ring-plovers, dunlins, snipes, golden plovers, and reeves besides certain varieties of seagulls and terns'. [4] The priest J.N. Wilse noted of the same island during a journey in 1776 that people went to it annually to take eggs, 'leaving a couple in each nest'. [5]

In his description of the State of Denmark in 1825, the statistician and historian, Fr. Thaarup, gave a general survey of egg collecting. 'Egg collecting on the wild bird islands is important. On List alone, at the northern tip of Sylt, it is reckoned that about 50-70,000 eggs, bigger and smaller, can be collected each year. They stay fresh for only a short time and should, therefore, be used as quickly as possible. They are packed in

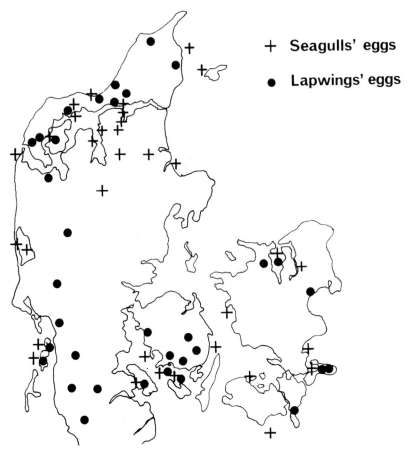

1. Distribution of reference points for the taking of seagulls' and lapwings' eggs.

moss in baskets and sent to the nearest market places. At the Limfjord and several other places, egg collecting is not without importance.'[6]

At that time, the island of Sylt was still part of the State of Denmark, like two other North Frisian islands, about which it was said in 1817: 'the quantities to be found can be judged by the fact that on Sideroog not only do they feed pigs with them, but also most of the poor people on Pellworm live on them throughout the summer, and besides this, great basketfuls are carried to Husum'[7]

These and other scattered references in the topographic literature give indications of the technique, extent, exploitation and importance of egg-collecting. A countrywide survey became possible, however, only after the circulation of a Questionnaire by the Danish Folk Museum in 1959.[8]

The answers to the section on egg collecting provide the basis for the following account. It should be noted that one of the answers indicates almost as great a quantity of eggs collected as in the *Danske Atlas*; it is, however, an exception. The answers concentrate on the eggs of lapwings, gulls and terns, and it is with these that the rest of this essay is concerned. [9]

The nesting grounds of the two bird types differ so much from each other that this has an appreciable influence on the way of collecting. Lapwings' nests are scattered on the meadows above the beach or on arable ground, whilst those of seagulls are packed so closely, nest alongside nest, on small islands, that it is almost impossible to walk amongst them. Great seagull colonies are to be found on the islands in the Kattegat, Øresund and the Great Belt, in the Limfjord and in Ringkøbing fjord. The most numerous and fullest Questionnaire answers come from these areas.

The early arrival of the lapwings in Denmark and their early egg-laying often meant that their nests on the arable land were in danger. Much of the information supplied tells that eggs were taken that would otherwise have been destroyed during field operations. Alongside such casual collection, however, there was also a more systematic form, though it never reached the proportions of seagulls' egg collecting.

Lapwings' eggs have always been regarded as a more exclusive food, because they came early in the year, were relatively scarce, and besides had a pleasant taste in comparison with seagulls' eggs, which many descriptions characterised as not particularly good: 'they have a fishy, oily, muddy taste', as a Drejø informant put it. In a note on lapwings' egg collecting, it was said that if they came upon seagulls' eggs, 'we did not touch them. It was told to us children that they were poisonous'. The informant added that this was due to the strong, fishy flavour.

A report from South Jutland [10] relates that the first lapwings' eggs were collected in the month of March. 'It was said at the time that the Iron Chancellor Bismarck had many lapwings' eggs sent to him to eat. It isn't known if the people who sent them got anything for them.' Such attention to one of the mighty members of society has parallels within the field of hunting, [11] but in general did not have an influence on collecting, which followed the same pattern as that for seagulls' eggs.

The systematic collecting of lapwings' eggs for sale is known, for example, from Als, where three boys from an artisan family in the village of Ulkebøl sold eggs to a merchant in the nearby town of Sønderborg, when they had a big enough number. Similar records refer to Drejø in the middle of the archipelago of Funen, and to Klim in the most northerly part of Jutland. In Klim, eggs were in part used in the household and in part sold to merchants. 'At one time you got a couple of coins for an egg, but from 1914-18 you got 25 coins an egg for the earliest, and later 5 to 6 coins' (an *øre*, about an eighth of a penny). The rise in price was due to the war. There is mention also of the export to England and Holland of lapwings' eggs packed in baskets, but without precise details. The export ceased when the import of collected eggs was forbidden.

In North Jutland it is similarly recorded that the herd boys collected lapwings' eggs and boiled them over a bonfire in which they roasted potatoes at the same time. To regulate the time for boiling without a watch, they counted to 300, which more or less corresponded to 5 minutes.

As already mentioned, seagulls and terns nest in great colonies, in which the results of collecting can be considerable in a short period. During the Second World War, collecting was so intensive that the bird colonies were reduced in size. Some statistics exist for the state-owned Klægbanke in Ringkøbing fjord, where black-headed gulls in particular nested. In 1938, an estimate of 20,000 pairs of nesting black-headed gulls was made, and of 226 common gulls. In all, 117,603 gulls' eggs were gathered in that year. Intensive collection continued in 1939, with the result that the stock of birds had fallen by 1942 to 982 and 94 pairs respectively, and the produce was reduced to 7,957 eggs collected. [12] Here, an overseer controlled the collecting of eggs.

Egg collecting, even on privately owned holms and islands, often happened also without reference to ownership rights. The owner could, of course, use the eggs himself, as happened, for example, on the estate farm of Anneksgård on Orø near Holbæk. The farm owned some small islands where gulls nested in their thousands. The informant noted: 'my brothers were with me collecting eggs and the owner and his wife were also there. They could drive out to the holms with a horse and wagon, when the tide was not too high. Then the boys collected eggs in baskets, and folk from the farm, along with the owner and his wife, packed them in boxes that were sent to Copenhagen. But when prices began to fall, the boys got a basket of eggs home with them. I think that was the pay they got'.

Some of the privately owned islands and holms had a house for an overseer and his family, who during the summer looked after grazing stock as well as the bird colonies. Of the little island of Lindholm, lying between Askø and Lolland, an informant relates that around 1890 there were masses of gulls' nests. 'In my boyhood people came from islands around to collect eggs for a bit of extra income. The island was owned by

Knuthenborg, but no attention was paid to ownership rights. Gulls' eggs could be sold to the bakeries. They were excellent for cakes.'

The island of Musholm in the Great Belt is owned by Mullerup farm, which grazes stock there during summer under the care of a permanently resident family which, in the author's youth, was always that of a fisher from Reersø. Gulls nest in thousands on the island's stony ledges. When a boat sails in to land, the seagulls rise like a vast, white cloud over it and their cries are deafening. At that time in the 1920s it was still the custom for people from Reersø, on the second day of Whitsun if the weather was good, to make a trip to Musholm to enjoy themselves and get seagulls' eggs to take home with them.

Two fishing boats were packed with children and adults. There was an accordion or two, and on the island there was dancing on the grass and the children played singing games. Later the food hampers appeared and there was competition to see who could eat most boiled gulls' eggs. The overseer had boiled a great potful. He was prepared for the invasion.

An appraisal of all Questionnaire answers gives the following more general impression: for the most part, only children are named as collectors, nearly always boys only. Old folk, and only men, may collect alone or along with children. In many cases the reason given for collecting wild fowls' eggs was that they were coveted at that time of the year either because the collectors were from poor homes where eggs never appeared otherwise, or because, as one answer said, 'it was hardly surprising, when you realised that the hens had not laid for the whole winter'.

Collecting also took place on a greater scale, above all from the bigger gull colonies, with the sale of eggs in mind. They were sold to local merchants, to the nearest market centre or to the capital. Bakers are often named as buyers, because the eggs were specially suitable for cakes. In one case, sale abroad is mentioned.

All answers show that eggs were also used in local households in traditional ways: hard boiled, as omelettes and—less often—fried. This corresponds to the meals in country districts in earlier times, and to complementary information in cookery books that reflect finer housekeeping.

Most interesting in this respect is Hagdahl's cookery book, translated into Danish and published in 1883. [13] It says that 'the fact that lapwings' eggs are considered a delicacy derives from the toothsome reputation they have got due to their rarity and the consequent price'. First it discusses hard-boiled lapwings' eggs, served with the end knocked off so that they can stand on a folded serviette. They were served with fresh butter and cress.

There was a more elaborate description of a dish called 'lapwings' eggs in a bird's nest' (oeufs de vanneaux dans un nid en beurre). For this 18 eggs were needed, with fresh butter and cress. The eggs were boiled hard. A rim of butter was laid on a dish in such a way that it resembled a bird's nest. The bottom of the dish was covered with a layer of cress, the eggs were cracked a little at the pointed end, and were built on in the form of a pyramid (Fig. 2).

2. Lapwings' eggs in the dish 'a bird's nest', from Hagdahl's cookery book (1883).

In the cookery book, *Contemporary Food,* that appeared in 1930 it is only said that lapwings' and gulls' eggs are found in limited quantities in the shops in spring and are considered a delicacy. There is no indication of how they were prepared. In 1934, a so-called *Kitchen Calendar* was published, giving recipes for main meals for every day of the year. [14] For 19 May the composition of the meal was as follows: Gull's eggs in a nest. Grilled veal with spinach. Meringue layer-cake. For the first dish ten eggs were needed, with lettuce leaves and mayonnaise. The hard-boiled eggs were arranged in a dish or basket lined with lettuce leaves. A dish of mayonnaise spiced with curry or French mustard was served with it.

In current recipes [15] details are given of hard-boiled gulls' eggs served with leavened bread, butter, salt and watercress or in the usual boiled form or as eggs in mayonnaise or in jelly.

Translated, A.F.

NOTES

1. *Kulturhistorisk Leksikon for Nordisk middelalder* XX (1976), 465-67 (äggrätter), 468 (äggtäkt).
2. G. Berg, Nordskandinaviskt-nordeuropeiskt. In *Rig* (1933), 119-20. For an earlier general allusion to the question, see S. Ekman, *Norrlands jakt och fiske*, Uppsala 1910, 194.
3. Olaus Magnus, *Historia om de nordiska folken* IV (Uppsala 1925), 141 (Swedish translation).
4. *Danske Atlas* V (1769), 523.
5. J.N. Wilse, *Reise-Iagttagelser* . . . V (1798), 190.
6. Fr. Thaarup, *Statistisk Udsigt over den danske Stat i Begyndelsen af Aaret 1825*, 198.
7. C. Kusz, *Grundrisz einer Naturbeschreibung der Herzogthümer Schleswig und Holstein*, Altona 1817, 145.
8. Nationalmuseets etnologiske undersøgelser (NEU), Questionnaire No.25: Jagt, fangst og ægsamling (1959).
9. There are 62 Questionnaire answers on egg-collecting, some short and some very comprehensive: 39 refer to the eggs of gulls and terns, and 37 to lapwings' eggs (i.e., some mention both). The period covered is 1890-1920.
10. At the time to which the data refer, this locality was part of Germany. It was annexed after the war of 1864, but re-united with Denmark in 1920.
11. G. Berg, Första lärkan och några andra förstlingsgåvor. In *Norveg* 29 (1986), 5 ff.
12. *Nordens Fugle i Farver*, IV (Copenhagen, undated), 46.
13. Ch.Em. Hagdahl (translated by A. Lütken), *Illustreret Kogebog*, Copenhagen 1883, 678 f. The author was Swedish.
14. Køkken Kalenderen. Middagsopskrifter til hver Dag i Aaret, Copenhagen 1934, 91.
15. For example *Mad fra A til Z*, No. 31, 849.

THE WOODCOCK AND ROYAL GAME

Grith Lerche

The grand old man of northern ethnology, Gösta Berg, has provoked me into considering the question of the first woodcock shot as a gift to the king. The following essay is intended to supplement the findings in his excellent article in *Norveg* 1986 [1] on the first migrating lark given to the Swedish king. Gösta Berg focused especially on the tradition connected with being honoured and rewarded for presenting 'the first', and so the extraordinary (bird, herring, salmon etc.), to the king.

The more evidence collected, the more complicated the subject becomes. The present essay, therefore, should be taken as a provisional presentation of a subject which I intend to investigate further in all its aspects, for example the importance of game in the royal household.

The *Woodcock* (Scolopax rusticola) is a wader and a migratory bird in Denmark. It is a breeding bird in Europe. It looks like a snipe, with an average weight of 300-350 grammes. It has big eyes and a very long bill (from 80mm down to 63.5mm). [2] It prefers boggy and wet areas and deciduous trees. [3] The majority of woodcock in Scandinavia migrate in a SW direction to their winter quarters in Western Europe (the British Isles, France, and Spain); some from Finland, Norway and Sweden migrate to the Balkans, Turkey and Italy. The Scandinavian woodcock seldom migrate as far as Africa. When they migrate they do so across a broad front. The woodcock breeds in Norway, Sweden and Finland, and increasing numbers are making their breeding grounds in Denmark, following the abolition of spring hunting in 1972.

The birds begin to move back to their breeding grounds in the first half of March. In Denmark they may arrive in early March, but some may overwinter in Denmark, depending on the severity of the winter.

Spring shooting

The main migration in spring occurs during the period 25 March-20 April and in autumn 20 October-20 November. [4] Until 1894 the shooting of the woodcock as a migratory bird was allowed all the year round in Denmark. Up to 1922, the shooting season for woodcock was from 1 August to 14 May. The length of the season was then reduced several times.

In the latest Game Act of 1967, it was from 1 March to 7 April, but after a five-year trial period it was totally prohibited in 1972 to hunt the woodcock during spring in Denmark. [5]

The yield of woodcock shot during the autumn hunting from 24 September till the end of December was, for example, 22,000 in 1976-77 and 27,000 in 1977-78, whereas that for pheasants in the same years was 724,000 and 739,000. [6]

The Year's First Woodcock

Over the last century many hunters' diaries, and short notes and articles in the hunting journals, [7] repeatedly mention the spring shooting of the woodcock with pleasure. From the hunters' point of view this was esteemed as a special hunt. It was the first hunt after the silent winter period. It was considered a test of skill as a hunter to be able to shoot the flapping woodcock in the twilight; but many 'real' hunters, who would never dream of shooting in the breeding period, even if they appreciated the woodcock spring hunt as such, themselves abstained from it and took part in the discussion that arose for or against such hunting of a migratory bird and its influence on the size of the breeding population in the neighbouring countries of Scandinavia. [8]

In his published hunting diary, W. Dinesen—the father of the well-known author Karen Blixen—mentions the woodcock many times:

'March 1888. We are in the woodcock season—according to the almanac, but the gun is still untouched on the wall . . .'

'April 1888. The woodcock migration is still waited, we have not yet heard about 'the first spring woodcock ' which is sent to the royal kitchen from the State forests and gives the lucky gamekeeper five Rigsdaler besides the honour; but the starling, the peewit, and the buzzard have arrived.'

'March 1890. The woodcock has arrived! It is already long since the sensational news passed the country. But it was a 'false alarm', though there was a bit of truth in it. The woodcock were there, being shot as you could be aware, and the state foresters had already in February sent the woodcock to the royal kitchen to get the desired reward of 10 DKr for the first spring woodcock; but the Chief-Cook or the Chief Lord in Waiting or the Chief Master of the Royal Hunt or the Chief Lord Steward of the household or whatever kind of authority it fell to within answered that not until 1 March was a woodcock accepted by the royal kitchen as a spring woodcock, and no reward was given. And he is right. It must have been wintering birds which are shot in the winter months . . . .'

Dinesen added that the reason why it does not breed here is less because of our climate than because it is sought out and hunted for pleasure because of its delicious flesh and beautiful appearance. [9]

Many other writers refer to this tradition of 'the King's woodcock'. [10] In Denmark the tradition of sending the first woodcock to the king and being the year's 'King of the Woodcock' was well known far beyond the hunters' circles. It was mentioned every year in the newspapers when the king had received the first woodcock.

How old is the tradition?

How old is the tradition that ended in 1972? It is documented within the last 100 years. [11] According to a personal communication from the late Lord of the Royal Hunt, Svend Rix, the tradition of giving the first woodcock to the king is well documented. He had discussed it with his predecessor, and it was a vivid tradition already during the reign of King Christian IX (1863-1906).

Other references indicate that the tradition was alive in the reign of the previous king, Frederik VII (1848-1863). [12] From Dinesen's remarks [13] it seems as if it was at that time, 1888, a tradition among the Royal forest staff, whereas later it seems to be that every eager hunter competed to be the one to send the woodcock and so get a letter of thanks from the king and be mentioned in the newspaper.

We thus have the tradition documented for the whole period of democratic rule in Denmark. According to the Danish Constitution of 5/6 1849, absolute monarchy was abolished. From 1/1 1850, the old custom of delivery of game to the Royal household was abolished and the Royal household had to pay for the amount of game delivered to the Royal kitchen. [14]

Before the establishment of the Constitution when the kings were sovereigns the title 'King of the Woodcock' was, according to Steen Steensen Blicher, not attached to the staff of the Royal forests and not even as a special title to the man who sent the first woodcock to the king. The custom of making this gesture as an act of freewill seems to have originated after the abolition of the sovereignty.

The hunting enthusiast and poet Blicher mentions the woodcock in his poem 'Trækfuglene' (The Migrants), first published in 1838. Blicher was a hunter who loved to wander in the vast Jutland moors. In his poem 'Sneppen' (The Woodcock) he says:

Fra morgenstund
til den mørke nat
med sin flint og sin hund
gennem skov, gennem krat;
Og har han tillige en fjer i sin hat.
af den første sneppe fra skoven baaret.
til *sneppekonge* da er han udkaaret.
Saa stolt som en konge, og langt mere glad
han staar som den første i jægerens rad. [15]

From light of dawn
To dark of night
With flint and dog
Through wood, through thicket;
And if in his hat he wears a feather
From the first woodcock borne from the wood.
Then they elect him woodcock king.
Proud as a king, and happier far
He stands as the first in the hunters' line.

This shows that the title 'King of the Woodcock' simply characterises the hunter as the first among equals.

The Royal Game

During the era of the monarchy, the snipe and the woodcock had, however, for long played an important role amongst the normal supply of wildfowl for the Royal table. The Royal supply of game and wildfowl is known to have been regulated in the most minute detail. According to Weismann, author of *The History of Game in Denmark*, before 1850 the only expense the Royal kitchen had for the obligatory delivery of game from the state forests and Royal game preserves was the reward, the 'shooting money' given to the ranger. The amount given was 15% of the selling price for fur-covered game and 25% for wildfowl. The amount of 'shooting money' is known to have been regulated several times previously, for instance in 1839 when it went up from two Marks to one Rigsdaler, and also earlier in the eighteenth century. [16]

In the eighteenth century letters and accounts in the Royal Household Archive on the delivery of game and wildfowl, the shooting money and rewards are often referred to because they were an important part of the staff's income. In this respect an important document often referred to later is the Royal instruction of 29 June 1722 by King Frederik IV on game delivery to the Royal household, and on 'shooting money' as well as the rate for calculating the division of game into dishes. This instruction, written to the Master of the Royal Hunt, Frederik von Gram, is quoted below:

> The necessary delivery of big game in the summer months should every week amount to 70 dishes. This is shared out thus:
>
> From Jægersborg Deerpark every Tuesday
>
> | | |
> |---|---|
> | 4 fallow deer of 5 dishes each | 20 dishes |
> | from the rest of Copenhagen county every Wednesday | |
> | 2 roe deer of 5 dishes each | 10 dishes |
> | from Frederiksborg county every Sunday | |
> | 1 stag | 8 dishes |
> | every Friday 1 fallow deer of 8 dishes | |
> | every Friday 2 roe deer of 4 dishes   16 dishes | |
> | every Saturday 1 roe deer | 4 dishes |
> | from Kronborg county every Thursday | |
> | 1 stag | 8 dishes |
> | 1 roe deer | 4 dishes |
> | total per week | 70 dishes |

These should be shot in the Royal preserves in due time, but in such a way that the stock of game would still be maintained. They should be delivered to the Royal kitchen against a receipt.

Concerning small game and wildfowl, as much as the Royal reserves could readily provide should be delivered against a receipt. This was also calculated in 'dishes' and a full list of the exact amount of 'shooting money', to be given as rewards for specific fowls etc. was listed.

Two amounts in 'skilling' ('shillings') are given in this 1722 document. The first appears to be the shooting money paid up till 1722. The second is the shooting money to be paid from then on, and as can be seen the reward is reduced. The list also specifies the small game needed to constitute one 'dish'.

From this it is evident that the foresters as well as the Royal Household before 1850 had been accustomed to settle their accounts for obligatory delivery of game (*leverancevildt*) by means of 'shooting money' (*skydepenge*). [17] I suggest that the king's letters of thanks to his subjects accompanying the 10 kroner or five Rigsdaler reward for the first arriving woodcock should be seen as a reminiscence of this older tradition in the Royal household, transformed to fit the more democratic behaviour that the new Constitution demanded.

	before 1722	after 1722	per dish
1 hare	28	16	1
1 pair of small greyling	28	12	
1 wild goose	16	12	1
1 pair big mallard	16	12	2 pieces
1 pair of teal	12	10	4 pieces
1 pair of partidge		32	
when they are here in			
Sept. and Oct.	24		5 pieces
from Oct. to Feb. when they are			
fed and kept in the lofts		48	
1 pair of plover	10	6	8 pieces
1 pair of curlew (numenius	16	12	8 pieces
arquata) or black-tailed godwit (limosa limosa)			
1 pair of second-rate snipe	12	12	8 pieces
1 piar of black tailed godwit	4	4	24 pieces
1 score of larks	24	16	
1 pair of wild pigeon	12	8	5 pieces
1 score of small sparrows	12	6	
1 pair or 3 black grouse	64	32	
1 pair of common snipe	32	16	
(Gallinago Gallinago)			
1 pair of *woodcock* in spring	32	28	5 pieces
but in autumn when they are best		32	
1 pair of reeves or other small			
jack snipe (Old Danish *brus kopper*)			
equivalent to the other			
second-rate snipe	12	12	6 pieces

Royal Game Reserves

In quoting the Act of 1722, I wish to draw attention to the importance of the Royal Game Reserves, named *Vildbaner*, which is a direct translation of German *Wildbahn*, an unfenced hunting district. This does not mean that the Royal Game Reserves were not demarcated. Already King Frederik II (1559-1588) was active in regulating and rounding off the hunting areas, especially those around the Royal Domains and Castles in North Zealand, West Zealand (Antvorskov), Northwest Zealand (Dragsholm), South Zealand (Vordingborg), Falster (Nykøbing), East Jutland (Skanderborg) and South Jutland (Koldinghus). They eventually became marked out by wooden poles at equal distances apart, especially during the reign of Christian IV (1588-1648), but after 1688 the wooden poles were successively replaced by decoratively engraved stone pillars of which a great many have been preserved. [18]

Hunting was, however, not only a Royal sport, but evidently still an important means of providing fresh meat to the King's household. [19] In the Middle Ages it was even more so, when a king had to move around in order to settle disputes and stay for a while on his domains. He and his counsellors and guardians (*hird* and *huskarle*) could draw upon local resources, but game and fish would be the most reliable sources of fresh meat.

In fact the terms *Wildbahn* and *Ban-Forest* mean areas whose exploitation has been 'banned' to anybody else without permission from the king, who claimed the ownership of all land that lay waste. There was no special capital of a country, and it was customary for the king to carry his 'chancellery' with him so that he could issue his Charters from the place where he stayed.

The practice of claiming the rights of the Royal Ban-Forest is already evident in the Laws of King Canute of England, when he laid a heavy fine on anyone who hunted in a district which he had set apart for his own pleasure. [20]

NOTES

1. G. Berg, Första lärken och några andre förstlingsgåvor. In *Norveg* 29 (1986), 5ff.
2. Ib Clausager, Age and Sex Determination of the Woodcock (Scolopax rusticola). In *Danish Review of Game Biology* (No.101 from Vildtbiologisk Station), 8:1 (1973), 13.
3. Ib Clausager, 1972. Skovsneppen (Scolopax rusticola) som ynglefugle i Denmark. In *Dansk Vildtundersøgelser* (Vildtbiologisk Station), 19 (1972), 7, 31.
4. Ib Clausager, Migration of Scandinavian Woodcock (Scolopax rusticola) with Special Reference to Denmark. In *Danish Review of Game Biology* (No. 122 from Vildtbiologisk Station) (1974), 13, 32.
5. Ib Clausager 1972, *op.cit.*, 5.
6. *Danmarks Natur* 10 (Copenhagen 1981) 324; *Jagt håndbogen*, Copenhagen 1945, 265-66.
7. *Dansk Jagttidende* 1884-1830 (D.J.T.)
8. Ib Clausager, 1972, *op.cit.*, and articles in *Dansk Jagttidende*, e.g. between 1884-1892.
9. W. Dinesen, *Boganis Jagtbreve og Nye Jagtbreve*, Odense 1976 (several editions 1890, 1892, 1966), 63, 67, 210.

10. S. Fleuron, *I Naturen med Bøsse og Stok*, Copenhagen 1907, 30-31; O. Vinding, *En Anden Verden*, Copenhagen 1958, 90; Trier Mørk, *Skovfogedens vildtretter*, Copenhagen 1969, 138; *Nyt Dansk Jagtleksikon* 1973, 1307; *Dansk Jagttidende* 4 (1928), 71.

11. Cf. Dinesen, *op.cit.*, 210; Fleuron, *op.cit; Dansk Jagttidende*, 1928.

12. Fleuron, *op.cit.*, 30; V.J. Brøndegaard, *Folk og Fauna*, 2, Copenhagen 1985.

13. Dinesen, *op.cit.*, 210.

14. C. Weismann, *Vildtets og Jagtens Historie i Danmark*. Copenhagen 1931, photographic reprint 1985, 382.

15. St. St. Blicher, *Digte og Noveller* (ed. J. Nørvig), III, Copenhagen 1964, (Trækfuglene, first published 1838).

16. C. Weismann, *op.cit.*, 317.

17. Records in the Danish State Archive. Forest and Hunting Journals 1722-41; records of game deliveries to the Royal Court Nos. 1-41. The quoted record is No. 21. Archive Reference: RA Rtk 333.671.

18. K. Høgsbro, Vildtbanepæle. In *Antikvariske Studier* (1977), 251-64.

19. E. Madsen, De Kongelige Jagter og Fiskerier i det 16. Aarhundrede. In *Fra Arkiv og Museum*, 4 (Copenhagen 1909-1911), 487-533.

20. F.M. Stenton, *Anglo-Saxon England*, Oxford 1945, 676.

BARRELS AND BUNDLES OF HERRING

Nils Storå

This essay deals with traditional methods of preserving fish as food. Fish is more easily spoilt than many other kinds of food and cannot be transported far from the fishing-ground without some kind of preserving measures. Fundamentally, preservation aims at preventing, slowing down or controlling the processes of deterioration caused by micro-organisms, enzymes (ferments), or through the influence of oxidation. The principal preservation methods have been few—mainly drying, fermentation, smoking and salting—but variations of individual methods, and varying combinations of several different methods, are numerous. Regional variations, above all varying natural conditions, are not unimportant when considering the circumstances affecting the choice of preserving method.[1]

In Scandinavian food ethnology fish preservation methods have been dealt with in particular by Gösta Berg, in many instructive articles. A number of Finnish ethnologists have discussed various aspects of fish preservation, above all Ilmar Talve, in his survey of traditional food economy in Finland, 1961. Another study which will be referred to here is Asko Vilkuna's study of Finnish popular fish names indicating methods of preservation, 1965. Although focused on traditional treatments of only one particular species of fish in Finland, the present essay will necessarily touch upon food preserving in general. Methods for preserving herring have of course been used for other species of fish, and also for meat. Nor are the methods discussed here primarily unique to Finland.

In spite of a rapid putrefaction, fish, in this particular case the Baltic herring, has even in early Scandinavia played an important part in trade, and also constituted an item of taxation. Sixteenth-century tax rolls, and other early records, not only list the amounts of fish, but also indicate how the fish had been preserved. A preservation method may, however, be subject to various changes over time. The 'salted herring' of early records may be very different from what we understand today by this expression. To some extent the measures listed for each kind of fish may give some additional information on the treatment, as for example *barrels* for salted and *bundles* for dried herring. The preserving methods cannot, however, always be clearly separated from each other. The same lot of fish may have been preserved in more than one way. According to Olaus Magnus, almost all the fish, which is dried in the open air, or smoked, is additionally salted, in order

76

to preserve its peculiar taste for a longer period.[2]

The Baltic herring

Compared to many other commonly used species of fish, the Baltic herring is, generally speaking, rather small in size, and fat. Biologically the Baltic herring is a variant of the 'ordinary' herring (Clupea harengus L.) of other northern seas. In the southern part of the Baltic, and north as far as the Swedish town of Kalmar, it is called, in Swedish, *sill*, which is the common name of the ordinary herring, but north of this town *strömming*, a term specifically referring to the Baltic variant, which is smaller in size. Within the *strömming* area, however, even other popular names occur for the Baltic herring, which blur the herring terminology.[3] Thus, the name *sill* has been used to denote particularly large-sized *strömming*, regarded as a separate species even in trade and taxation. The term *häring*, related to *herring*, was also known and, until the beginning of the twentieth century among Swedish-speaking fishermen in SW Finland, used to denote a particular race of *strömming*.[4] The original uses of these terms, established as it seems in the Middle Ages, cannot be fixed. It is, however, interesting to note that these terms seem to point out certain characteristics of the herring-fishes, i.e. their appearance in shoals and the fact that they lack scales. They indicate that herrings are 'shoal-fish' and 'skin-fish'. In Finnish the term *haarkala* (*haar*-fish, derived from the Old High German form of *Hering*) has been used to denote 'skin-fish',[5] i.e. a group consisting of *sill*, *strömming*, and sprats (Clupea sprattus L.). *Skin-fish* (Sw. *skinnfisk*) and *scale-fish* (Sw. *fjällfisk*) both occur as terms for example in connection with trade, but seem to reflect old religious practices rooted in antiquity.[6]

A major reason for the ambiguity of herring terminology is the fact that separate names have been used for herring in a fresh and preserved state. An indication of this is given by the two Finnish terms for *strömming*: *haili* denoting the fresh fish, and *silakka* the salted or otherwise preserved fish. As shown by Finnish linguists,[7] the latter term contains the Swedish word for herring-brine, *sillake* (=sill-lake), a result of old trade contacts.

Although there are several races of the Baltic herring, ichthyologists usually separate only two major groups, one spawning in spring, the other in autumn.[8] Seasonal variations in the herring shoals have also been observed by the fisherman. According to an investigation from the beginning of the twentieth century,[9] archipelago fishermen in Finland used to distinguish three, or sometimes four, kinds of herring, according to the seasons: spring, autumn and winter herring, or spring, summer, autumn and winter herring. The differences observed between herring caught in spring, summer, autumn, and winter are mainly concerned with the size and the fatness of the fish. According to the fishermen, *spring herring* is in general lean and of large size, *summer herring* rather fat and varying in size, *autumn herring* is fat and growing in size towards late autumn, and *winter herring* is decribed as large and fattest of all. As can be seen, the differences are by no means clear, and there were, according to this investigation, some regional exceptions. When spring herring is generally described as lean, this was not the case with herring caught in Åland Island waters, where the spawning occurred later. Regarding the preservation methods, variations in fatness are particularly important. As a whole, the Baltic herring must be regarded as a very fat fish, its fatness sometimes compared to that of salmon or eel.[10]

Traditionally in Finland, spring and (early) summer herring have been caught with collective seines, from about the middle of the nineteenth century, but then to an increasing degree with nets (Sw. *skötar*), and later still with bow-nets (Sw. *ryssjor*). The traditional fishing tackle for autumn herring is nets, for winter herring special winter seines and, with local variations, also nets. In general, the same kind of fishing tackle was used in catching the large herring, called *sill*, but in this case, the nets were made with larger meshes. That these nets were made exclusively for this herring race is also clear from their Swedish names, *sillskötar* and *sillkrokar*. The seasons for this fishing in Finland have been in spring along the south and southwestern coasts, in spring and autumn in the Åland Islands, and in autumn and winter further north on the coast of the Gulf of Bothnia.[11] This calendar, however, refers to conditions at the beginning of the twentieth century. What changes might have happened in the movements of the herring shoals in the course of time seems very difficult to decide. Judging by eighteenth-century writers,[12] the diminishing catches of Baltic herring at that time depended on the fact that the fish had moved further out into the sea, abandoning its former waters in inlets closer to the shore.

Fresh and frozen

The possibility of selling fish fresh was limited to districts not very far from the fishing-grounds. In their well-vessels Stockholm fishmongers, and also Finnish fishermen, transported pikes and other 'scale-fish' alive from SW Finland to the fish market in Stockholm. With the aid of special hands, called *sumprunkare* (=smack-rockers), the water in the hold could be stirred and the fish kept alive for a longer period.[13] This was one common way of keeping fish like pike (Esox lucius L.) and perch (Perca fluviatilis L.) fresh during sea transport. For the fresh fish market the appearance of railways meant a considerable enlargement of the sales areas,[14] particularly for fish caught during the seasons of open water. In Finland the railway to St. Petersburg, completed in 1870, started a new era of fish export,[15] involving fresh as well as frozen winter herring. In the tax rolls fresh fish is measured in *bags* (Sw. *kassar*), as well as in barrels. In sixteenth-century Finland a bag equalled three (Swedish) pounds, or approximately 25 kilos.[16]

According to Olaus Magnus large quantities of naturally frozen fish were brought in winter to Stockholm and other Swedish towns, 'like stone or timber', in horse-drawn sledges. He also tells us how fish 'frozen hard as wood or stone' is to be thawed. Such frozen fish would keep even four or five months in frost without any salt, says Olaus Magnus.[17] No doubt the fish was deep-frozen, apparently fairly large, and, unless preprocessed in some way, caught in late autumn or in winter. Herring caught with winter seines could be easily frozen, which partly explains the intensity with which this fishing has been carried out, particularly in SW Finland. The fish was simply spread out on the ice to freeze. This was the method also used by Russian and Ingrian fish buyers, who until the beginning of the twentieth century, used to visit the winter seine-fishing sites along the southern coasts of Finland more or less regularly.[18] This frozen fish was transported by horse, later even by train, to St. Petersburg and other towns. A sudden rise in temperature in the spring could cause a destructive thaw, and, in general, towards spring the conditions for natural deep-freezing grew more complicated. In purchase the frozen herring was measured by the piece, i.e. in thousands, an amount which was apparently estimated with a basket of a fixed size.

A special kind of preserved fish, in Finnish called *pantiokala*, indicates that fish could be treated before being frozen. This was fish of a small species (Coregonus albula L.), which was caught in late autumn, and according to two eighteenth-century writers,[19] put into a vessel made of laths bound together, and there packed tight with weights. Before the fish was put into the vessel it was gutted, and according to one of the writers, also parboiled. In this state the *pantio*-fish was kept in a cold place until it froze. Essentially this fish is spoken of as frozen, but when packed unsalted into a wooden 'cage' (Fi. *pantio*) as early as September and October a preceding fermentation process could not be avoided. This was a combined process, used above all in the inland lake districts of Finland. Here, frozen fish was an article of trade in winter, consumed boiled in a kind of gruel. The 'frozen fish' occasionally mentioned as special items in sixteenth-century tax rolls for (inland) Finland [20] may have been of this very type.

From about the 1870s fishing consultants started urging the use of ice in cellars for storing fish, and in summer for keeping the fish catches fresh during transport. This did not, however, become a more common practice until the end of that century.[21]

Dried and smoked

Above all people here eat dry fish, says Olaus Magnus when considering the use of fish in the northern countries, and mentions as examples pike, pike-perch (Lucioperca l. L., Sw. *gös*), bream (Abramis brama L., Sw. *braxen*), burbot (Lota l. L., Sw. *lake*) and lavaret (Coregonus lavaretus L., Sw. *sik*). When dried, this fish is 'piled up like logs in a woodpile' and sold by length or weight. Olaus Magnus speaks of 'drying in the sun', but gives no description of the drying process.[22] On the other hand he gives good information on how dry fish is eaten, either soaked in lye, or clubbed, before cooking. The common use of dry fish is also indicated by the occurrence of professional women 'fishsoakers' (Sw. *fiskblöterskor*), whose task it was to soften dry fish.[23] From the tax documents we learn that, besides the species of fish mentioned by Olaus Magnus, perch, roach (Leuciscus rutilus L., Sw. *mört*), ide (Leuciscus idbarus L., Sw. *id*), herring, smelt (Osmerus eperlanus L., Sw. *nors*), flounder (Pleuronectes), and even a fat fish like the eel were also dried.[24] Included in the taxation is also 'dry fish', unspecified and measured mostly by weight, sometimes by barrels. The dry fish in barrels had apparently been salted down. There were also other measures for dry fish, as indicated by Olaus Magnus.

Both *strömming*-herring and herring of the large type (Sw. *sill*) are mentioned among the dried fish, the latter called *krampesill* and measured by *bundles* (Sw. *knippen*) of 1,000 herrings each. There were 5,000 dried herrings, or five bundles, to a barrel of 120 litres, at least in Finland as far as scanty sources show.[25] Dried herring was thus measured in thousands, like frozen winter herring. Both large and small herrings were, as dried, counted in thousands, equal to bundles. The excess number is indicated in hundreds, for example three barrels four hundreds,[26] which stresses the importance of a reckoning in numbers. The bundle-measure, however, seems to have been used only for dried fish of the *sill*-herring, and there were bundles tied either with one or two strings of bast. Since the herrings could be dried hanging from a string of bast, the same was probably used for tying the bundle together.[27] Other kinds of dried fish that were measured in bundles were smelt, pike, perch, flounder, and roach. The dried *strömming*-herring were measured in thousands, but as early as the sixteenth century increasingly in barrels.[28] The larger herrings continued to be preserved through drying, but gradually in taxation measured also by barrels or weight. Herring bundles occur in Finnish tax accounts from the earliest documents of the 1530s occasionally until the 1680s. There was from the beginning of the seventeenth century a remarkable drop in the price paid for this kind of fish,[29] which also indicates a diminishing interest in herring preserved in this way. Various other kinds of dry fish contained in the state taxation accounts for Finland are usually measured by weight, with the exception of ides, which are measured by the piece, and of the fish called 'spitfish' (Sw. *spettfisk*), estimated by a *klova* of 200 fishes or simply by the piece.[30] Apparently, the 'spitfish' was fish dried on a spit, as illustrated by Olaus Magnus.[31]

Fish to be dried could be spread out on a flat rock or fixed to the wall of a building. The use of particular scaffolds, so common for the drying of cod in Norway, has not been unknown in Finland, but confined to the Åland Islands and possibly other parts of the archipelago of SW Finland.[32] The best season for drying fish in the open air is in the spring, when the temperature is not yet too high. Spread out on flat rocks, fish could be dried even later in summer. In general, a northern climate has favoured this preserving method.[33] It might be thought that this method mainly applied to fish of little fatness, but there seem to have been ways of preparing even fat fish like salmon and eel so that they could be dried. The fish could be split in halves, spread out on sticks, or even sliced in order to facilitate the drying process. For fish caught in late summer and in the autumn, open-air drying was not possible. In these cases the fish could be dried inside the houses in the stoves. This method of preserving has recently been practised only in eastern and northern Finland,[34] but, in former times, seems to have been known also in the western part of the country. The piece of bark, and other material on which the fish was laid in the stove, have given rise to a number of Finnish terms for fish dried in this manner.[35]

Fish is still being dried in Finland to some extent, but for purposes other than human consumption. It was a very convenient way of preserving fish—and meat—and was therefore in general use. The loss of weight was, for transport purposes, a highly important factor. It is estimated that fresh herring could lose as much as 70% through the drying process. Weather conditions were a crucial factor, greatly affecting the result. According to fairly recent estimates, 5-6kg of herring under favourable conditions produce 1kg of dry fish. When conditions were unfavourable, however, more than 10kg were needed for the same amount of dry herrings.[36]

According to Olaus Magnus *smoked* fish is much appreciated, salmon being the best of all in quality. Salmon is particularly eaten by travellers, since even as a raw dish it is in high esteem. Among other fish that are smoked he mentions bream, lavaret, pike-perch, herring, and lampret.[37] To judge by Olaus Magnus, smoking has been a common way of preserving fish as well as meat. Very little is known from old sources, however, that would clearly refer to the smoking process. The scarce source material rather suggests that smoking to the extent that it occurred was combined with other processes, in particular drying, and perhaps therefore rarely mentioned directly. In the sixteenth-century accounts of Finland,[38] whitefish seems to be the only fish explicitly mentioned as smoked. Smoked (and also dried) whitefish was measured in a *ryncke* of 300 fishes.[39] There are also references to unspecified 'smoked fish' and, frequently, to salmon called, in Swedish, *spickelax*. This salmon may have been smoked but more likely it underwent a combined process of smoking and drying, 'smoke-drying'.[40] In the accounts the *spicke*-salmon are measured by units as is smoked whitefish. These salmon are in the accounts clearly separated from 'salted salmon', measured in barrels.

When discussing the process of smoking, particularly with regard to herring, two different practices must be separated, i.e. smoking in 'cold' and in 'hot' smoke.[41] Cold-smoking implies smoking in a room filled with smoke, for 1-4 days, whereas hot-smoking is a much faster method, 2-4 hours in the heat (120-140 C) of a smoke oven.[42] Cold-smoking, implying to some extent even a simultaneous drying process, preserves food for a much longer period. Hot-smoking, which is the method by which herring is commonly treated today, keeps the fish only for a period of a week or therabouts. The hot-smoked herring (Sw. *böckling*) does not seem to be a very old phenomenon in Finland, although there are occasional indications in sixteenth-century sources. The method was not generally accepted until much later among the people.[43] In Sweden hot-smoking of herring was originally confined to eastern coastal provinces and above all to towns and large estates.[44] The *böckling*, whose name is borrowed from German, was very likely in former days cold-smoked, or preserved through the combined process of smoking and drying.[45] This method thus was formerly a kind of 'smoke-drying', a term occurring among the old Swedish population in Estonia.[46] It appears that Olaus Magnus when talking about fish that Germans call *Bucking* means dried herring.[47]

Judging by a single reference, in 1582, to 12 barrels of 'charcoal herring' (Sw. *kolströmming*, apparently a direct translation of the Finnish *hiilisilakka*) in SW Finland (the province of Åbo), herrings at that time were to some extent also grilled on gridirons, a method of treating herring very much in use in Finland to-day.[48] Obviously this is also a method of preservation, although grilled herring cannot be saved for more than a couple of days. The *barrels* of charcoal herring mentioned in 1582 were hardly intended for immediate consumption. The difference between methods for short-term preservation and food preparation is by no means always clear.

Fermented and salted

Although historical documentation is scarce for fish preserved through fermentation (souring) in Finland, this widespread method [49] was still fairly common in the eighteenth century. [50] It has also been proved that the modern Finnish names of two species of small fish (Coregonus albula and Clupea sprattus) have the original meaning of 'sour fish'. [51] In recent times fermented fish has been used in the eastern and northern parts of the country until the latter half of the nineteenth century, and to some extent even later. [52] This occurred mainly in inland districts, where species of fish other than herring were concerned. There were several ways of treating fish in order to start—and stop—the fermenting process. Salt was used either very little or not at all. Rye flour was sometimes put into the vessels, which were open, to further the process. [53] With regard to the herring the fermentation method has not, however, in Finland had an industrial development as in N Sweden, where fermented herring (Sw. *surströmming*) is still consumed, as a delicacy. [54] However, fermented herring still occurred in SW and W (the province of Vasa) Finland at least about the middle of the eighteenth century, and further north on the Bothnian coast even much later. [55] At that time fermented herring was used on both sides of the Gulf of Bothnia. When in 1755 the Chamber of Commerce published a decree concerning how Baltic herring was to be properly treated and salted, herring from West and East Bothnia is mentioned as particularly bad, being sometimes even 'sour'. [56] Whether this statement implied fermented herring, or simply herring that had accidentally turned sour, cannot be decided.

The exact way in which the herring in Finland was fermented is not known. We may believe this was done in the same way as the *surströmming* in Sweden. In this case the fish was slightly salted before it was put into a tightly closed barrel, where the process started. Fermented salmon has maintained what is probably the oldest way of fermenting, i.e. by putting fish unsalted into earthen pits, in order to make a kind of fermented fish. A more recent kind of fermented fish, in Swedish called *gravlax*, 'dug-down salmon ', has a name referring to this old method. [57] The *pantio*-fish mentioned earlier should probably also be considered in this connection.

Salt herrings occurred in many parts of Western Europe as early as the twelfth century, [58] although their condition was not what is known as salt herrings today. In the sixteenth-century taxation records, there are frequent references to barrels of unspecified 'salt fish', whereas barrels of salted salmon and lavaret are mentioned separately. The barrels of herring are not explicitly noted as containing *salted* fish, although this is very likely. The omission could simply indicate that the herring accepted as a tax item was as a rule salted, even with the Crown's own salt. The amount of salt used in preservation naturally varied. Light salting could be sufficient for short-term preservation, but had to be combined with other measures, such as drying or smoking, to keep for a longer time.[59] Various kinds of salt showed differences in quality. That the traditional methods were maintained among ordinary people long after salting had become the dominant method of preserving herring, may to a large extent be explained by the cost of the salt.[60] Salt was brought to Finland from the west, over the Åland Islands, from Reval and other eastern Baltic ports, as well as from the shores of the White Sea. It was known and used in the Finnish countryside at least as early as the fourteenth century.[61] Not until much later, however, did the use of salt become a common practice. In the sixteenth century both Gustavus Vasa and his son Johan III were still making considerable efforts to increase salting in fish preservation.[62] As previously mentioned, the fish obtained through the tax collection was salted with the Crown's own salt. According to the 1755 decree of the Chamber of Commerce the proper amount of salt was one fourth of a herring barrel. This was, however, a decree issued in order to reduce excessive use of salt, the usual amount of salt having been one-third of the barrel. A barrel of salt was needed for three barrels of herring.[63]

Although the methods of salting fish have been varying in many respects,[64] two major categories may be observed, i.e. 'dry-salting' (Sw. *torrsaltning*), and 'brine-salting' (Sw. *laksaltning*). Since Baltic herrings consists of nearly 80° water,[65] the salt added to fresh fish, under normal conditions, dissolves to brine even in 'dry-salting'. In this case, however, the herrings were tightly packed into the barrel with only a small amount of brine. There are numerous examples of how the barrels of herring intended for the eastern, and, in particular, the Estonian markets had to be packed with herrings so as to contain as little brine as possible. The herring intended for these markets was usually bartered for rye, implying that a certain amount of herring equalled an amount of rye; at times a barrel of herring equalled a barrel of rye. Under such circumstances the buyer, or rather the bartering partner, would not want any excessive brine. His main concern was the amount of fish.[66] In this case the brine was regarded as an unnecessary supplement, at least at the time of the barter. That this is also a matter of taste will be shown later. As for 'brine-salting', this method implied putting the herrings into barrels of readymade brine, sometimes even into *blood-brine*, i.e. brine which had been used before. It is interesting in this connection to note the different Finnish words for Baltic herring in a fresh state, *haili*, and in the case of the salted herring, *silakka*, the latter being derived from Sw. *sill-lake*, 'herring brine'.

The salting of herrings implied the use of wooden vessels or wooden barrels, since the Middle Ages made in a stave construction. As a measure for salted fish, a barrel roughly equalled 120 litres.[67] Traditionally, the best barrels have been made in SW Finland, and in the northern tar-burning districts. In the islands, there has been a shortage of the raw materials used in barrels, such as pine or spruce. It seems to have been a common practice to re-use the barrels in which the salt was imported. In some districts of Finland even barrels used for tar were burnt out and re-used for salted herring, above all in the eastern parts of the Gulf of Finland, where, until the beginning of the twentieth century, the making of fish barrels had not been developed.[68] This was not, however, due primarily to lack of handicraft skill, as has been maintained. From this district the herring trade was solely directed towards the market places of Russia, Ingria and Estonia, where the buyers were not interested in brine. Since the herrings were packed tight into the vessels, by letting the brine out, there was actually no need of vessels that could hold the brine. Almost any wooden vessel would do, even a barrel that had been filled with tar. Herrings could also be sold by weight, as 'dry', taken out of the vessel with the brine.[69] In this case the brine could be used for salting another quantity of herrings.

The original way of salting herrings seems to have been merely to shove the fish into vessels measuring a barrel or even larger vessels, holding as much as 5-8 barrel measures each. The herrings were hardly even gutted. Herring caught in the spring lay in vessels filled with brine until the autumn, which was the main market season. From the large vessels, the herring was then moved into smaller vessels, containing one-half or one-fourth of a barrel. A more careful way of treating the herrings seems to have been introduced to Finland by Åland fishermen, who according to tradition learned this skill from fishermen of the Swedish island of Gotland. To the fishermen in the Åland islands the preservation of herring was far more of a necessity, because of the long distance to the markets west and east. Whereas the fish intended for the eastern market could be shoved into the barrels, in traditional manner, the herring for the Swedish market had to be handled with much more care, every layer of fish in the barrel being neatly arranged to keep the fish undamaged. In this case the herrings, after they had been gutted and cleaned, were immediately salted into the small vessels in which the fish was sold. The result was a herring of a better quality, for which a higher price could be obtained. In the Swedish market a differentiation of the salted fish took place much earlier than in the eastern markets. At what time this 'new' method of treating herring was introduced is not known. Towards the end of the nineteenth century, however, this method, known in Finland as the 'Åland method', had gradually been introduced also to other parts of Finland.[70]

The choice of preserving method

As we have seen, fish was often preserved through combined methods. There were also variations of the methods in respect of the 'degree' of preserving, such as semi-drying and mild-salting, that affected in different ways the taste, the smell, the consistency and also the colour of the fish.[71] Even if salting as a method of preserving is not as old as drying and fermenting, salt has also in Finland been used since the Middle Ages, at first mainly as a supplementary measure. Since salt has been used both as a preceding and a following part of the preservation process, the primary preservation method is often difficult to determine.

In summing up the traditional preserving methods, with special reference to fish, the Norwegian ethnologist Astri Riddervold distinguishes three major categories: preservation 1) through the use of natural, external factors such as temperature and wind, 2) by using preserving media such as salt, smoke and acid, and 3) biological preservation, with enzymes and microbes.[72] Riddervold rightly points out that 'most often' combinations of two or more techniques were used. As regards the Baltic herring, examples have been given of methods in all three categories. Natural freezing and drying in the open air could be referred to the first category, salting and smoking to the second category, and fermenting apparently to the second as well as the third categories. Less common techniques such as drying in the oven, and grilling on charcoal, which had to be combined with salting, seem more difficult to relate to one of these categories.

Several different circumstances have influenced the choice of method for preserving fish, such as the size and fatness of the species, the actual quality of the fish, the season of the catch and the equipment used, the transport and storing conditions, the market, and, in general, the duration of the preservation time intended. To what extent even different tastes were taken into account is a more complicated question.

Olaus Magnus seems to imply that salting in addition to the drying or smoking of fish was aimed at preserving its particular taste for a longer period. The buyer and the fisher did not always represent the same tastes, and what would today be regarded as 'putrid' fish is likely to include fish preserved through some of the processes common in the old days. Also herring could be preserved without using any, or just a small amount of, salt. As early as the sixteenth century there was a development of taste towards more strongly salted fish, at first, at least, contrary to the taste of ordinary people. Whether people held on to less salted fish because of taste or economic necessity, since salt was expensive, is difficult to decide. At any rate, common people were for a long time much in favour of traditional preserving methods like drying and fermenting. Thus, in 1759 still, the medical officer of the province of Åbo in his medical book, referring to herring and lavaret, writes about the fermented or 'putrid' salt fish that people eat, quite commonly, as it seems.[73] The rapid disappearance of fermented herring in Finland, apparently towards the end of the same century, is difficult to explain. The lack of fermented herring in tax rolls seems due to the difficulty of controlling the process, which made fish preserved in this manner a bad item of taxation. Even in the Russian market salted fish was not very much in favour,[74] although fish during the many fasts constituted the main foodstuff.

In spite of the fact that drying and fermenting continued to be used in preservation, salting gradually became the dominant method, even after hot-smoking had been introduced. In 1898, the total amount of Baltic herring reaching the market in Finland was estimated at 250,000 barrels (120 litres each), and all containing salted herring.[75] The first half of the twentieth century was marked by a growing dislike of salted herring, usually explained by the rising standard of living. The railway and other fast means of transport had already widened the market for fresh fish, which reduced the interest in salted fish and caused a change in taste. For preserving Baltic herring, canning has been of little importance.

NOTES

1. C.L. Cutting, *Fish saving* (London 1955), 1-3; A. Riddervold, Saltet mort og lubbesild, gamalsei, spekelaks og rakefisk. In *Dugnad* 11, No. 1 (Oslo 1985), 32.

2. Olaus Magnus, *Historia de gentibus septentrionalibus* (Romae 1555), *Historia om de nordiska folken* (I-IV, Uppsala and Stockholm, 1909-25, V, commentary by J. Granlund, 1951), book XX: chap. 27.

3. J. Bernström, Sillfiskar. In *Kulturhistoriskt lexikon för nordisk medeltid* (=KLNM) XV (Helsingfors 1970); Chr. Hessle, The Herrings along the Baltic Coast of Sweden. In *Publications de circonstance* No. 89 (Copenhague 1925), 12-48; cf. N. Storå, Finländskt strömmingsfiske. In *Norveg* 22 (Oslo 1979), 140.

4. Storå, *op. cit.*, 138.

5. Bernström, *op. cit.*.

6. Granlund, *op. cit.* (cf. ref. 2), 498.

7. E. Itkonen and A.J. Joki, Suomen kielen etymologinen sanakirja IV. In *Lexica societatis fenno-ugricae* XII No. 4 (Helsinki 1969), 1023; cf. A. Vilkuna, Kalannimistä kulttuurintutkimuksen lähteenä. In *Suomi* III No. 2 (Helsinki 1965), 32-33.

8. Cf. V. Sjöblom, Wanderungen des Strömlings (Clupea harengus L.) in einigen Schären- und Hochseegebieten der nördlichen Ostsee. In *Ann. Zool. Soc. 'Vanamo'* 23 No. 1 (Helsinki 1961), 3-4.

9. Cf. Storå, *op. cit.*, 167-168.

10. Cf., e.g., O.Reuter, Om saltning och annan konservering af strömming. In *Fiskeriföreningen i Finland* IV (Lovisa 1902), 4.

11. Storå, *op. cit.*, 141-165.

12. U. Rudenschöld, Berättelse om ekonomiska o.a. förhållanden i Finland 1738-1741. In *Todistuskappaleita Suomen historiaan* VI (Helsinki 1899), 52, 86-87; cf. E. W. Juvelius, Silakansaaliin vaihteluista Uudenmaan rannikolla ja saaristossa 17-sataluvun puolivälissä. In *Suomen kalatalous* 1916-1917, No. 4 (Helsinki 1917), 103-104; N. Storå, Strömmingsfiskets betydelse för skärgårdsbefolkningen. In *Fiskerimuseiföreningens publikationer* 3 (Hanko 1986), 53-56.

13. S. Erixon, Stockholms sumpfiskare och fiskköpare. In *Folk-Liv* X (Stockholm 1947), 61; J. Gardberg, Fiskhandel och bondeseglation i Åbo skärgård. In *Svenska kulturbilder*, N.F. 5 (Stockholm 1937).

14. Cutting, *op. cit.*, 217.

15. K. Forsström, Om strömmingsfisket och fiskens behandling vid Träskö i Kimito. In *Fiskeritidskrift för Finland* 1893 No. 1 (Helsingfors).

16. Finlands årliga inkomster under 1500-talets senare hälft. In *Todistuskappaleita Suomen historiaan* IV (Helsinki 1899), e.g. 18; K.R. Melander, Muistiinpanoja Suomen mitta- ja painosuhteista. In *Historiallinen arkisto* XI (Helsinki 1891), 128.

17. Olaus Magnus XX: 14 and 24.

18. U.T. Sirelius, *Suomalaisten kalastus* II (Helsinki 1907), 238; V. Ruoppila, Kannakselaisten Pietarin-kaupasta. In *Kotiseutu* 1952 No. 5-7, 125-126; Storå, *op cit.*, 51; V. Voionmaa, *Hämäläinen eräkausi* (Porvoo 1947), 397-398, 412.

19. Rudenschöld, *op.cit.*, 51; V. Voionmaa, *Hämäläinen eräkausi* (Porvoo 1947), 397-398, 412.

20. Voionmaa, *op.cit.*, 398.

21. Reuter, *op.cit.*, 32; T.H. Järvi, *Suomen merikalastus ja jokipyynti* (Porvoo 1932), 70.

22. *Olaus Magnus* XX: 24.

23. G. Berg, Rökt skinka, torkade gäddor och surströmming. In *Mat och miljö* (Lund 1970), 168-172; *idem*, Lutfisken. In *Gastronomisk kalender* 17 (Stockholm 1976), 20, 27; S. Ljung, Fiskblöterska. In KLNM IV (Helsingfors 1959).

24. Finlands årliga inkomster (cf. ref. 16), 13, 18, 85, 138, 147.

25. Storå, *op. cit.* (1979), 137; cf. J. Teitt, Klagomålsregister emot adeln i Finland år 1555-1556. In *Todistuskappaleita Suomen historiaan* V (Helsinki 1894), 215.

26. Finlands årliga inkomster, 57.

27. Storå, *op. cit.* (1986), 48.

28. Melander, *op. cit.*, 128; *idem*, Sillin eli suurhailin kalastuksesta maassamme 1500-luvulta alkaen. In *Historiallisia tutkimuksia* XII (Helsinki 1931), 24-26.

29. Melander, *op. cit.* (1931), 24, 35, 217-218.

30. Finlands årliga inkomster, 13, 61 *et passim*; Melander, *op. cit.* (1891), 127-128.

31. Olaus Magnus XX: 26.

32. I. Talve, Kansanomaisen ruokatalouden alalta. In *Suomi* 109 No. 4 (Helsinki 1961), 12.

33. O. Hasslöf, *Svenska västkustfiskarna* (Stockholm 1949), 347-349.

34. Talve, *op. cit.*, 13.

35. Vilkuna, *op. cit.*, 47.

36. Cf. Storå, *op. cit.* (1986), 48-49.

37. Olaus Magnus XX: 26.

38. Finlands årliga inkomster, 65, 70 *et passim*.

39. Melander, *op. cit.* (1931), 198.

40. A. Ropeid and K. Vilkuna, Speking. In KLNM XVI (Helsingfors 1971); Berg, *op. cit.* (1970), 166-168; Talve, *op. cit.*, 24-27; Vilkuna, *op. cit.* (1965), 29-32.

41. Cutting, *op. cit.*, 284-287.

42. Hasslöf, *op. cit.*, 371; Berg and K. Vilkuna, Rökning. In KLNM XIV (Helsingfors 1969); Ropeid and Vilkuna, *op. cit*; G. Norsander, *Salt sill* (Lund 1976), 71-73.

43. Talve, *op. cit.*, 27; cf. also Cutting, *op. cit.*, 285.

44. Berg, *op. cit.* (1970), 163; Norsander, *op. cit.*, 72.

45. Talve, *op. cit.*, 25-28.

46. *Ibid.*, 29.

47. Olaus Magnus XX: 26; cf. G Berg, Sill som föda. In *Norveg 22* (1979), 180.

48. Finlands årliga inkomster, 94.

49. Berg, *op. cit.* (1970), 172-174; Talve, *op. cit.*, 7-11; K. Eidlitz, Föda och nödföda (Kristianstad 1971), 130-132.

50. I. Manninen, Vanhan ruokatalouden alalta. In *Suomen museo-Finskt museum* XXV (Helsinki 1918); U.T. Sirelius, *Suomen kansanomaista kulttuuria* I (Helsinki 1919), 308.

51. Vilkuna, *op. cit.* (1965), 23-27.

52. Talve, *op. cit.*, 9.

53. Manninen, *op. cit.*, 48-49.

54. G. Berg, Gravlax och surströmming. In *Gastronomisk kalender* 2 (Stockholm 1962), 53-59.

55. Manninen, *op. cit.*, 48-49; K. Vilkuna, Varsinaissuomalaisten kansanomaisesta taloudesta. In *Varsinais-Suomen historia* III No. 2 (Porvoo 1935), 166; Sirelius, *op. cit.*, 308.

56. *Underrättelse om strömmingens ansande och saltande* (Stockholm 1755).
57. Berg, *op. cit.* (1962), 49-52.
58. Cutting, *op. cit.*, 57.
59. *Ibid.*, 2-3; G. Mathiesen, Salt—et konserveringsmiddel i folkelig hushold-ning. In *Dugnad* 11 No. 1 (Oslo 1985), 49.
60. B. Lorentzen, *Salt* (Bergen 1952), 48-50; Cutting, *op. cit.*, 45-48; Norsander, *op. cit.*, 11-15.
61. G. Kerkkonen, Salthandel (Finland). In KLNM XIV (Helsingfors 1969).
62. Melander, *op. cit.* (1931), 190-192.
63. Underrättelse (cf. ref. 56); O. Vollan, Fisketilvirkning. In KLNM IV (Helsingfors 1959).
64. Hasslöf, *op. cit.*, 355-356; Cutting, *op. cit.*, 53-69.
65. A. Haapala, Saltning av strömming. In *Fiskeriföreningen i Finland* XI (Helsingfors 1926), 14, 23-24.
66. Cf. N. Storå, Öståländskt krokskötsfiske. In *Folk-Liv* 1967-68 (Lund 1970), 30-31.
67. Berg, *op. cit.* (1979), 184-185; T. Nilsson, Tunnan—containerns föregångare. In *Kulturen* 1987 (Lund), 42-43.
68. O. Reuter, Konservering af fisk. In *Vårt land* No 12 (Helsingfors 1898), 11-12.
69. *Ibid*; A. Forsberg. Om åländska strömmingskonserveringen förr och nu. In *Fiskeritidskrift för Finland* 1898, No. 7 & 8 (Helsingfors), 126.
70. Forsberg, *op. cit.*, 126-127; Reuter, *op. cit.* (1902), 10-17.
71. Cf. Norsander, *op. cit.*, 65-73; Riddervold, *op. cit.*
72. Riddervold, *op. cit.*, 33.
73. Cf. Vilkuna, *op. cit.* (1935), 166.
74. Ruoppila, *op. cit.*, 126.
75. Reuter, *op. cit.*, 9.

SWEDISH BUTTER FIRKINS

Nils-Arvid Bringéus

The Swedish author Frans G. Bengtsson (1894-1954) recounts in *Den Lustgård som jag minns (The Paradise I Remember)* (1953) what he learned from a woodman employed on the Rössjöholm Estate in north-western Scania. This was a man of the old-fashioned stamp, who knew the qualities of different types of wood and saved timber for future use. Frans could not understand why the woodman was sawing up a hawthorn tree that had been uprooted by a storm. The woodman was no less surprised that young Frans, 'who was after all going to the learned school', did not know that the wood could be used to make teeth for rakes:

I was then given a detailed lecture about the specific qualities that distinguished different kinds of wood. Beech had its properties, as did hornbeam, and even larch, even pear and cherry had their qualities, which distinguished them from other types of wood. Ash was the best for pitchfork shafts because of its toughness, something else was best for axe-shafts, and even aspen, which was otherwise of little use even as firewood, was the best for people who made matches. For wheelwrights there were at least three different sorts of wood they had to use if the wheel was to last. And the coopers, who make butter firkins, must have beech and nothing else, like the kind we cut up for them down in the sawmill.

As a young ethnologist I had similar lessons from rake-makers in northern Scania and Gotland.[1] Beech, which grows only in the southernmost part of Sweden, was of no use for either house timber or tool making. It was, however, excellent for butter firkins, since it did not impart any taste to the butter.

The word translated here as firkin is *drittel*, a Danish measure for butter originally denoting one 'third' of a *tønde* ('tun') or 37.33kg. When butter was exported to England, the size of the *drittel* was increased to equal one English hundredweight (50.8kg). It is not recorded when the packing of butter in Sweden changed from the large tun to the smaller firkin. Torvald Nilsson has recently conjectured that the change took place in association with the growth of the creamery-based butter trade.[2] This is highly probable. The Dictionary of the Swedish Academy has no example of the word *drittel* before 1882; it has a definition cited from a 1903 agricultural publication: 'firkins are small, bulging barrels of beech, held together by four pairs of withies'.

Cutting the staves

Like the barrel, the firkin is a staved container with the top and bottom (the heads) set in a groove cut near the ends of the staves. The storage of butter in barrels must have been common ever since containers like these began to be made in the Middle Ages, following continental models, and since the export of butter on a larger scale was made possible by the addition of salt.[3]

In Frans G. Bengtsson's native parish of Tåssjö there was a village called Stavershult. The name is attested as far back as 1524 in the cadastral rolls for Helsingborg County and probably refers to the staves which the area provided.[4] During the seventeenth century there were extensive exports of barrel staves from Helsingborg, as customs records show.[5] In 1748 there was still a considerable export of barrel staves to Copenhagen.[6] A county customs register from Båstad surviving from 1798 allows us to locate the source of the beech staves in the Rössjöholm region. This comprised primarily the two Scanian parishes of Tåssjö and Örkelljunga, together with the parish of Våxtorp on the other side of the provincial boundary in Halland. From Tåssjö staves for *fjärdingar* ('quarter-barrels or firkins') were supplied to Ängelholm, where there were a few cooperages. In the neighbouring parishes of Fagerhult and Hishult, where the pine forests were better than the beech, the local craftsmen made tubs, chests, and other wooden articles.

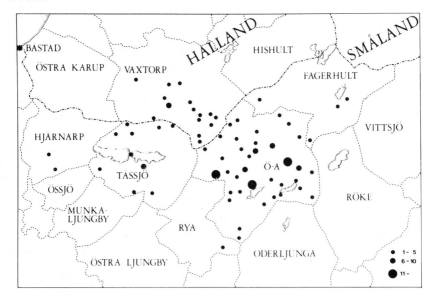

1. The location and number of suppliers of beech staves, according to the Båstad county customs register for 1798. From Bringéus 1983:72.

The customs register from 1798 records no fewer than 198 suppliers of barrel staves to Båstad from 72 different villages (Fig. 1). Deliveries came in every month of the year, although there were low periods at seedtime and harvest. Practically all the casks passing through the customs were full-sized barrels (228,550 of them), whereas the number of half-barrels (3,000) and quarter-barrels (4,200) was not nearly so impressive.[7] The customs register provides an explanation for an enigmatic contemporary observation by C. A. Ehrensvärd during a visit to Örkelljunga in 1795: 'In general the peasants earn their living from working with trees. They are thus craftsmen and therefore let the land rest until the forest is exhausted'.

In actual fact, the forest had by this time been considerably reduced north of the boundary with Halland. Dean Osbeck of Laholm wrote in 1796: ' . . .over twenty years ago one could constantly see barrels made by our own peasants being driven to Båstad, Laholm, and other places. Barrel staves now come to Båstad, Laholm, and other places. Barrel staves now came to Båstad in considerable numbers from the Scanian parishes of Örkelljunga and Tåssjö'.[8]

According to Pehr Osbeck, stave cutting and barrel making were mainly intended to meet the need for herring barrels. This is confirmed by Anders Gustaf Barchaeus in his notes from a journey through Halland in 1773: 'Herring barrels are made in large quantities in Varberg by four coopers, who buy staves of beech from the rural peasantry. They are transported to Gothenburg, where they fetch a price of 4½ to five copper dalers each. The peasant receives eight styvers per barrel and can transport 30 to 36 of them in a wagon drawn by two horses. The peasant sells the barrels on the cooper's behalf and on return hands over the money to the cooper, who then gives him his payment'.[9]

The great extent of stave cutting in Halland and northwestern Scania must be viewed against the background of the herring boom in Bohuslän between 1747 and 1808. There was a huge demand for herring barrels, and it was to meet this that the Crown on 17th March 1748 issued a prohibition against the purchase of finished staves and stave timber abroad. As in Viksdalen in Norway, the need for barrels for herring salting on the coast led to the growth of a regional craft at a relatively long distance inland.[10]

Reports from Norra Åsbo Hundred in the transactions of the Kristianstad County Agricultural Society in 1817 and 1833 still mention stave cutting as an ancillary occupation. Barrels of beech staves were used for, among other things, the transport of potash, which was burnt in large quantities in the far north of Scania and here and there in Halland.[11]

The market that disappeared along with the Bohuslän herring appears later to have been captured by Norway. In 1876 we learn that 'what is left of

the beech and oak forests is exported every year in the form of staves, princi-
pally to Norway'.[12]

There are still those in Örkelljunga who remember characters like
'Stave-Pär' of Bälinge, with his red hair and his hearty appetite, and Jöns
Ljunggren and Per Nilsson, who were cutting staves at Lärkesholm right
up to the First World War. These peasant craftsmen did not own any forest
themselves, however, but bought standing timber at auctions on the
Lärkesholm Estate. Staves were manufactured mostly during the summer
half of the year, while wooden drains were made during the winter.[13]

From Huseby in southern Småland we learn that stave cutting at the
turn of the century was carried on practically the whole year round, and
that deliveries to the coopers were made in units known as 'great thousands'
(12,000 staves), packed together in sixes. The bulk price in 1900—1905 was
30 kronor per great thousand, delivery included.[14]

At this time a new use for beech staves had arisen as a result of the more
rational handling of milk products in the newly established creameries; this
was the butter firkin. Norra Åsbo Hundred in 1866 had creameries 'almost
exclusively at the so-called manor houses.'[15] By 1892 no less than 123
creameries had been established in Kristianstad County alone.[16]

When stave cutting boomed once again around the turn of the century,
there were thus several factors: increased butter production, availability of
beechwood for the firkins, an old tradition of craftsmanship, and private initiative.

Butter production and export

Butter production by the creameries increased steadily at the beginning of
the twentieth century, at the same time as there was a decline in rural butter
making on the farm, which in 1932 amounted to 25,000 tons. In 1956 the
creameries were producing 82,406 tons and the farms only 1,300 tons.

The increased butter production exceeded the needs of the nation, so
Sweden exported significant quantities of butter. In the pre-war years of
1937-1939, Swedish butter exports amounted to approximately 25,000 tons
per annum, of which slightly more than half went to England and the rest to
Germany. Since 1935 all butter export has gone through the National
Association of Swedish Creameries, which came into being in 1932.

When war broke out in 1939, the export of butter was interrupted, and
with its resumption in 1949, the English market was closed to Sweden ow-
ing to long-term agreements which England made with Denmark and the
Commonwealth. Exports of butter from Sweden therefore went mainly to

West Germany, East Germany, Switzerland, France, and North Africa.[17] The foundation of the European Common Market had significant consequences: in 1986, only about 8,000 tons of butter were exported, of which some 4,500 tons went to Morocco and 2,000 to Switzerland.

Keeping pace with the rising production and export of butter at the beginning of the century came the increased need for butter firkins. Production by craftsmen on the old basis was no longer sufficient; instead it had to be rationalised through the establishment of special stave factories where the coopers could order finished staves and heads. The coopers' own work was thus reduced to the assembly or 'raising' of the firkins.

Creamery production of butter brought with it a demand for higher quality, as a result of which regulations for the control of butter were enacted in 1896. Butter which was found to meet certain quality requirements at the testing stations was given a special stamp of approval, known as the 'rune brand'. This was branded along with the number of the local creamery on one of the staves of the butter firkin, the 'brand-stave' that was supplied direct to the coopers by the butter-testing stations (Fig. 2).

2. Brand-staves for butter firkins in Charles Olsson's cooperage. Photo: Sven Hjalmarson, Örkelljunga.

For butter firkins made by local craftsmen there had been allowances for marginal differences in the capacity of the casks, but the rune-branding system involved a thoroughgoing standardisation. Butter firkins of beech were nevertheless unsurpassed, so the new stave factories were situated in the beech forest areas of Southern Sweden. Examples of places with stave factories include Knobesholm east of Falkenberg, Stehag, Åstorp, Mala by Hässleholm, Bjärnum, and Östra Ringarp in Örkelljunga Parish. It is the stave production at the latter factory that we shall study more closely here.

Stave manufacture

Östra Ringarp could boast splendid beech forests at the end of the nineteenth century. Thanks to steam-powered saws it was now no longer necessary to locate factories near sources of water power. Yet it did require personal initiative and capital.

Denmark was a pioneer in the handling of milk produce, and it is evident that the idea for a stave factory in Ringarp came from there. A property registered as nos. 1-11 in Östra Ringarp was bought on 1st October 1892 by Jens Christian Hansen, a director from Copenhagen. One year later he sold it to Carl Christian Hansen, a manufacturer, and Leander Thorvald Wittus Thorlund, a wholesale merchant, both from Copenhagen. From a deed for the sale of part of the land, dated 4th February 1895, we learn that a sawmill had been erected. That the manufacture of butter firkins had begun is evident from a photograph (Fig. 3) which must have been taken some time between 1893 and 1897. The photograph shows the two Danish owners in the stave factory along with six workers.

On 30th August 1897 the freehold in Ringarp was sold by the two Danes to the farmers Johannes Bengtsson of Ekholm and Johan Peter Bengtsson of Skogen. On 16th January 1899 the latter became sole owner of the entire freehold; he then sold the freehold to his sons Albert and Josef Johansson, the sale being legally ratified on 14th February 1899. By 3rd November of the same year the land on which the sawmill stood, some 2½ acres, was parcelled off and five-sixths of it sold back to the father, J. P. Bengtsson, along with Alfred Andersson, Olander Bäck, Arvid Persson, and Gustaf Persson. A company to run the factory was thereby formed by Albert and Josef Johansson and these five purchasers.

Part of the agreement was that Albert and Josef Johansson should sell each year all the beechwood on the freehold in such a way that every year there would be felled 100 cords of 'six-foot high, six-foot wide, two-foot long' timber. No block was to be less than six inches at the top end. The

3. Interior of the stave factory in Östra Ringarp. Photo: Gollmann & Hansen, Store Strandstræde 6, Copenhagen, *ante* 1897.
From left to right: August Svensson of Östra Ringarp, the owners Hansen and Thorlund, Elof Eriksson of Östra Ringarp, Magnus Nilsson of Bälinge, August Johansson of Ånhult, August Eriksson of Östra Ringarp, and Gustaf Pålsson of Bälinge. The last owned the photograph and set it in a frame which he made himself. The picture was donated to the Örkelljunga Local History Society after the death of his daughter, Tora Pålsson.

blocks were to be well lopped down to the trunk, reasonably straight, and completely healthy. In addition, they were to sell annually five-sixths of 35 cords of beech blocks, to be supplied in various lengths, evidently for the manufacture of heads for the casks. Payment was calculated at nine kronor per foot length, including delivery to the sawmill. By this agreement Albert and Josef Johansson became the main suppliers of raw material to the stave factory. However, they were not allowed to supply timber other than that felled on their own freehold. All other timber buying had to be done by the owners of the company together.

Josef Johansson appears later to have bought up his brother Albert's share of the stave factory, and he then sold his holdings in the autumn of 1918 to Gustaf Persson of Västra Ringarp and the widow Petronella Bengtsson of Östra Ringarp. These were now the sole owners of the sawmill, but they in their turn sold out to Axel Bengtsson, Johan Persson, and Nils Johansson of Västra Ringarp. These three together ran the stave factory until the end of 1940, when Johan Persson (nephew of Gustaf Persson) became sole owner. The break-up of the three-man partnership may have been the result of financial difficulties. At the same time, the war had interrupted butter exports, with a reduced demand for butter firkins. The account books for the spring of 1941 show that the factory had started producing 'car wood', i.e. wood and charcoal for gas-powered vehicles; during the war years this was no doubt as important a source of income as stave production. Johan Persson continued running the factory until 1968, when there was no longer a market for butter firkins.

According to the deed of sale of 1899, the factory contained, besides a boiler and a steam engine, a cross-cut saw, one large and one small circular saw, a machine for planing the staves, and an emery-grinder. When the business changed hands in 1929, the deed of sale listed not only a cross-cut saw, a circular saw, and a planer, but also a stave saw, a trimming saw, a stave-jointing machine, a bundling machine, an overhead and thickness planing machine, a drill, and a round sawing machine. There is still no mention of a crozing machine, but the accounts for 1938 book the cost of this, 2,352 kronor. Before this, crozing (the cutting of the grooves for the heads) had therefore been done by hand by the coopers themselves.[18]

In the spring of 1913 the factory was razed to the ground after catching fire from sparks from the steam engine. The factory was rebuilt later in the same year with the somewhat larger premises that are still standing (Fig. 4). The entire machinery (with the exception of the steam engine) is still intact, although the stave factory is now used as a warehouse.

4. The Östra Ringarp stave factory rebuilt in 1913.

When the factory started production, the workers were not permanently employed, being taken on only when there were orders to fill. During the high season there was shift working for up to 12 or 14 hours. With an annual production of 25,000 butter firkins by the 1920s, the Ringarp factory was one of the biggest in the country.

One of the factory staff is still alive. Charles Olsson, born in 1913, started to work there at the age of 15 and stayed on until production stopped in 1968. We visited his former workplace together, and it is his reminiscences which form the basis of my account, along with a ten-minute long 16mm black-and-white film made by the photographer Sven Hjalmarson of Örkelljunga at a time when stave production was still flourishing.

The working day in Charles Olsson's time lasted from 7 a.m. until 5 p.m., with an hour for lunch and two coffee breaks. The engineer, however, had to start one hour earlier in order to build up the pressure in the steam engine.

The steam whistle sounded on Saturday at noon to indicate the end of the working week; it was then the workers received their pay. The hourly wage when Charles started was 30 öre, which was eight öre more than when a cooper in Osby started making butter casks in 1902.[19] Charles Olsson's pay when the factory closed in 1968 was no more than 10 kronor per hour.

Neither Charles nor any other worker at the factory was unionised. The sense of community among the workers was good, and there were no conflicts with the owners of the stave factory. The frequent changes of ownership around the turn of the century testify to a wave of financial speculation, but the owners were nevertheless, like many other small farmers and peasant craftsmen, profoundly Christian people.

Since heating was not installed before the 1940s, the factory was a very cold place in which to work. The men had to warm themselves by the steam engine during the breaks. In the summer they sat on the grass outside the factory. In Charles Olsson's early days the factory was lit during the dark winter hours by means of paraffin lamps (as seen in Fig. 3).

The timber-felling season began in November and lasted well into spring. Timber was initially bought from the owners of the Östra Ringarp estate and the farmers of Örkelljunga, Oderljunga, and Röke, and later also from forest owners on Söderåsen, where there was good beech timber.

A trolley was used to transport the two-foot long beech blocks on narrow rails to the saw, where they were cut into four inch thick planks. The width varied depending on the thickness of the wood. From these planks the stave blanks were then cut into thicknesses of 12mm.

When the stave blanks were cut, the timber was taken out in wheelbarrows to the base of spruce logs on which they were stacked for drying. They were piled, not directly on top of each other, but on the skew—to allow air to pass freely—in stacks which could reach heights of 150-170cm and lengths of 30-40m.

After being seasoned outdoors for three months, the undressed blanks could be brought into the factory, where they were cut by twin circular saws to lengths of 57cm, eight to ten at a time.

They were then fed by a roller to the stave plane with its conical blades, which planed them concave on the top and convex on the bottom and trimmed them to a thickness of approximately 7mm. The next stage was the 'listing' or dressing of the edges to give them their slightly bulging shape, broadest in the middle and narrower at either end. The edges were given exactly identical forms by means of a wooden template on the plane, but the width of the staves varied.

The next stage of the job was to croze (*krösa*) the staves by cutting a groove on the inside about 2mm wide and the same depth, near the top and bottom edges of the stave. This groove is known in Swedish as *lagg*. The crozing machine at the same time bevelled the inside ends of the stave.

The staves were now ready to be packed, a job often done by an old pensioner. The staves were piled side by side in two stacks, each about 325cm; this was equivalent to the number required for five firkins with a circumference at the belly of 130cm. In Ringarp it was usual to reckon on 20 staves for each butter firkin and 100 staves in each pack. The staves were sorted into first and second grades, and then a home-made bundling machine was used to tighten an iron band around them.

Cask bottoms could be made of slightly poorer timber, but the lids had to be of pure white wood. The edges of the undressed boards were shaved square with an overhead planer, after which one side was smoothed with a thickness planer. They were then nailed together by a nailing machine, which drove two nails into each board. It had previously been the practice to drill holes for dowels.

After nailing, the other side was planed, and then the heads were taken to the round sawing machine. Here they were cut round with a circular blade, which was slanted to bevel them on one side, at the same time as a plane bevelled the edges on the other side. Twenty-five lids and the same number of bottoms were bound together in one pack.

The staves were at first transported by horse and wagon to the railway, which opened in 1894. Later the coopers hired lorry drivers who picked them up direct from the factory. Second-grade staves were sent to coopers in Northern Sweden, while first-grade staves were intended for casks for export. Accounts surviving from 1930 show that many coopers bought staves from the factory in Östra Ringarp year after year. The main customers were Karl Svensson of Hillarp (Munka-Ljungby), C. D. Törnkvist of Björka, Nils Hansson of Sösdala, Erik Henningsson of Hasslöv (southern Halland). A major customer for several years was G. V. Lindkvist (later called Wecke) of Lund, and there were also deliveries to wood-processing factories in Stehag and Åstorp (Johansson's). In the 1930s the stave producers joined together to form the Association of Stave Manufacturers Limited, and from 1937 most deliveries were made to this association.

Assembling the butter firkins

Coopering was originally a guild-based craft and thus concentrated in the towns. However, casks were also made by peasant craftsmen. The coopers in Kristianstad complained in the eighteenth century in a petition to the Board of Trade that peasants in the Göinge region were supplying the

5. 'The Cooper', from a series of pictures of craftsmen, painted on linen by Johannes Nilsson of Breared, Halland, in 1804. Nordiska Museet, Stockholm, no. 48061. Another wall hanging by Johannes Nilsson depicts the cooper's plane (see further Bringéus 1975: 40, 74, 82; Bringéus 1982: 20 ff.).

Scanian countryside with casks and thus spoiling the market for profession-al coopers.[20] As we saw above from Dean Osbeck's description from Laholm in 1796, herring barrels at this time were being made 'by our own peasants' (Fig. 5). The county customs register for Båstad for 1798 shows that, as well as staves, full-size barrels, half-barrels, and quarter-barrels were being brought in from six different villages in Örkelljunga Parish, and the same was true of Våxtorp and Tåssjö.

In Norra Åsbo this manufacture had older traditions. In a report from the county governor of 1740 it is recorded that 'those peasants who live in the Northern Hundred, where there are forests of oak, beech, and alder, can earn some money by the making of wooden vessels'.[21] Gillberg also mentions 'all manner of coopering work' in the northern parishes of the hundred in his description from 1762.

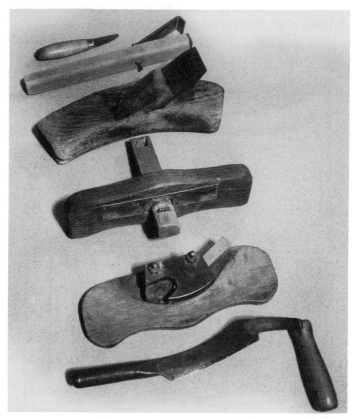

6. Old coopering tools in Charles Olsson's workshop. The knife, the hoop lever and the topping plane (at the top of the picture) can still be used when needed. The draw knife at the bottom was used to smooth the grooves in which the heads of the casks were set. The two other tools were used to cut the grooves.

The manufacture of staves and finished firkins continued in Örkelljunga after the arrival of the stave factory in Ringarp. The last man to run the factory, Johan Persson, also made butter firkins, together with his brother-in-law Gunnar Olander. According to the account books, Johan Persson began buying staves from the company in ever greater quantities from 1935 onwards. During the war and in the post-war years he regularly supplied butter firkins to the nearby creameries of Örkelljunga, Röke, and Heljalt (in Oderljunga), and from 1949 also to the creamery in Hjärnarp.

Charles Olsson also learned the skill of raising casks at the stave factory. When production ceased in 1968, he bought some of the remaining stock of staves and heads, and in the past twenty years he has carried on the making of butter firkins in a little workshop under the general store in Hjelmsjö, a few miles from the stave factory. His collection of tools includes some older cooper's implements that are no longer used, such as the *krösa* or croze (Fig. 6) which was used to cut the grooves for the heads.[22]

Charles Olsson begins the assembly of the firkin by placing the 'raising-up ring' on a stool 20cm high. The bottom hoop of the ring is 34cm in diameter (Fig. 7). The brand-stave and about 19 others with a belly width varying between 3 and 7cm are set around the inside of the ring. When the staves are in place, the ring is slowly raised (Fig. 8). Then the cask is turned upside down and a hammer is used to drive the lower truss as far as possible towards the belly of the cask. In the film, Gunnar Olander uses the older coopering method of working from the top with the raising-up ring around

7.　　　　　　　　　　　　　　　　　　8.

7-17. Charles Olsson raising up and hooping a butter firkin in his workshop in Hjelmsjö, 14th September 1987. Photos: Sven Hjalmarson.

the upper ends of the staves. To help hold the staves upright the raising-up ring had a little iron rim set at an angle on the inside (corresponding to the wooden flange on the type formerly used by coopers).

Next the cooper threads an iron cable around the splayed ends of the staves, pulling them together with a windlass (Fig. 9), thus making the top end of the cask tight (according to the film this was previously done with a rope pulled tight with the help of a pulley mounted to a bench). Once a truss is put around the staves, the cable can be removed, and there is now an open cask without heads (Fig. 10).

9.   10.

Now the cask has to be given its bottom. Two stout truss hoops are hammered down with an iron *drev* 'driver' (Fig. 11). Then a ready-nailed bottom is forced down into the groove with the aid of the hammer shaft (Fig. 12). Sometimes it may be necessary to loosen the outer hoop to get the bottom into the groove. Then the ends or chimes of the staves have to be smoothed at top and bottom with a topping plane (Fig. 13).

Next the cask has to be bound with withies which have been softened in water. About 10cm from one end a notch is cut down to the middle of the withy (Fig. 14). This is then wound round the cask and the cooper measures for the notch at the other end, which is cut on the opposite side of the withy. When the ends are overlapped, the notches slot together to 'lock' the hoop, which can be forced over the top of the cask and pushed down as far as

11.

12.

13.

possible towards the bulge with a wooden driver (Fig. 15). This first withy is fixed in place with two pins at the joint. Then a new withy is prepared in the same way and pushed down towards the first. To keep it in place it is held by small pins all round the cask. When the hoops are fixed in place the protruding ends of the withies are cut off with a sharp knife.

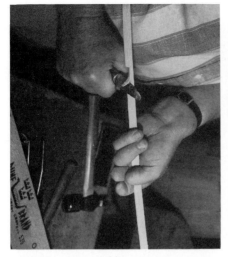 

14.   15.

The same procedure is repeated around the lower bulge of the cask, as well as around either chime, sometimes with the aid of the hoop lever (Fig. 16), so that the firkin has a total of eight hoops sitting in pairs.

16.   17.

When the cask is hooped it holds together without the assistance of raising-up rings and truss hoops. The firkin is now finished (Fig. 17).

On average a cooper could assemble twenty firkins in an eight-hour day. In the days when the cooper himself had to dress and croze the staves and nail the heads together, a deft and tenacious cooper could at most produce five or six butter firkins in a ten-hour working day.[23] Whether the finished cask was perfectly tight or not was of minor importance, since it was intended for storing butter and was lined inside with greaseproof butter paper. The lid was only loosely fitted by the cooper, and was not finally nailed fast until it was filled with butter at the creamery.

Butter firkins for new uses

The old way of selling butter in the shop—loose by weight direct from the cask—gave way in the 1930s to the sale of rune-branded butter wrapped in half- and quarter-kilo packs.[24]

Development, however, did not proceed so quickly outside Sweden. A picture of a cold store from 1957 shows butter firkins for export being stacked using pallets and fork-lift trucks.[25] However, the price of beech was

18. Charles Olsson's stock of finished firkins and half-firkins in Hjelmsjö. The firkin in the centre foreground is made entirely of brand-staves. In the top row to the left there is a firkin which has been given a patina with a blowlamp and bound with brass hoops. On the far left is a cask of stouter wood intended for beer. On the shelves in the background there are some headpieces. Photo: Sven Hjalmarson. Butter firkins exactly like these can be seen in the Nordiska Museet in Stockholm (from Urshult in Småland and Falkenberg in Halland).

too high and the firkin became too expensive a form of disposable packaging, so in August 1970 firkins were replaced by 25 kg cartons.[26] The firkin had had its day in Swedish butter distribution. The remaining stave factories had to close down or change to the production of other articles.

A butter firkin can be used for things other than butter, however. From his stock of staves and heads, Johan Persson and after him Charles Olsson of Örkelljunga began to make casks for ornamental use. They could, for example, be fitted with lids and used to store wool or other goods (Fig. 18).

These new functions involved certain changes. The firkin was rather too large a cask for ornamental purposes, so 'half-firkins' were made instead, although these are not exactly half the volume: they can hold 35 kg of butter instead of 50 kg.

The casks were now decorated with two rune-branded staves, something which never existed during the days when butter was exported in them. Since there were only brand-staves for firkins and not for half-firkins, they had to be shortened at both ends. Other changes were forced by shortage of materials: the withies formerly bought from Poland and Germany have been largely replaced by hoops of cane, which is suppler and easier to work with.

Another consequence of the production of ornamental casks is that these are smoothed with rasps and files to remove any roughness; this was unheard of in the past. Some buyers have wanted their casks varnished or even given a patina with the aid of a blowlamp, all with the intention of making them look more antique.

In the same way as baskets of juniper wood, the Örkelljunga butter firkin has been transformed from a package into a souvenir or a symbol of an old craft. The firkin is not thrown away or chopped up for firewood as used to be the case with this disposable pack.

The casks are no longer sold on a commercial basis. By donating a firkin to the church sewing club auction—where it can fetch a price of up to 500 kronor—this form of handicraft attracts an attention that can lead to new orders. Charles Olsson has also demonstrated the manufacturing process a few times at the local history society in Ingeborrarp.

Charles Olsson is the last practitioner of a craft which has long provided a living for the people who live by Hallandsåsen. The occupation of stave cutter, cooper, and firkin maker was never highly esteemed. When a street in Örkelljunga was named *Bödkaregatan* 'Cooper Street' a few decades ago, it was not considered respectable enough by one industrialist who lived there. Yet today Charles Olsson's butter firkins can even be seen at the local library as a reminder of the old craft of the region. Perhaps, amid all the learning amassed on the shelves, these artefacts can still tempt young people to think about the question that Frans G. Bengtsson poses in *The Paradise I Remember*: 'Why do people become better, the less they do with their hands?'

NOTES

1. N.-A. Bringéus, Gotlandsräfsan. In *Gotländskt arkiv*, 1963; Från bondehantverk till småindustri. Ett räfsmakeri under tre generationer. In *Skånes Hembygdsförbunds årsbok*, 1964.

2. T. Nilsson, Tunnan—containerns föregångare. In *Kulturen*, 1987, 46.

3. *Kulturhistoriskt Lexikon för Nordisk Medeltid* XVI (1971), s.v. *smör, smörhandel, smörskatt*.

4. N.-A. Bringéus, *Resekörare och besekrämare. Om handeln i Örkelljungabygden*, 1983, 75.

5. B. Boëthius and E. Hecksher, *Svensk handelsstatistik 1637-1737*, 1938, 104, 313, 563.

6. B. Hanssen, *Österlen. En studie över socialantropologiska sammanhang under 1600- och 1700-talen i sydöstra Skåne*, 1952, 163, 225.

7. Bringéus 1983, *op.cit.*, 70ff.

8. P. Osbeck, *Utkast till beskrifning öfver Laholms prosteri 1796*, 1922, 94, 364.

9. A.G. Barchaeus, *Underrättelser angående landthushållningen i Halland, samlade under en resa—1773*, 1924, 48.

10. R. Kloster, Håndverksbygden og bygdehåndverkeren. In S. Svensson, ed., *Nordisk folkkonst*, 1972, 130.

11. A. Sandklef, Hallands folkkultur. In *Hallands historia 2* (1959), 1003.

12. *Topografiska och statistiska uppgifter om Kristianstads län* (Generalstabens Topografiska afdelning), 1876, 34.

13. Bringéus 1983, *op.cit.*, 74.

14. *Nordiska Museets hantverksundersökningar.*

15. *Historiskt-geografiskt och statistiskt lexikon öfver Sverige*, VII (1866), 595.

16. *Sveriges mejeriväsen*, 1892 (printed 1893), 12ff.

17. *Svensk mejeriindustri. Svenska mejeriernas riksförening 1932-1957*, 1957, 76ff.

18. C.F. O[lsson], Tunnbinderiet—ett yrke som försvinner. In *Ystads Allehanda* 18/3 (1950).

19. T. Brogårdh, *Kring en gammal riksgräns*, 1971, 28.

20. A.-M. Nylén, *Hemslöjd. Den svenska hemslöjden fram till 1800-talets slut*, 1968, 376.

21. Bringéus 1964, *op.cit.*, 82.

22. Brogårdh 1971, *op.cit.*, 27.

23. *Ib.*, 28.

24. B. Conradson, Vår förpackade historia. In *Kulturen*, 1978, 29.

25. *Svensk mejeriindustri 1967, årsredovisning för Svenska mejeriernas riksförening*, 1 (1968), 77.
26. S. Johansson, Smör. In *Mejerilära utgiven av SMR:s personal- och utbildningsgrupp*, part 5 (1979), 65.

THE PLUNGE CHURN FROM IRELAND TO TIBET

Janken Myrdal

Introduction

Just as travel abroad teaches you to know your own country better, so also can you better understand your own culture and its peculiarities through relating it to a broader geographical context.

Taking this as my goal, I shall here deal with questions about one of the more important implements in the material culture of Europe: the plunge churn. This was in most cases a women's tool, milking being a feminine duty. The plunge churn belongs both to the sphere of food production and to the sphere of domestic duties. Churning was usually done in the kitchen area or in a separate milk chamber.

In its typical form the plunge churn is a high and narrow vessel with a plunger, the churn staff, which terminates in a cross or a round disk. The vessel is most often made of wood and stave-built, with a height usually between a half and one metre. The disk, and sometimes also the cross, at the end of the churn staff normally has holes. During churning the grease particles in the milk or cream are stirred until they coagulate into butter. The churn staff is worked up and down to make the liquid spurt through the holes or pass alongside the cross or the disk. The method is efficient and the same principle is used in modern churns.

This type of plunge churn can be found over most of Eurasia from the Atlantic coast in the west to Mongolia in the east. The classical questions in research on material culture can be raised: where, when and how did it spread, and why?

The general survey of the geographical distribution given below refers mainly to the last period before industrialisation, the end of the nineteenth and the beginning of the twentieth century. My point of departure is Sweden; I shall then pass on to the rest of Europe and to Asia, leaving the New World aside.

Sweden

Stave-built plunge churns dominated in the entire country. The vessels were occasionally wider at the bottom, but more often were of uniform width.

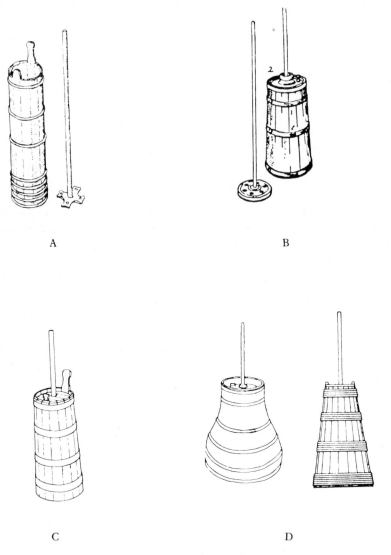

Fig 1. A: Dalecarlia, Sweden, from L. Levander, *Övre Dalarnas bondekultur*, 3 (Uppsala 1947), 358; B: Yorkshire, England, from M. Hartley and J. Ingilby, *Life and Tradition in the Yorkshire Dales* (London 1968), 18; C: Westfalen, Germany, from Siuts 1982, Taf. 75; D: Flanders, Belgium, from Lindemans 1952, 381 and Weyns 1974, 904.

The staffs were provided with crosses or disks, crosses being more common in North Sweden. Two informants considered that a staff with a cross is less effective when used in cream that is not sour and thick. A churn of just on 50cm height was reckoned as small, the size partly depending on the number of cows kept on the farm. Cream for one churning could be gathered over a whole week, but churning could also be done several times a week.[1] The cream was often fairly sour when churned. Milk from cows was the basic liquid for butter making, more rarely milk from goats or sheep.[2]

That cream was skimmed from milk, that churning was done once a week or somewhat more often, that the size of the plunge churn was related to the number of cows and that cow milk dominated, are facts valid for the main part of Europe, but in some regions milk from sheep played a greater role in butter making.

Some churns in Sweden had a small hole, with a tap, near the bottom of the vessel. Occasionally fresh milk was poured into the churn immediately after milking, and the skimmed milk could eventually be drained off through the hole, leaving the cream in the churn. More common was to use such holes to drain the buttermilk after churning. In Denmark some churns had similar holes for draining.[3]

In southernmost Sweden, in Scania, small vessels of earthenware exist as a sub-group among plunge churns. The diffusion of these pottery vessels is primarily due to a scarcity of wood, but their small size is also explained by the less developed cattle breeding and dairying in the corn-growing plains of Scania.

Besides staved vessels there are also some cut out of a single log. The existence of this type is dictated mainly by the wood supply, and it cannot be held as an older type. The stave-building technique was known in north-western Europe from about the birth of Christ, before the plunge churn was introduced.

A totally different type is the shake churn, which existed as a relict in a small region of Western Sweden, Northern Värmland, up to the nineteenth century. It was used by descendants of Finns who, arriving in Sweden in the sixteenth century, had preserved an old-fashioned material culture. Their shake churns were small cylinders of birch-bark held with both hands when shaken.

To shake or whip the cream is the most rudimentary way to make butter. This method was used all over Sweden for smaller amounts of cream, for instance by poor people. Only in Northern Värmland was a special implement used for shaking the cream; it was not an occasional solution but much more a typological and partly chronological forerunner of the plunge churn. As we shall see, the shake churn was not typically Finnish, but existed in all the fringes of the area where the plunge churn dominated in Europe.

Already in the pre-industrial society the plunge churn was beginning to be replaced by more effective types. In Sweden the barrel churn became the most widespread new type, and butter-cradles also existed (they had to be filled with a lot of cream to be fit for use). But the diffusion of the more modern types falls outside the scope of this survey.

Europe

Westward from Sweden, in Denmark and Norway, the same conditions are found. The staved plunge churn predominated. In Denmark pottery vessels with churn staffs also existed. One difference between Nordic and Continental churns is that the former more often do not have lids.

In Germany stave-built plunge churns dominated. The churn staffs normally end in crosses or holed disks. Other types of churn staffs exist, but they are always mere variations of the two main types. Rather big pottery vessels existed as a sub-type.[4]

Even in the British Isles staved plunge churns were the major type. Estyn Evans' account of the different types in Ireland has shown that churn staffs with crosses were more common in the western parts of the island. In Shetland and Orkney plunge churns without lids were used.[5]

In Ireland and Wales shake churns existed as a relict. The type was a wooden vessel hung from a rope or on a pole in such a way that it could be rocked back and forth. In the Hebrides pottery vessels or even skin bags were used in much the same way.[6]

In the Netherlands a rich variety of churns existed, but the stave-built plunge churn dominated. The more developed barrel churn was in use already in the seventeenth century, and spread extensively in the nineteenth. Some of the staved churns in the Netherlands had a curved, bulging form, and the same type can also be found for instance in Wales and Ireland. Otherwise the churns nearly always had straight sides, which is also in line with the stave-building technique.[7]

Even in France plunge churns were used, but in the southernmost part of the country butter was of less importance. The plunger type existed only in parts of this region, and then as a late introduction during the nineteenth century. Before that shake churns were used. These were leather or skin bags which were set in motion in different ways. They could be found in use up to modern times in northwestern Spain.[8]

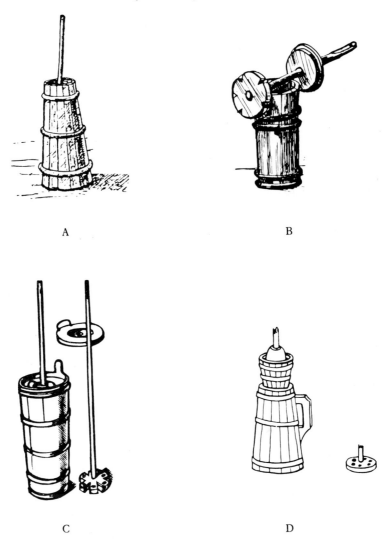

Fig. 2. A: Central France, from W. Egloff, *Le paysan dombiste* (Paris 1937), 25; B: Switzerland, from Weiss 1941, 145; C: Northern Italy, from Scheuermeier 1943, 32; D: Austria, from Gaál 1969, Taf. 33.

We have now reached those parts of Europe where olive oil replaces butter as the fat in cooking. Cattle were kept mainly as a source of traction power and meat. Milk from goats and sheep was used for cheese-making. The highly developed cheese culture in Southern Europe is thus partly in contradiction to butter-making; it is especially concerned with the making of cheeses with a high fat context. In northern Europe skimmed milk was most often the basis for cheese-making.

In Italy we again meet this cultural border between butter and olive oil as fat for cooking purposes. Butter-making occurred only in the northernmost part of the country, bordering Switzerland, and there the plunge churn was in use. Already on the coast around Genoa and Venice butter was rare, and in these regions cream was shaken or whipped to make butter.[9]

In Switzerland dairy production was well developed and the stave-built plunge churn was the dominating butter-making implement. In this territory we can also already in the sixteenth century find an early mechanisation of churning, with a lever to work the churn staff.[10] Similar arrangements also existed in other parts of Europe in the eighteenth and nineteenth centuries.

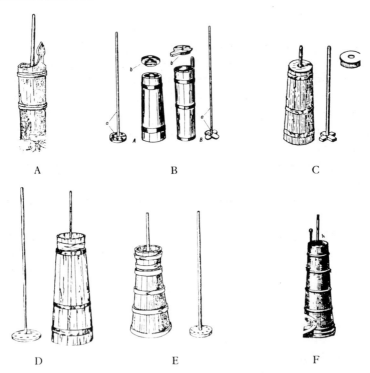

Fig 3. A: Finland, from Grotenfelt 1906, 29; B: Lithuania, from *Lietuviu kalbos atlasas 1: Lexika*, (Vilnius 1977), 143; C: White Russia, from *Narody Evropejskoj casti SSSR*, 1 (Moscow 1964), 794; D: Poland, from Kowalska-Lewicka 1970, 120; E: Bohemia and Moravia, from L. Kunz, Die traditionelle Milch- und Käsewirtschaft in Mittel- und Westmähren. In *Viehwirtschaft und Hirtenkultur* (Budapest 1969), 717; F: Albania, from F. B. Nopcsa, *Albanien: Bauten, Trachten und Geräte Nordalbaniens* (Berlin 1925), 99.

Even in the main part of Austria staved plunge churns existed. But in the southeastern part of the country small earthenware vessels were used as plunge churns up to the late nineteenth century, when the larger stave-built churn was introduced in connection with the passage from production for home use to production for the market.[11]

In Finland the stave-built plunge churn was universal. Even in Estonia plunge churns were in use, but the shake churn existed as a relict. If we continue southwards, we find the plunge churn in Latvia and Lithuania. In Poland the stave-built plunge churn was predominant, but high pottery vessels especially made as churns were also in use.[12]

The plunge churn was dominant in Czechoslovakia. In Hungary it came into use rather late over the whole country. The shaking or whipping of cream to make butter was earlier dominant in large regions.[13]

In Russia we find a totally different method of butter-making. Here the cream was heated up in an oven until the butter fat was precipitated. Sometimes the butter was worked slightly, but it was not churned. The plunge churn was introduced as a novelty especially in White Russia but also in parts of Greater Russia in recent times. [14] Among cattle-breeders east and south of the Russians this method, the separating of butter grease through heating, was known[15] (but shake churns were also used by nomadic tribes east of the Russians, and further to the east and south, plunge churns).

This method had its counterpart in one of the procedures for preserving butter. In West Europe the common way to preserve butter was to salt it down. But in parts of East Europe it was melted and then left to stiffen. This means of preparing the butter made it very durable, and the method was used not only in Russia, but also in, for instance, Moravia, Hungary and Yugoslavia. Presumably there is some connection between the diffusion of this type of butter preparation and the Russian method of making butter, where the preparation method could be the older one. (In India, too, butter is melted, and clarified to *ghee* before being consumed.)

In the northern part of Yugoslavia, in Slovenia, pottery vessels were earlier used as plunge churns, but later a change to stave-built wooden churns occurred, as in adjoining southeastern Austria. In the Serbo-Croatian parts of the country the plunge churn is known, but in some regions on the coast shake churns, skin bags, were used instead. The plunge churn is also distributed in the southern part of Yugoslavia, the Macedonian area, as in adjoining Albania.

In Rumania and Bulgaria the stave-built plunge churn exists, but here we cross another border. In older times in Rumania it was common to churn the whole milk, without first separating the cream. The milk was allowed to get sour and thick to be churnable. In Bulgaria cream was seldom used in butter-making, and instead sour milk or even yoghurt, with its special bacterial culture, was churned. In Bulgaria and Rumania we also find the shake churn particularly among the cattle herdsmen.

According to the ethnologist Zelenin it was not common in the Ukraine to make butter in the Russian way. The plains north of the Black Sea had an exchange of different cultures, with periods of settled farming with little emphasis on cattle-breeding, followed by periods of growing nomadism and the dominance of cattle-breeders. The plunge churn was no doubt in use, at least periodically, in large parts of Southern Russia.

In the northern parts of Caucasia, for instance, the Nogai Tartars had stave-built plunge churns. Like other nomadic peoples, their history starts with migrations, but from the thirteenth century they were settled in the region between the Black Sea and the Caspian Sea. If we turn south to the Caucasus we cross the southern border for the extension of the plunge churn and reach the huge territory where the shake churn predominates. In Georgia, plunge churns in pottery vessels can still be found, but in Georgia and Armenia as a whole shake churns of wood and earthenware, hung up and rocked, were standard.[16]

Before we continue into Asia, a short summing up of the European extension may be given. The plunge churn was distributed throughout most of the continent. In the central parts the plunge churns were retreating in the face of newer and more effective types like the barrel churn; but at the same time the plunge churn was spreading in the outer regions of its extension, as in the Pyrenees where it replaced the shake churn, or in White Russia where it replaced butter-making through heating.

In the southeastern corner of Europe cream was not the basic liquid for butter-making. Instead, whole milk was churned when sour and thick. This relates to a wider Asian territory where the churning of whole milk was dominant.[17] (Buttermilk played a more important role when the whole milk was churned.)

In the rest of Europe the separated cream was used for butter-making, but the churning of whole milk existed as an older cultural layer. The Finnish ethnologist Sirelius mentions that it existed as a relict in Finland, and Evans demonstrates the same for Ireland. In England butter could be made of whole milk in the seventeenth and eighteenth centuries, but the skimming of cream was more common.[18] Even in the Netherlands, with its highly developed dairy production, butter-making from whole milk existed, but the method was used only by poor peasants owning one or two cows.[19]

Butter churned from whole milk resulted in a less pure butter, with a lower concentration of butter fat, and in most parts of North and West Europe the method was totally unknown in the period immediately preceding industrialisation. The separation of cream is a more recent and more developed method. The climate can have been of importance for the spread of this method. If the milk is not kept cold it will become sour and coagulate before the fat can rise to the surface. Separation of cream thus needed greater effort in a hot climate than in a cold one.

Asia

If we continue southward from Caucasia to West Asia we find shake churns everywhere. Whole milk was shaken in skin bags or pottery vessels until the butter could be collected from the buttermilk. An instructive description of the process is given by Gustaf Dalman in his work on Palestine.[20]

Before continuing to the east we can have a look at the south and west, where cattle breeders all over North and East Africa make butter. The shake type was universal in this area, and in wide regions of East Africa calabashes were used as churns.[21]

The shake churn dominated from West Asia over the plateaux of Iran up to Afghanistan. Nomadic cattle breeders mainly used hanging skin bags, and among more settled farmers pottery vessels were often used. In Anatolia and Caucasia wooden vessels can also be found.

Pottery vessels, probably used as shake churns, have been recorded from archaeological sources in Sogdiana, south of the Aral Sea, from about the eighth to the tenth century.[22] In this area the plunge churn was later to dominate butter making.

In Afghanistan the three most important types of vessel for the making of butter meet.[23] In the north plunge churns are used, in the west shake churns, and in the south-west the milk was whipped to butter with rotary drill churns. The last-mentioned types dominated in India and Pakistan. A cord is laid round a staff standing in a pot. When the rope is drawn to and fro the staff turns. This churn with a rotating stick or staff, here called a drill churn, functions like the simplest type of drill. This rather efficient technique has been used for a long time. A drill churn is mentioned already in Indian mythology datable to about the birth of Christ.

Returning to the plunge churn, we find it again in northern Afghanistan. In Afghanistan, as in isolated cases in Iran and also in

E

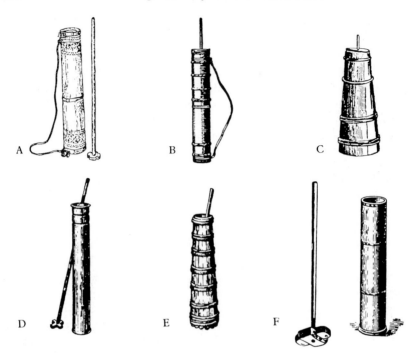

Fig. 4. A: Tajik SSR, from *Narody Srednej Azii i Kazachstana*, 1 (Moscow 1962), 559; B: Kazakh SSR, *ibid*; C: Uzbek SSR, from *Archeologi cheskie i etnografi cheskie raboty Xorezmskoj ekspedicii 1945-1948* (Moscow 1953), 360; D: Kashmir, from *Narody Južnoj Azzi* (Moscow 1963), 360; E: Tibet, from R. Kartuz, *Die Völker Nord- und Mittelasiens* (Stuttgart 1925), 57; F: Buryats, *ibid.*, 65.

Anatolia, butter could be made through churning with a staff furnished with a cross in a big skin bag. This form must be regarded as a sub-type of the plunge churn.

The staved plunge churn also existed along the river Amu Daria (Oxus) up to the Aral Sea, as in the rest of Uzbek SSR, and in Tajik SSR. In these regions pottery vessels used as plunge churns also existed. Among the Uzbeks and Tajiks shake churns and drill churns also existed.

In Kashmir, bordering Tibet, the stave-built plunge churn was in use, as in Tibet. In the last-mentioned country the plunge churn had, and still has, a central role in the material culture. [24]   Butter is important as food, especially in the much used butter-tea, a kind of soup made of tea mixed with butter. Butter is also important in the Lamaitic ceremonial, and huge amounts are used as fuel for temple lamps.

In the mountain highlands of Inner Asia the yak replaces ordinary

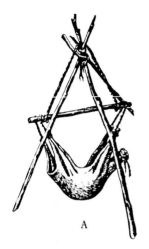

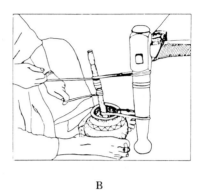

A   B

Fig. 5. A: Shake churn from Central Asia, from *Narody Srednej Azii i Kazachstana*, 1 (Moscow 1962), 599; B: Indian drill churn, from M.-C. Mahias, *Délivrance et convivialité: Le système culinaire des Jaina* (Paris 1985), 166.

cattle, and the base for butter-making was yak milk, which had a higher percentage of fat.

The common plunge churn in Central Asia looked very much like those in Europe. Generally they were staved and the churn staff ended in a cross or a disk with holes. A certain difference is that churns in Tibet and adjoining parts of Central Asia frequently were more narrow than those in Europe, although they had about the same height. Possibly this made the Central Asian churns easier to transport. In Tibet the churns often had a carrying strap.

Churning related in this area to whole milk, as elsewhere outside Europe, and the cream was seldom separated.

If we continue to follow the extension of the plunge churn to the east, we find it in Mongolia, for instance among the North Mongolians, the Buryats. Their churns were stave-built and not as narrow as the churns in Central Asia.

East and south of Tibet and Mongolia the limit for the extension of the plunge churn is set by the Han-Chinese aversion to all kinds of milk products; the same holds true for the peoples of Southeast Asia. This aversion has to a certain extent purely biological reasons. The Chinese people generally do not have the enzymes necessary for breaking down the lactose (in cow milk) to glucose, a biological divergence that in the longer perspective has its basis in the cultural history of mankind.

In the arctic parts of Eurasia the economy and activities were mainly concentrated upon hunting and fishing, and butter played a minor role or none at all. Amongst some of the Lapps in North Scandinavia reindeer milk could be used for butter-making in shake churns. Even among the Sojots in the middle of Siberia shake churns were used to make butter from reindeer milk.

An interesting case is the Yakuts living in the region around lower Lena. Their economy was dominated by horse- and cattle-breeding, and both mares and cows were milked. Simple churn staffs with a hollowed disk were used for the preparation of koumiss, made of milk from mares.[25]

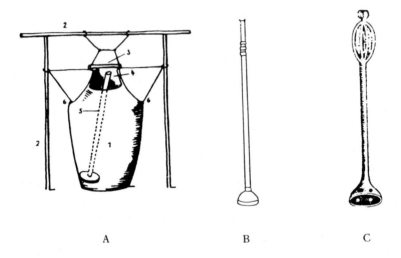

A   B   C

Fig. 6. A: Leather sack with churn staff for koumiss-making, from J. Schubert, *Paralipomena Mongolica* (Berlin 1971), 176; B: Yakutian churn staff for koumiss-making, after Levin and Potapov 1964, 256; C: Kalmukian churn staff for butter, from Martiny 1895, 28.

The remotest extension of the plunge churn in eastern and northern Asia is rather uncertain, at least for me, and the diffusion map is thus more uncertain in its outlines for Asia than for Europe.

The Kalmuks, a cattle-breeding people spread from western Mongolia to the east of the Caspian sea, had plunge churns, and at least in some cases the end of the churn staff was of a bulging shape and hollow form, and was thus similar to the churn staffs the Yakuts used for koumiss making.

Koumiss is a fermented liquor prepared from mare's milk. To the nomadic peoples of the Eurasian steppes it was culturally as well as economically very important. The making of koumiss plays a certain role for our understanding of the diffusion of the plunge churn.

Mare's milk turns sour faster than cow's milk, and has to be fermented to make it keep. Old milk could be added to hasten the process. To disperse the fermentation as evenly as possible the liquid must be stirred with a staff. The end of the staff could be hollow in form, like the Yakut ones, but it could also end in a cross or a disk with holes like the ordinary churn staff for butter-making.[26] There must have been some interaction between these two implements, used side by side from Mongolia to Hungary.

Koumiss is mentioned already by Herodotus in a text concerning the Scythians living north of the Black Sea. He describes the process, and reports that the liquid was stirred, but does not mention any churn staff.

In the middle of the thirteenth century the Dutch monk William of Rubruck went as a diplomatic envoy to the Mongols. He describes how the nomads living in the territory controlled by the Golden Horde made koumiss. He tells that the mare's milk was poured into a skin bag or a vessel and that they 'set about churning it with a stick prepared for that purpose, and which is as big as a man's head at its lower extremity and hollowed out'.[27]

The staff seems to be similar to the churn staff later used by the Yakuts for the the same purpose.

The association between the implements for koumiss and butter-making also emphasises that the plunge churn actually belongs to two different economic systems. In Central Asia it was used by nomadic herdsmen and in Europe by settled farmers.

Because of our European point of departure, it is necessary to relate at least some of the characteristic features of the nomadic culture. It is obvious that the nomads do not move around at large. Every tribe had its more or less formally delimited regions where their grazing grounds were situated. During winter, the nomads tended to be more stationary than in summer, when they sought to exploit as wide grazing areas as possible. As the climate was mainly dry, a second type of economy often developed: intensive agriculture with irrigation. The exchange between farmers and nomads was of great economic and cultural importance.

Several divisions of the nomadic economies have been suggested. The classifications are, as a rule, based on the degree of sedentarisation.[28] At one extreme, groups roam around all the year, without staying for long at any site, even if their route or grazing areas could be fairly stable. An intermediary type is groups that are more settled for a part of the year, i.e. in winter, and nomadic for the rest of the year. At the other extreme are peoples whose wanderings are concentrated on a shorter period of the year. The first are the true full-nomads, the second are here called semi-nomads (even if they too must be regarded as true nomads), and the third are close to the kind of transhumance which can be found in Europe.

Full nomadism is especially common in the most arid parts of Inner Asia, and was carried on, for instance, by some tribes in the north in Kazakhstan and in the south in Turkestan and also in Mongolia. In this type of nomadism sheep and horses as a rule totally dominate. Cattle are less well adapted to perpetual movement. Full nomadism is normally not immediately linked to any corn-growing.

Around Pamir we find instead a type of cattle-breeding rather similar to the form of transhumance in Europe with rather short migrations with cattle, in summer.

The use of the plunge churn was mainly limited to the semi-nomads and those engaged in transhumance. The most important reason for this is that the full nomads did not have access to cow's milk, which nearly everywhere was the base for butter-making. They had therefore no need for butter churns. The spread of the plunge churn was thus not unbroken over the steppes. In the most arid regions around and north of the Aral Sea, butter was not much used by the nomads.

This does not, however, allow us to speak of two separate regions of extension for the plunge churn. A strong cultural interchange existed over the steppes north and east of the Caspian Sea. In times of war and famine nomadic tribes could migrate to distant regions. Even more important for cultural interchange were the trade routes linking east and west. The extension of the plunge churn follows the silk road with its connections north of the Caspian Sea.

If the plunge churn was an innovation from one region to another, this ought to have happened during periods when trade contacts were flourishing and the caravan routes were protected by strong states.

How old is the plunge churn as a technical innovation in Asia? Three different sources of information are at our disposal: written sources, pictures and archaeological material. The last-mentioned must be, for a simple implement such as the churn and for earlier periods, our main source, and for Asia I am going to look only at this source. Archaeology that provides organic material is essential not just for the study of churns but for the whole cultural history of pre-industrial times, because the basic material was then in most cases wood.

An utterly arid climate in parts of Inner Asia has preserved wood for ages. The conditions for preservation of organic material are in these regions as good as along the coast of the North Sea, but for totally different reasons, since in Northwestern Europe wood is preserved in waterlogged sites. The wood material from Inner Asia could, if it was presented and summarised, give us a good picture of the history of material culture in this region of outstanding importance for cultural interchange in Eurasia.

A few well-known publications already exist, for example by Aurel Stein, and those concerned with the excavations led by Sven Hedin. The archaeological material presented covers the period from slightly before the birth of Christ to the centuries immediately after A.D. 1000. At a site in the Edsen-Gol region, in the eastern part of Inner Mongolia, on the northern route of the silk road, a probable plunge churn disk has been identified. It is datable to c. A.D. 1000-1200. Bo Sommarström has characterised this find as unique, and it has no counterpart in the older wooden material stretching back to the first century B.C.[29] An alternative interpretation is that this plunger was used for koumiss-making.

Before we return to Europe it may be appropriate to give a short summary of the extension of the plunge churn in Asia. It was an implement of central importance in Tibet and adjoining parts of the Asian steppes. The southern border of its spread follows approximately the Himalayas and the Kara-Kum desert to the Caspian Sea and Caucasus.

The form of the Asian plunge churn is similar to its European counterpart, even down to being staved and having a staff with a cross or a perforated disk. Everywhere whole milk was churned, and cow's milk (or yak milk) was the normal base for the production. At what time the plunge churn was introduced into Asia is still an open question; but the above-mentioned finds of shake churns in Sogdiana and of a plunge churn in Inner Mongolia together with William of Rubruck's report of churn staffs for koumiss hint at a breakthrough for the churn staff and perhaps also for the plunge churn for butter in Asia around A.D. 1000. If this is true, it coincides with a period of growing trade and cultural contacts between Asia and Europe from the Crusades to the Mongols.

Calling attention once again to the cultural interchange between East and West, I return to Europe, trying to establish when the plunge churn was first introduced there.

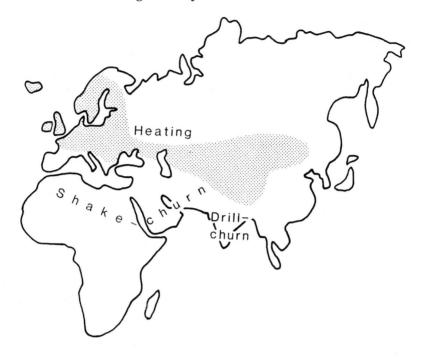

Fig. 7. The main techniques for butter-making in the late nineteenth century. The spread of the plunge churn is marked with dots. It is striking how this more elaborated technique is spread in between the less effective and older techniques in north and south. The shake churn was in use also for instance in the Hebrides, North Scandinavia, Esthonia, Hungary and Siberia. Shaking is the primordial way to make butter and for thousands of years dominated everywhere.

The Breakthrough in Northwestern Europe

Compared with earlier methods, and especially with the use of the shake churn, the plunge churn led to more effective butter-making, but it also required a larger amount of liquid to be usable.

Authors of classical antiquity mention on several occasions that the barbaric tribes in the north were using butter. Pliny gives a detailed description of the production, and tells that butter was made in wooden vessels shaken back and forth, i.e. in shake churns.[30]

The archaeological material from Northwest Europe is rich and well published. Along the southern coast of the North Sea large amounts of wood have been preserved, as mentioned above, in waterlogged sites from the first millennium A.D. [31] The same is valid for Slavic defensive works from the second part of the first millenium and many excavated towns in Western and Northern Europe from the High and Late Middle Ages.

The plunge churn is rather easy to identify. The cross or the holed disk at the end of the staff can be singled out from most other forms in the material culture of Northwestern Europe. An object similar in size and form is a type of spoon holder, but this is most often semi-circular and has larger holes than the disk on the churn staff.

The most important excavation with wood material from the first half of the millennium is Feddersen Wierde on the coast outside Bremen, with material from about A.D. 100-500. This excavation has been published in its entirety, but none of the objects can be interpreted as a part of a plunge churn. In other published excavations from contemporary sites along the southern coast of the North Sea, of which van Giffen's excavations at Ezinge in Holland are the best-known, no plunge churns can be identified.[32]

Bog finds marking large-scale sacrifices from about the same time, for example in Thorsbjerg, Vimose and Nydam in Jutland, have produced many wooden objects but no plunge churns. In these deposits household utensils play a minor role.

If we look at the second half of the first millennium, Norwegian burial mounds of the Viking Age, such as the Oseberg find, have produced large amounts of wooden objects including household utensils but no plunge churns.[33]

In Ireland excavations have been made on several *crannogs*, settlements on islands and datable to the seventh to the ninth centuries. These excavations have brought to light a lot of wooden objects, but none can be interpreted as a plunge churn. An excavation of a monastery in the Inner Hebrides in Scotland produced many wooden objects from the early seventh century, but no plunge churns.[34] In an Irish site a staved vessel with two iron rings attached on the outer side was found; it has with good cause been interpreted as a shake churn. It is probably datable to the ninth or tenth century.[35]

If we turn eastward, much wooden material has been excavated and published from Slavic fortified sites and settlements from the later half of the first millennium A.D., such as Behren-Lubchin and Gross Raden, but any parts of plunge churns have not been published.[36]

The evidence has so far been negative. But in research about implements proof of non-existence is as important as the contrary, and gives the earliest appearance of the implement a correct proportion.

The earliest evidence for plunge churns is from the excavation in Elisenhof on the west coast of Southern Jutland, with wooden material from the eighth and ninth centuries. The excavation is as important for the Viking age as Feddersen Wierde is for the earlier period. Both villages were situated in marshes on the coast, and the villagers concentrated on cattle-breeding. From Elisenhof we have as many as three disks with holes and a lid with a central hole. The plunge churn must have been rather common in this village. Also in Hedeby, the contemporary and neighbouring town, from which came a huge amount of excavated wooden objects, two parts of plunge churns have been identified.[37]

If we step a few centuries ahead we find plunge churns in archaeological materials from all over Northwestern Europe, in town excavations. For instance, a plunge churn was found at Tiel in Holland from the twelfth century.[38] Early evidence also exists from several town excavations in Scandinavia, for example from the eleventh or twelfth century in Lund and from the thirteenth century in Lödöse and Uppsala in Sweden. But in a rather large assemblage of wood material datable to around A.D. 1300 from a farm in Dalecarlia, no plunge churn could be identified. One explanation may be that this innovation had not then spread as far as North Sweden.[39]

In the enormous range of wooden material from Novgorod plunge churns have been found, datable to the fourteenth or perhaps even the thirteenth century. The excavator, Kolcin, points to high and narrow staves as a main criterion for identifying plunge churns. I agree that this is a rather good criterion, few other stave vessels having the height and narrowness of churns, but there are also some churns that are rather low. The high churn staves in Novgorod are datable at the earliest to the fourteenth century. In his publication Kolcin also presents holed disks, which he interprets as spoon holders. I am inclined (just having seen the pictures) to say that they can be interpreted with greater probability as disks for churn staffs (which is supported by the existence of staves for churns). The earliest of them are datable to the thirteenth century.[40]

The churn staff with a holed disk seems to be the oldest type in Northwestern Europe, but about A.D. 1300 the cross form appears in Lödöse and Uppsala, and perhaps already in the eleventh century in Oslo in Norway. [41]

Turning to pictures, the earliest drawing of a plunge churn is in the Utrecht Psalter of c. A.D. 800, probably made in Northern France.[42]

In medieval art from after A.D. 1000 there are several pictures of plunge churns. Particularly rich is the material from the later Middle Ages in Northern Europe: North Germany, Denmark, Sweden and Finland. On wall paintings in churches the legend about the devil helping a woman to steal milk and to make butter is described. This legend was popular even in later folk belief, because butter was one of the most valuable products made. The pictures always show large staved churns to emphasise the amount of milk stolen.[43]

Mainly on the basis of the archaeological evidence, a timetable for the breakthrough of the plunge churn can be established. Up to about the seventh century, only shake churns were in use in Northwestern Europe, and this continued to be the situation for most of the region until about or after A.D. 1000. The plunge churn was first introduced in an area along the coast of the North Sea from Northern France/Netherlands to southern Jutland. Soon after the turn of the millennium the innovation became more widely diffused in the rest of Northwestern Europe.

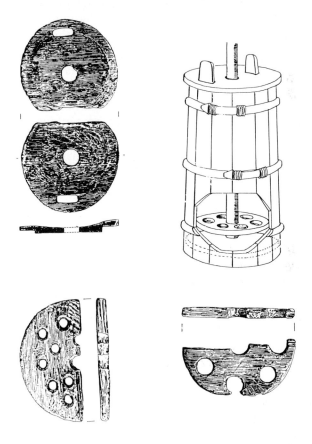

Fig. 8. Disks and lid to plunge churns (with reconstruction) from the excavation in Elisenhof, Jutland, dated to eight or ninth centuries. From Szabó, Grenander-Nyberg and Myrdal 1984, 82, Taf. 16-17.

Etymological data concerning the age of implements are to be handled with great care. A technical innovation can adopt a word already existing in the language, and on the other hand linguistic changes can occur without corresponding changes in tools and artefacts.

In the case of the plunge churn, however, linguistic data provide an interesting contribution. The words for butter are different in the European languages, but the words for the plunge churn are more unified. They derive from a Teutonic stem, in the forms *churn, karn, kirne, kärna*, etc. in English, Norwegian, Icelandic, Danish, Swedish, Dutch, German (with dialects), and among non-Teutonic languages in Polish, Finnish, Estonian, Lettish and even in Lithuania (along the coast). This diffusion of the word indicates that the word has followed a new implement: the plunge churn. Kustaa Vilkuna has asserted that the linguistic form of the word in Finnish means that it, and the plunge churn, was taken over from Sweden to Finland during the Middle Ages after c. A.D. 1000. The etymological data are thus congruent with the archaeological.[44]

It is of interest in this context that butter in Europe was made of separated cream. This resulted in a higher percentage of fat, and in this respect in a butter of higher quality. There does not have to be any connection between the introduction of the plunge churn and the separating of the cream, but it has been suggested that the word *churn* originally stems from a word for kernel (Sw. *kärna*), which should point to the cream as the kernel of the milk.

Pottery vessels with a spout near the bottom have been interpreted in Germany as vessels for separating cream from skimmed milk. The earliest vessels of that type are from the first half of the first millennium A.D.[45] If this interpretation is correct, the cream separated (if it was meant for butter) certainly must have been shaken or whipped to make butter. In later periods the most common way to separate the cream was to take it off with a spoon or to hold back the cream when the skimmed milk was poured away. The phrase *renna mjólk* in Old Icelandic (i.e. running milk) indicates that the method of pouring out skimmed milk when holding back cream was in early use.[46]

Conclusion

An investigation of the spread of the plunge churn in time and space leads naturally to the question of why the invention spread.

It may be appropriate to start explanations with a diffusionistic approach. Was the plunge churn developed separately in Central Asia and Europe, or was it transferred from one of the regions? (To assume more than these two regions of origin is certainly out of the question.) In my opinion the similarities in the typical form of the plunge churn in east and west argue against the assumption of two different places of origin. This does not mean that the process of diffusion was a simple one from a single starting point. More probably the innovation was developed through an interchange within the technical development in different regions. Trade and cultural contacts between east and west were from time to time quite intense along the caravan routes.

I shall sketch here the outline of a possible process. The making of koumiss was certainly of great importance, and the churn staff was perhaps first used for this purpose. In that case the churn staff was the contribution from the east in the development of the plunge churn. But it was probably from the west that the stave-building technique was introduced. With this the vessel could be made in its perfect form around the disk or the cross, and staved vessels are well suited for keeping liquids. This sketch of a possible interaction between east and west is still a hypothesis, to be verified (or rejected) when the oldest Asian material has been brought together and examined. But if the breakthrough of the churn staff and the plunge churn even in Asia occurred about A.D. 1000, the spread of the invention was rather fast.

Diffusion cannot explain the limits in extension of a certain object. If we turn to ecological factors instead (which determined economic factors), we will find some fundamental features in common in the area of extension. The plunge churn was spread over the Eurasian plains with surrounding mountain regions around 40° to 50° of latitude. Cattle-breeding was of great importance everywhere, and in some regions transhumance with cattle was well developed as in the Nordic countries, in the Alps and around Pamir.

But differences were also important. In Europe settled farmers lived in a rainy climate, in Central Asia nomads dominated cattle-breeding and the climate was arid. Furthermore a one-sided ecological approach cannot explain why a technological innovation is introduced at a specific time.

The following discussion about chronology will be limited to Northwestern Europe, for which a fairly certain date of introduction of the plunge churn has been established.

The plunge churn must be set in a wider technological complex as a part of cattle-breeding and dairying. One of the most decisive changes in cattle-breeding before modern times was the introduction of cattle sheds.

The earliest cattle sheds in Northwestern Europe have been found in Holland, dating from the Bronze Age. In Denmark they are known from about 500 B.C., and in Northern Germany and most of Scandinavia they came into use in the centuries around the birth of Christ. [47] (In England and France cowsheds were not introduced on a general scale until the High Middle Ages.)

Before that cattle were kept out of doors the whole year round. In winter, smaller amounts of fodder could be given, but the keeping of cattle indoors led to the greater importance of harvesting fodder, and especially hay. The introduction of the cattle shed caused an intensification of cattle-breeding, and the possibilities of milking must have increased. It became more desirable to keep mainly milk cows.

However, the keeping of cattle outdoors in winter and summer can very well be combined with the milking of cows, as shown, for instance, by the nomadic tribes in Asia who have no cattle sheds, but for whom cow's milk is a basic food.

Also in Europe it can be shown that dairying is much older than the keeping of cattle in cowsheds. Evidence can be got from osteological material, pictures and changing forms of pottery. In an interesting survey Andrew Sherratt considers that the milking of cows probably came into wider use in the third millennium B.C.[48]

Among early pottery vessels some are interpreted as shake churns, and there are also vessels perforated with holes and interpreted as having been used in the making of curd. Originally curd certainly played a dominant role in dairying. Its production follows naturally from the coagulating of milk, and when dried it is a rather durable product. Gustaf Ränk among others considers that it belongs to the oldest layers in folk culture. [49] Butter was certainly made in the millennia B.C., but in Northwestern Europe had not attained the dominant position it was later to achieve.

The advantage of butter compared with other dairy products is not primarily its preserving qualities. The principal aim with butter-making was instead to separate the fat and to get a product with a concentrated volume and a high calorific value. The butter had to be preserved through special processes like heating or salting.

The plunge churn was a more effective implement than the shake churn for larger amounts of liquid. Where butter was of limited importance, there was no need for a change from simple shake churns to plunge churns.

The introduction of the plunge churn could thus be connected with a more widespread need for the production of butter. In a nomadic culture, a concentration of fat in milk can be practical, thereby facilitating transport and movement. But in the settled farming culture of Europe this advantage seems to have been of less importance, if butter was not used in trade. And this, the usage of butter as a commercial product, is in my opinion a major cause of the general spread of the plunge churn in the West.

Between the ninth and eleventh centuries an economic change started in Europe. Trade routes were established, and towns like Dorestad, Hedeby and Birka evolved. The centre for this development was Frisia. Simultaneously, a general economic expansion started with land reclamation and a growing population, combined with a gradual introduction of technological inventions in agriculture. Around A.D. 1000 this economic expansion entered a new phase of rapid development, into what has been called the medieval agricultural revolution. This also had consequences for trade and commerce. Between A.D. 1000 and 1250 a number of towns were founded and a regional division of labour developed in North Europe, with the textile-producing Flanders as its centre, a centre that had to be provided with food.

The plunge churn had its breakthrough in this period of change, at first along the southern coast of the North Sea, and then in the whole of Northwest Europe. In written sources butter features more prominently than before, and it became one of the main components in interregional trade.[50] Transport over long distances was required, and the concentrated percentage of fat in butter became a great advantage.

Another important component in the growing trade was salt. This was used for all sorts of conservation, and to a great extent for butter. Salting was a necessity if the butter had to be transported for a long period. Growing interregional trade thus provided both the need and preconditions for an expanding butter trade.

At this period Europe also underwent a fundamental social change. A social structure that could be called feudal was firmly established, and all the peasants were subjected to the landowning nobility and the church either directly or through the state, and they had to pay rents and taxes. This meant that a greater amount of surplus production went to the ruling groups, which also promoted the production of such an easily transportable and valuable product as butter. Over large regions butter became an important article in the tributes the peasants had to pay.

These factors gave butter its dominant role in the dairy production of Northwest Europe, and also provided a stimulus for an innovation such as the plunge churn.

Butter was, during the High Middle Ages, established as a luxury article of great importance. Both in the Middle Ages and in later times peasants produced but seldom ate butter. Their consumption of butter was limited to festivities, when it was given a central place at the table.

More recent support for the connection between a growing degree of commercialisation and a change in churn types is provided by the above-mentioned development in Southeastern Austria. Large staved churns replaced smaller pottery vessels in connection with the changeover from the production of butter for home use to production for the market.

Perhaps the separating of cream, which raises the quality of butter, spread more generally at the same time as the plunge churn achieved its breakthrough. Even if there are no connections in technical terms between the two methods, the same general causes could have promoted both.

To conclude this discussion of the spread of the plunge churn, I shall use the three classical dimensions propounded by the Swedish ethnologist Sigurd Erixon: time, space and social context.

The spread of the plunge churn can partly be explained through a time-directed, diffusionistic, approach: the innovation developed and spread through a technical interchange between centres of innovation, and this occurred especially during times of intense trading contacts.

The extension can also be partly explained from an ecological point of view, with a space-orientated starting point: the spread of the innovation is limited to around the same degrees of latitude in Eurasia, and to regions where cattle-breeding and the milking of cows were of special importance.

But the social (and economic) context has also played a decisive role: in Europe the general introduction and breakthrough for the plunge churn can be connected with a social and an economic change which meant that the peasants had to deliver the best of their production, which included butter.

The form of the staved plunge churn appears to have fitted it well for its purpose, and in Europe it remained the dominating implement in dairying for about three-quarters of a millennium.

NOTES

1. E.O. Arenander, *Die altertümliche Milchwirtschaft in Nordschweden*, (Stockholm 1911); I. Söderlind-Myrdal, Att kärna smör. In *Fataburen*, 1977.
2. G. Berg, Fåret som mjölkdjur. In *Rig*, 1949, 50.
3. O. Højrup, *Landbokvinden* (Copenhagen 1975), 75.
4. A full bibliography of German literature on butter churns is given by H. Siuts, *Bäuerliche und handwerkliche Arbeitsgeräte in Westfalen* (Münster 1982), 132-

144, 404-405.

5. E.E. Evans, *Irish Folk Ways* (London 1967), 95-97; A. Fenton, *The Northern Isles: Orkney and Shetland* (Edinburgh 1978), 440-441.

6. I.C. Peate, *Tradition and folk life: A Welsh view* (London 1972); cf. Hugh Cheape's article in this volume.

7. J. Weynes, *Volkshuisraad in Vlaanderen*, 3 (Antwerp 1974), 916-917 with a map of the distribution of barrel churns, cradles and plunge churns in Flanders. The oldest evidence for barrel churns is given in the somewhat obsolete but still fundamental work by B. Martiny, *Kirne und Girbe* (Berlin 1895), 110.

8. F. Krüger, *Die Hochpyrenäen 2: Hirtenkultur* (Hamburg 1935), 70-74. Concerning the border between different cooking fats, see map in L. Febvre, Repartition géographique des fonds de cuisine en France, in *Travaux du I:er congrès international de folklore* (Paris 1938). For the same border on a European level, see E. Schmitthenner and H. Schmitthenner, Speise und Trank in Europa. In *Wissenschaftliche Veröffentlichungen des Deutschen Institut für Länderkunde*, NF 17/18 (Leipzig 1960), 142-143.

9. P. Scheuermeier, *Bauernwerk in Italien, in der italienischen und rätoromanischen Schweiz* (Zürich 1943), 31-33.

10. R. Weiss, *Das Alpwesen Graubundes* (Zürich 1941), 144-146.

11. K. Gaál, *Zum bäuerlichen Gerätebestand im 19. und 20. Jahrhundert* (Vienna 1969), 129-130.

12. G. Grotenfelt, *Bidrag till kännedom af mjölkhushållningens utveckling i Finland* (Kuopio 1906); I. Manninen, *Führer durch die ethnographischen Sammlungen* (Tartu 1928), 76-77; A. Kowalska-Lewicka, La production traditionnelle du beurre en Pologne. In *Ethnologia Slavica*, 1970.

13. Central and East Europe have been covered in several articles concerned with traditional dairy production in *Viehwirtschaft und Hirtenkultur* (Budapest 1969), with articles by C. Vakarelski about Bulgaria, V. Novak about Yugoslavia, N. Dumare about Rumania, Keszi-Kovács about Hungary and L. Kunz about Moravia.

14. D. Zelenin, *Russische (Ostslavische) Volkskunde* (Berlin 1927), 127-128; K. Moszyński, *Kultura ludowa Słowian* (Krakau 1929), para. 277.

15. For example, W. Radloff, Die Haustiere der Kirgisen. In *Zeitschrift für Ethnologie*, 1879, 300; U.T. Sirelius, *Suomen kansanomaista kultuuria*, 1 (Helsinki 1919), 328.

16. A. Byhan, Kaukasien, Ost- und Nordrussland, Finnland. In *Illustrierte Völkerkunde* (G. Buschan, ed.), 1 (Stuttgart 1926), 649, 849, 853.

17. E. Kisbán, Die historische Bedeutung des Joghurts in der Milchverarbeitungssystemen Sudosteuropas. In *Viehwirtschaft und Hirtenkultur* (Budapest 1969), 518-519.

18. Sirelius 1919, *op. cit.*, 189; Evans 1967, *op. cit.*, 97; G.E. Fussell, *The English Dairy Farmer 1500-1900* (London 1966), 206.

19. P. Lindemans, *Geschiedenis van de landbouw in België*, 2 (Antwerp 1952), 381-382.

20. G. Dalman, *Arbeit und Sitte in Palästina*, 4 (Gütersloh 1939), 296-302.
21. An instructive survey of African dairying is P. Göbel, Alles dreht sich um die Milch: Ein Kapitel Hauswirtschaft der afrikanischer Viehzuchter. In *Hirtennomaden und Viehzüchter* (Leipzig 1973).
22. E.M. Peśćereva, *Gonćarnoe proizvodstvo Srednej Azzi* (Moscow 1959), 63- 64.
23. K. Ferdinand, Nomadism in Afghanistan: With an appendix on milk products. In *Viehwirtschaft und Hirtenkultur* (Budapest 1969), 155-156. In this article a presentation of literature about butter churns in West and Central Asia and also in Africa is given.
24. About the central position of butter in Tibet, see for example M. Hermanns, *Die Nomaden von Tibet* (Vienna 1949), 63-64.
25. M.G. Levin and L.P. Potapov, *The peoples of Siberia* (Chicago 1964), 248- 250; A.P. Okladinov, *Yakutia before its incorporation into the Russian state* (Montreal 1970), 241-243.
26. S.I. Rudenko, Studien über das Nomadentum. In *Viehwirtschaft und Hirtenkultur* (Budapest 1969), 27-28. Rudenko here also gives a general survey of nomadic people's dairy production.
27. W.W. Rockhill, ed., *The journey of William of Rubruck to eastern parts of the world 1253-55* (London 1900), 66-67. To churn is in William's originally Lat in version written: 'concutere cum ligno', F. Michel and T. Wright, eds., *Relations des voyages de Guillaume de Rubruk . . . Publiées en entier* (Paris 1836), 31.
28. See, for example, A.M. Khazanov, Characteristic features of nomadic communities in the Eurasian steppes. In *The nomadic alternative* (Paris 1978); B.C. Karmyśeva, Versuch einer Typologisierung der traditionellen Formen der Viehwirtschaft Mittelasiens und Kasachstans am Ende des 19./Anfang des 20. Jh. In *Die Nomaden in Geschichte und Gegenwart* (Berlin 1981).
29. M.A. Stein, *Ruins of desert Cathay*, 1-2 (London 1912); B. Sommarström, *Archaeological researches in the Edsen-Gol region, Inner Mongolia*, 1-2 (Stockholm 1956-58), 1, 158, Pl. 40:11. I want to thank Bo Sommarström for help with the Asian material.
30. Concerning written evidence from antiquity, see Martiny (1895); Pliny, *Natural History, with an English Translation*, 8 (London 1963), 94-95.
31. A general survey of excavations with organic material is J. Coles, *The Archaeology of Wetlands* (Edinburgh 1984). Here also literature about excavations involving wood from earlier periods, like the lakeside sites in Switzerland or Glastonbury in England, is presented. But there is no evidence for plunge churns amongst these wooden objects.
32. W. Haarnagel, *Die Grabung Feddersen Wierde* (Wiesbaden 1979); A.E. van Giffen, Der Warf Ezinge, Provinz Groningen, Holland und seine westgermanischen Häuser. In *Germania*, 1936.
33. A.W. Brøgger and H. Shetelig, eds., *Osebergsfundet*, 2 (Oslo 1928).
34. H. Hencken, Ballinderry Crannog no 2. In *Proceedings of the Royal Irish Academy (PRIA)*, 47c (1941-42); H. Hencken, Lagore Crannog: An Irish royal residence of the 7th to 10th centuries A.D. In *PRIA*, 53c (1950-51); J.W. Barber,

Excavations on Iona 1979. In *Proceedings of the Society of Antiquaries of Scotland*, 111 (1981). An excavation of a similar crannog in Moynagh Lough in Ireland, from the eight to the ninth centuries, has produced much wood but, according to information from Niall Brady, no plunge churns.

35. G. Bersu, The Rath in Townland Lissue, Co Antrim. In *Ulster Journal of Archaeology*, 1947, 53-54; compare E.E. Evans, 1967, *op. cit.*, 96-97.

36. E. Schuldt, *Behren-Lubchin: Eine Spätslawischen Burganlage in Mecklenburg* (Berlin 1965); E. Schuldt, *Gross Raden: Ein slawischer Tempelort des 9./10. Jahrhunderts in Mecklenburg* (Berlin 1985).

37. M. Szabó, G. Grenander-Nyberg and J. Myrdal, *Elisenhof in Eiderstedt: Die Holzfunde* (Frankfurt am Main 1985), 79-82. In the present exhibition at Hedeby, Schleswig, a holed disk and a lid with a central hole are displayed and I have studied the disk in the unpublished catalogue of the finds.

38. J.M.G. van der Poel, De landbouw in het verste verleden. In *Berichten van de Rijksdienst voor het oudheidkundig bodenonderzoek*, 1960-61, 181. A perforated wooden disk for a plunge churn has been found in the recent excavations at York, England, but unfortunately it is undatable; R. Hall, *The Viking Dig* (London 1984), 34-36.

39. J. Myrdal, Medeltidens boskapsskötsel (manuscript); J. Myrdal, Träföremäl. In *Vardagsliv i en medeltida bondby: Fynd från Västannorstjärn i Leksand, Dalarna* (Leksand 1984).

40. B.A. Kolcin, *Novogorodskie drevnosti: Derevjannye izedelija* (Moscow 1968), 25, 27, 85.

41. The find from Oslo according to information from Birte Weber.

42. D. Diringer, *The illuminated book, its history and production* (London 1958), 165.

43. J. Wall, *Tjuvmjölkande väsen*, 1 (Uppsala 1977), has a full presentation of pictures with this motif in Northern Europe.

44. See Martiny, 1895, *op. cit.*, 23. Concerning etymology, see E. Hellquist, *Svensk etymologisk ordbok* (Lund 1966), 547-548, 1008-1009; K. Vilkuna, Smör: Finland. In *Kulturhistoriskt lexikon för nordisk medeltid*, 16 (Malmö 1971), 316-317.

45. O. Erich, Tongefässe in der Milchwirtschaft. In *Volkswerk*, 1941, 230-231.

46. A. Olsson, Mjölkhushållning. In *Kulturhistoriskt lexikon för nordisk medeltid*, 11 (Malmö 1966), 663.

47. J. Myrdal, Elisenhof och järnålderns boskapsskötsel i Nordvästeuropa. In *Fornvännen*, 1984.

48. A. Sherratt, Plough and pastoralism: Aspects of the secondary products revolution. In *Pattern of the past* (Cambridge 1981).

49. G. Ränk, *Från mjölk till ost* (Stockholm 1966, reprint 1987); V. Cheke, *The Story of Cheese-making in Britain* (London 1959).

50. M.M. Postan, The trade of medieval Europe: The North. In *Cambridge economic history of Europe*, 2 (Cambridge 1952), 121.

WOODEN MILK VESSELS IN THE SWISS ALPS: TRADITIONAL SHAPES AND DECORATIONS

Arnold Niederer

Wooden dairy utensils have remained longer in use in the Alps than in the plains. Although it would have been more simple and time-saving to use metal utensils, they went on being manufactured from wood in those regions where geographic isolation had created an economic system based on self-subsistence. The value attributed to this type of economy contributed to its continuing to be effective, even though new transportation means, together with better possibilities for earning an income, had rendered self-sufficiency less imperative. It may be that the shortage of cash was conducive to a selective use of industrially manufactured utensils. Wood was very inexpensive and the work involved was not as yet measured in terms of the hours involved. Under these conditions, wooden utensils remained in use particularly in alpine dairy-farming,[1] in spite of their manufacturing and their maintenance being relatively work-intensive. Nowadays, of course, metal and plastic containers are popular everywhere. They cost little and are light; mountain peasants who often have to carry their utensils to their next place of work soon understood that they were useful. The old coopered or turned wooden vessels are now used to decorate restaurants or the comfortable lounges of middle-class people—that is, when they did not finish up in the lumber-room or as firewood. A few have been kept in some of the numerous local museums which have been opened recently. What we describe in the following refers to the period around the Second World War and applies to a few regions of the Swiss Alps.

The traditional milk vessels and their handling have survived longest in regions where some families exploit an alpine dairy on a private basis during the summer, i.e. produce their own cheese and butter. In this type of dairy-farming milking is done manually. The milking vessel is a coopered pail in which the milk will then be carried to the cheese cauldron, to be poured into it through a milk sieve. During the winter, which the cowherds and their herd spend in the permanent settlement down in the valley, it is usual for the milk to be brought to the village dairy cooperative; is it then processed and the produce is sold. On the alp, the milk cannot always be processed just where the cows were milked. Pick-a-back vessels are used to carry the milk from a remote spot to the alpine dairy; the same vessels are used in the winter to bring the milk to the village dairy cooperative.

The Milking Pail

A wooden milking pail containing five to eight litres is most commonly found in the alpine regions. There are two basic types in existence (with numerous variations): 1. A coopered round pail where the staves are held together with wooden hoops. The pail widens uniformly towards the top and has a movable handle which is made of wood or of metal (Fig. 1). Buckets which are narrower at the top are used whenever the milk has to be transported, thus preventing the milk from slopping over (Fig.3). 2. A coopered, round or oval pail with an extended vertical stave which includes an opening for carrying the pail and a hole for hanging it up (Fig. 2).

The round vessel with a movable handle is common in Eastern Switzerland and the Grisons, whereas round or oval containers with an extended stave are to be found in Western and Central Switzerland. According to the importance of dairy-farming in the different regions of the Swiss Alps, the milking vessels are more or less carefully manufactured and decorated (for example straight or bulged vessels, vessels with one colour of wood or with alternating light and dark staves, smooth or carved vessels). The most simple shapes are found in regions where dairy-farming plays less of a role, coexisting with corn and wine growing and serving mainly to satisfy the local demand (Southern Grisons, Valais and Ticino). Milking pails are more elaborate in regions with large areas of meadowland and an important milk production (Appenzell, Toggenburg, Emmental, Bernese Oberland, Gruyére). The white cooper [2] trade became important and respected only in regions where cattle-breeders had attained a certain wealth through the production of cheese which was sold and exported; in those regions, cattle-breeders came to constitute a specific class of people.

White coopers in the poorer regions of the Central and Southern Alps were mostly village carpenters or laymen from families in which a talent and a taste for crafts had been transmitted over the generations. They worked on wood which had grown slowly and which had to be cleavable and free of knots. Woods common in the alpine regions were preferred, such as stone pine (Pinus cembra), spruce, larch and sycamore maple; the wood from these trees was not sawn, but rather chopped, along the radius of the trunk. The manufacture of the hoops requires particularly flexible and resistant wood. Mountain sycamore maple was used, but the wood of larches growing on meadows outside the forests was equally good, although only that part above the ground up to a height of about two metres is suited for the manufacture of hoops for vessels. The staves for the walls of the containers are first cut roughly; they are then worked

Fig. 1.　　　　　　　　　　　　　　Fig. 2.

Fig. 3.

Fig. 1. Coopered milking pail with moveable handle, containing 7 litres. Prätigau, Grisons. (Photo: Paul Guggenbühl).

Fig. 2. Milking pail with extended stave and holes for handling and hanging. Rossinère, Vaud (Photo: Paul Guggenbühl, about 1960).

Fig. 3. Cowherds setting out for milking outside Grimentz, Valais. (Photo: Charles Krebser, about 1930, courtesy of the Archives Cantonales du Valais, Sion).

on with a plane and carved into the conical shape of the milk pail with its narrower bottom. The cooper cuts a groove into the inside of the staves and then inserts the floor of the pail. The most difficult part of the work is that consisting in manufacturing and affixing the hoops. The cooper fixes both ends of small boards—which have been cut to the right length and width—into a shaving-horse; he then smoothes them with a draw-shave. The ends of the hoops, which are lapped over each other, are locked by interlocking notches (Fig. 4). The hoops are soaked in water for a long time, in order to be made resilient, before they are bent. Once the hoop is closed, it is hammered onto the conical vessel.

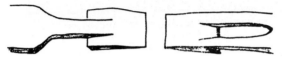

Fig. 4. Ends of flat hoop cut out for interlocking.

Milk Sieves and Basins, Cream Ladle, Cream Pail

In regions where cheese and butter are being processed, the milk is carried in milk pails to the milk cellar; this cellar is normally situated within the alpine chalet. It contains flat basins in which the cream is allowed to form on the surface of the milk and which are aligned on stands. They are round wooden basins, with a height of about 15cm and whose walls are made of staves held by wooden hoops (Fig. 5). Basins made of tin-plated copper or of aluminium are also in use. The creaming vessel used by Appenzell cowherds is a basin made of one piece of turned wood.[3]

A cone-shaped coopered sieve is used to filter the milk while it is being poured from the milking pail into the creaming vessel; it has an extended stave with a hole for carrying it and holds the dirt particles back (Fig. 6). The bottom end of the sieve is blocked with a ball of clean root-fibres, green spruce or juniper twigs, or sometimes with a thin woollen rag; those are changed daily. Nowadays, however, metal sieves are used. In order for the sieve not to have to be held, it is put on a small stand. It is interesting to note in passing that the cone-shaped sieve is also used as a speaking-tube by the cowherd when chanting his evening prayer (the 'Betruf').[4]

A large spade-shaped wooden ladle is used to skim the layer of cream which has formed after about 24 hours (Fig. 7). The skimmed cream is first put into a special cream pail whose shape is similar to that of the milking pail and which normally has a lid (Fig. 8).

Fig. 5. Coopered basins in which the cream is allowed to form; height 15 cm, diameter 40 cm. Lötschental, Valais. (Photo: Walter Scheiwiller).

Fig. 6. Sieve with support over basin in which the cream forms; height 18 cm, upper diameter 20 cm, diameter at the base 5 cm. Simmental, Bern.

The Pick-a-back Milk Vessel

Pick-a-back vessels are, apart from milking pails, the most characteristic vessels used in alpine dairy farming; they are manufactured in all sizes— even for children. They are carried on the back, the arms and the hands of the carrier remaining free for other tasks. This allows him to manage the obstacles he might meet on his way, or to take an animal along, or even to knit or to smoke, etc. The pick-a-back vessels for milk and other

Fig. 7. Spade-shaped wooden spoon for skimming the cream in the basin. Lötschental, Valais. (Photo: Paul Guggenbühl).
Fig. 8. Cream pail, 15 cm high, 15 cm diameter. (Photo: Paul Guggenbühl).

liquids have an elliptical shape, with one side flattened in order to feel comfortable against the back of the carrier. They are narrower at the top, so as to prevent the milk from splashing over (Fig. 9). Their manufacture requires great care, since they have to be made well enough for liquids to be transported over large distances. Whenever possible, the cooper uses wood from the stone pine (Pinus cembra); this wood is soft and has the advantage of absorbing water easily. A vessel which leaks after being used for a long time may be rendered waterproof again by letting the wood swell in water. It is also said that milk put into wooden vessels, and especially into those made of the strongly scented stone pine, has a better taste.[5] The pick-a-back vessel is equipped with a lid which closes tightly and has an extension for lifting it. The lid has a small hole, so that, whenever the vessel is submitted to shaking, the air may escape and the lid will not be pushed open. The wooden carrying straps are made of the same wood as the hoops of the vessel. They have to be bent into shape over many days, in order to be adequately curved. The carrying straps are attached to the top and the bottom of the vessel with cords or with small chains.

The milking vessel and all other containers used in a dairy require constant cleaning after use. Natural wood is easy to brush and to keep

Fig. 9. Pick-a-back vessel for milk, containing 30 litres. Lötschental, Valais. (Photo: Paul Guggenbühl, 1959).

clean. In dairies where cheese is manufactured, the hot whey from the milk is used for cleaning; a layer of whey forms progressively which—it is believed—acts as a preservative.[6] In regions where hot whey is not available (e.g. in the Lötschental), sand is used. The sand is kept in a small, square sandbox; women clean their vessels at the village well, pressing a woollen rag into the sand and scrubbing the wood (Fig. 10).

The dairy cooperatives and the milk-collecting centres played an essential role in having wooden dairy utensils supplanted by vessels made of other materials. In the thirties, they forbade the dairy farmers the use of wooden vessels, declaring them unhygienic. Only the small farmers and alpine exploitations continued to use the traditional wooden vessels, since they went on processing their own milk; but they eventually changed to using aluminium or plastic pails. The white coopers therefore could no longer count on being commissioned by milk producers; they partly succeeded in surviving by manufacturing vessels to be used for decoration.

Fig. 10. Lötschental women cleaning the milk vessels at the village well. To the right is the sandbox. (Photo: Albert Nyfeler, 1935).

Decorated Milk Vessels

Dairy vessels made of stone pine or spruce may be looked on as folk art, even when they are not decorated; their hoops are joined with decorative locks, holding the staves together, and their shape is tastefully balanced. In a few regions of Switzerland in which dairy farming plays an important role, the white cooper trade developed a tradition of richly decorated vessels. In the Bernese Oberland, in the Toggenburg and in the Appenzell region, milk pails, hand and pick-a-back vessels with carved ornaments, plants or other figurative patterns were manufactured. Beautifully carved dairy utensils were to be found in the Bernese Oberland during the eighteenth and nineteenth centuries, when the cattle and the cheese trades reached their zenith in that region. The alpine cattle-breeders and cowherds had many ways of showing their wealth. Their comfortable houses had carved and painted façades demonstrating wealth.

But also, the richer a mountain peasant's milk vessels and dairy utensils were, the wealthier he was considered to be. Skilled white coopers produced the objects of this decorative folk art, their modest existence depending on commissions given them by wealthy cattle-breeders. The decoration of dairy vessels consisted in incised drawings (Fig. 11) or in chip carving; both techniques were often used simultaneously on the same object (Fig. 12). A few craftsmen created utensils which had embossed carved surfaces (Fig. 13). Another form of art consisted in inlaying pieces of brightly coloured wood from fruit trees into the pale pinewood of the staves (Fig. 14). Traditional vessels from the Bernese Oberland may be seen in the Bern Museum of History. Their decoration is partly ornaments (zigzags, waving lines, six-pointed stars, swivels), partly patterns from the plant world (leaves or flower tendrils, often tulips). Cows are mainly used as figurative motives, but pictures of cowherds are also to be found. It is usual for the name of the owner and the year of manufacture to be carved into the utensil. Sometimes aphorisms are inscribed, such as: 'Die Kuh ist ein nützliches Tier, man bezieht Milch, Käs und Butter von ihr, darum sei dem Höchsten Lob, Preis und Dank derfür' (The cow is a useful animal, it gives milk, cheese and butter, the Lord should be praised, prized and thanked for it) (Fig. 15).

Fig. 11. Coopered milk pail with incised drawings, dated 1748. Bernese Oberland. (Photo: by courtesy of the Bernisches Historisches Museum, Bern).

Fig. 12. Coopered milk pail in spruce wood. Incised design of flowers, bear and alphorn player. Name of the owner in chip-carving, dated 1740. (Photo: by courtesy of the Bernisches Historisches Museum, Bern).

Fig. 13. Cream pail of spruce and sycamore wood, beginning of the nineteenth century. Embossed carving in a tulip pattern and incised motto. (Photo: by courtesy of the Bernisches Historisches Museum, Bern).

Fig. 14. Pick-a-back vessel of spruce-wood with inlaid figures in fruit tree wood. Simmental, Bernese Oberland, eighteenth century. Hoop made of sycamore wood. (Photo: by courtesy of the Bernisches Historisches Museum, Bern).

Fig. 15. Milk pail, beginning of nineteenth century. Embossed wood-carving showing a cowherd and his cow. (Photo: by courtesy of the Bernisches Historisches Museum, Bern).

While the white cooper trade slowly disappeared from the Bernese Oberland because metal dairy vessels were being used by more and more farmers, it managed to survive to this day in the Appenzell region and the Toggenburg, thanks to the custom of the ceremonial leading of the herds to the higher pastures. The cowherds who lead their herd to the alp in the Spring are carrying, as a kind of class symbol, their milking pail (Figs. 16-17) slung over the left shoulder, so that the carvings on the outside of the base are clearly visible. Circular paintings used to be affixed to the bottom of the pail for the ascent to the alp. The picture was always of the same motif: the herd together with the herdsman in ceremonial dress, with a milk pail slung over his shoulder. In order for the paintings not to be destroyed when the pails were being washed, they were removed upon arrival on the alp, to be attached again for the descent from the alp in the autumn.[7]

The traditional ascent of the herds in the Appenzell region and in the Toggenburg was not just a show for the tourists. The whole population participated in it. The objects manufactured by white coopers and used on that occasion are also appreciated by amateurs who use them for decoration or as gifts on special occasions. They also constitute rustic souvenirs purchased by tourists, whereby miniature versions of the traditional vessels are often produced (Fig. 18).

Fig. 16. Profusely decorated milking pail for ceremonial use during the 'ascent' to the high pastures. Toggenburg, Saint-Gall. (Photo: Paul Guggenbühl, 1963).

TOKAY WINES: TYPES AND PRODUCTION

Iván Balassa

Foreigners with an average education know very little of Hungary, but a relatively high proportion of them have heard about *Tokay wine*. Not so many have actually tasted any of its varieties, and even fewer foreigners are familiar with the way the grapes are grown and the way the wine is made. This method, developed in the course of centuries and having adopted certain standards, is rooted sometime in the late Renaissance, a period of great intellectual effervescence which had a fertilising effect not only on the arts but on agriculture as well.

1. Grape harvest at Tokay, nineteenth century. C19108.

Both in Hungary and abroad there are many false beliefs about Tokay wine, even in professional literature, and, naturally, much more so among men in the street.

First of all, this wine is not produced in a single place, in a single town called Tokay. This little town at the crossing of the Rivers Tisza and Bodrog merely marks the threshold of the so-called *Hegyalja* ('foothill') which has encompassed between twenty and thirty small towns and villages at different historical periods, including Sárospatak which, with its Calvinist College, has spread intellectual, and in many respects also material, culture. The local name of the wine producing area, *Hegyalja*, was difficult to translate into foreign languages. Since there was a need to refer to it in such a way that merchants coming from several countries (Germany, Greece, Russia, Poland, Scotland) could all understand and remember it, it was named Tokay District after the small town at its southern 'gate'. The people living in this area call their 'narrow homeland' Hegyalja even today, whilst the official language connects the two names and uses *Tokay-Hegyalja* both in speech and in writing.

Another mistaken belief is that the most characteristic wine of the region, called *Tokay Aszú* (Old Tokay),[1] was discovered around 1650 and first made by Minister Máté Laczkó Sepsi for the Transylvanian Princess, Zsuzsánna Lorántffy, who was a frequent visitor to Sárospatak. In fact, its name appeared around 1570[2] and it was referred to several times in the first half of the seventeenth century.[3] This legend appeared in the second half of the eighteenth century and it has kept recurring in agricultural and ethnographic professional literature up to the present day. That is why it is important to investigate the question in greater historical perspective.

Beginning in the fourteenth and fifteenth centuries, an economic boom exerted a significant influence on the structure of society, especially in the southern part of Europe. It was, in particular, in the city states of Italy that a social level of citizens appeared, that gave an impetus to industry, agriculture and above all commerce, as a consequence of which the different branches of art began to flourish as well. This class looked upon the culture of the Roman age as an example to follow in every respect. When printing facilitated the spread of the works of ancient writers to a wider circle, those dealing with agriculture exerted a very fertile influence. Consequently, the agricultural literature of the European nations frequently referred to Latin authors, and adopted a great many things from them. In Hungary this trend began in the second half of the sixteenth century, but Latin works were often mentioned in the first half of the nineteenth century too.[4]

In the fifteenth century, especially in the period of King Matthias, 1458-1490, Hungary belonged to the vanguard of the European nations in many respects and maintained close contacts with Italy, even with its southern part. The intellectual surge was maintained by the Reformation, though in a somewhat different direction, in the sixteenth century. Although the Turkish invasion, beginning in 1541, split the country into three parts,[5] this only slowed down and differentiated the surge. Regions lying between the three parts were able to develop further, though not in an undisturbed manner. One such region was the Tokay-Hegyalja or Tokay-District which was never invaded by the Turks, but was constantly kept uneasy by their incursions. The family estates of the Transylvanian princes lying here linked this region primarily to Transylvanian areas of Protestant character. The Calvinist College of Sárospatak started to spread Latin culture and also engaged in disseminating Latin agricultural literature.

It is well known that already the Greeks made some kind of wine from dry grapes. The method has been handed down to us by Roman authors in considerable detail. Columella, however, described the Italian method: 'When the grapes have dried, they must be picked and placed into a barrel, then they are to be covered by must (grape-juice) of the highest available quality. When the grapes have become saturated with must, on the sixth day they are to be placed into a basket and pressed, and then the raisins are to be taken out. Then the raisins are to be trodden upon, and filled up with must again: then it may be left alone to ferment'.[6]

This method was continued in medieval Italy, as we know from the work of Crescentius.[7] This was the so-called *raisin wine* whose name originates from the town of Malvasia (cf. 'malmsey') in Southern Greece. It was actually a small island which in the Middle Ages came under the supervision of Venice, and its famous wine was transported by the

2. Selecting the dry grapes on a flat board at Sátoraujhely, about 1900. C19105.

merchants of that city. As early as 1358, the Hungarian King Louis the Great received thirty barrels of it as a war indemnity. Later on it was to be encountered on the tables of the king and magnates.[8] In the fifteenth and sixteenth centuries it reached the tables of the citizens of the Hungarian towns too, but its import was increasingly hindered by Turkish rule, and afterwards it could only be obtained through Vienna. For this reason, attempts were made in Hungary too to produce wine similar to that mentioned by the Latin writers.

These wines involved dry grapes in one way or another, and experiments may have started some time in the second half of the sixteenth century. It was in a list of words put together around 1570 and used as a textbook in the College of Sárospatak that the two most characteristic types of wine, *main wine* and *dry grape wine (Aszú)*, appeared for the first time.[9] As to their production methods, we have indirect evidence as well. It is worth mentioning some of them.

Although in this region of the County of Zemplén grapes had been grown and wine had been made earlier, it failed to gain national fame. In the middle of the sixteenth century, however, at the request of the County, the royal family allowed it to use an escutcheon in which two angels held a bunch of grapes. The heraldic significance was that this region produced grapes much above the average in quality. [10] At this time, too, the manner of grape cultivation changed; the main innovation was that the soil was hoed three times instead of twice, as had been the practice before [11] . Attempts were made to introduce types of grape which ripened late and turned dry. Among them the greatest significance was attached to *furmint* which has held a dominating role up to the present day. Its Italian or French origin is still subject to debate. [12]

At the third meeting of the Council of Trent, the Bishop of Pécs, György Draskovics, representing the Hungarian king, offered the Pope some wine originating in one of the famous towns of the Tokay-Hegyalja District, *Tállya*. The Pope, used to Italian wines, noted the excellent quality, taste and fragrance of the wine and expressed his gratitude with a Latin poem composed by a contemporary poet:

> Gratulor ergo mihi Papa dicit, talia nobis
> Vina, Petrem Sanctum Tallia vina decent. [13]

This involves a pun based on the rhyming of *talia* 'vina' and the name of the town: *Tállya*. The mythical atmosphere of the anecdote definitely indicates that at this time some kind of high-quality wine was being produced here.

Amongst the indirect evidence is the fact that grape harvests were started late, from the second half of the sixteenth century. Late fifteenth-century records mention grape-harvesting in the first half of October as a rule, but in the second half of the sixteenth century the day of Simon of Judaea (28 October) was considered the first day of the grape harvest, which in many cases lasted till the end of November, or even the beginning of December. It also happened that the bunches were collected from vine-stocks covered with snow. [14]

These changes relate to the increasingly greater significance of quality wines based on the dry grape (Aszú) in one way or another. In the mid-seventeenth century, the Diet passed a law, according to which serfs were not obliged to give one-ninth and one-tenth of their dry grape production to the landlord and the church, respectively. This encouraged the serfs to collect the dry grapes and sell them separately, or less often, to manufacture them themselves [15].

By the beginning of the 1700s a system of Tokay wines had been established, which has essentially survived up to the present day. This was explained in 1726 by an excellent expert, a wine merchant, a 'Hungarus' of German origin from Upper-Hungary, living in Poland, as follows:

> The quality of the wines depends also on their treatment during the grape gathering: if you only take very green bunches of grapes you get the ordinary table-wine: if the green berries are mixed up with the dry berries you get what we call a main wine, a kind (of wine) which is always delicate and lasting: if the green and the dry berries are picked, they are trodden under foot into a pulp and filled up with the best must to ferment together in tubs; when the skins and seeds of the dry berries float to the surface, the dry berry wine is ready. With a strainer they filter all skins and seeds out and fill it into tubs and barrels: if the whole juice flows quite freely (without pressure) out of a quantity of dry berries and is collected like honey and put into barrels, it is called wine-essence: both of these sorts are the most delicate kinds and the longer they are seasoned the better they get and the more they reveal their delicious aroma and purity: *Unfortunately in recent times all too much dry berry wine and essence-wine has been produced, so that only a few ordinary main-wines are available.* The variety of the ordinary table-wines is very changeable, so that the whole wine-growing area falls into great discredit.' [16]

The three types of wine whose basic material or partial material is the dry grape Aszú are: *main wine* (Szamorodni), *Aszú* and *Essence*.

Naturally, in the Middle Ages there had been types of grape on which the berries turned dry. No special attention was then paid to them: they were simply used together with the rest of the berries for making wine. The berries did not turn dry every year, therefore significant differences were to be observed for individual years, as the different sources indicate as well. However, once the wine made from dry grapes (Aszú) appeared, the wine in which the dry grapes were manufactured along with the rest of the berries, received a separate denomination, *main wine*.

This name was first written down in 1570. Its Latin form, *primae notae, generosum*, demonstrated that its quality was exceptionally high. [17] There are frequent references also in different records in the next century. In 1618, for example, it was mentioned in the cellars of two magnates. Moreover, a distinction was made between table wine (ordinarium) and main wine [18] . This area generally produced white wines, but it seems that in the seventeenth century red wine was also made since it was mentioned in 1632 that 'main wine of red colour was filtered from black grapes'. Such red wine may be traced in the eighteenth century too but we suddenly lose track of it in the nineteenth.

Main wine slowly lost ground in the eighteenth century, but regained popularity in the nineteenth especially through Polish merchants who were glad to buy it. That is how its acquisition of a Polish name, *Szamorodni*, may be accounted for. This is a compound word, *Samo+rodne* 'selfgrown', i.e. a wine which was ripened together with the dry berries Aszú [19] This denomination is used today as well and its *sweet* and *dry* versions are differentiated. The latter is consumed by those fond of strong but dry wines.

The making of *Szamorodni* is discussed in a work published in Hungary in 1867 and translated into English also:

> It is prepared from those grapes which have not been deprived of the sweet berries. These grapes are put into sacks, and pressed in vats: the juice is made to run into casks, but the skins and stalks remaining in the sack are put into tubs, from which they are again taken out, and then strongly trodden down by the bare feet of men; the must, which was already expressed, is again poured upon it and the whole is allowed to stand for several hours, that is, until fermentation begins. After having been stirred up several times and kept lightly covered, it finally is again put into sacks, is again trodden down in them, and the must thus obtained is put into casks.
>
> From this mode of proceeding it is evident that the quality of the Szamorodni depends upon the greater or lesser quantity of dry berries which are found among the grapes and upon their more or less perfect formation, and it is this difference that generally determines the character of the Ausbruch (Aszú), and there exist instances when the Szamorodni is found better than the Ausbruch grown in bad years [20] .

In the first half of the seventeenth century the *dry grape wine* (Aszú) is frequently encountered, primarily in the cellars of princes, magnates and prelates. Among the economic documents of the Prince of Transylvania, Gábor Bethlen, there are records of the quantity of the *uva passa* dating back to 1620 [21] . It seems that the estates of the Transylvanian Prince Gyorgy Rákóczi I were the centres for making this wine in the second quarter of the seventeenth century. In 1632 there were barrels of Aszú in the cellar of the Castle of Sárospatak. In 1635, seven barrels and two *átalags* (half barrels) were recorded, and about the same amount in 1639. That quantity far exceeds simple experimenting, since it amounts to about 1-2% of the total production [22] . At this time Aszú was kept not only in barrels, but also in bottles, as appears from a record of 1640, when Prince György Rákóczi needed a bottle of Aszú [23] .

Referring to an earlier example, a detailed grape regulation was made in 1641 which, among other things, declared: 'Under pain of punishment by caning, the harvesters may not take home with them even one bunch of grapes in their baskets or in any other way, but it is even more strictly forbidden to take along just half a handful of dry grapes (Aszú)'. [24]   This prohibition was later repeated on several occasions, so demonstrating the high value of the Aszú grapes, the price of which far exceeded that of raisins imported from Italy.

The method of making Aszú was formulated as early as the second half of the seventeenth century and did not differ in essentials from the mode used in the second half of the last century:

> At the time of the vintage, the dry berries are selected from the grapes, and the grapes thus selected are placed upon oblong boards, provided with a ledge, in order that the grapes of inferior quality may be separated from the good ones. The mass of dry grapes is accordingly poured into vats, and here stamped by men's feet, or pressed by a machine, till it is reduced to a complete jelly; it is then transferred to other vats, and into them the requisite quantity of must is poured. It is left to stand for a longer or shorter space of time according to the temperature of the weather; in cold weather 48 hours, in warmer weather 12 hours and it is stirred up a few times: and finally this mixture is strained through pressing sacks, and the Aszú thus obtained is poured into a cask. [25]

Beginning in the second half of the seventeenth century, the Tokay Aszú became an increasingly popular product, attracting German, Polish, Greek, Russian and Jewish merchants from faraway lands. With their help, raising its price two- or threefold, this wine found its way to several countries of Europe and became well-known not only as a beverage but even as a medicine. The layer of producers was not only formulated, but was stratified as well. In addition to the local and foreign merchants and brokers, a great significance was also attached to the carriers who trans-

3. Breaking the grapes at Erdöbénye, 1956. Photo: I. Balassa. 53/50/70,74.

4. Treading out wine at Tokay, about 1900. C19106.

ported the wines for distances of hundreds of kilometres, up to the middle of the nineteenth century when the first railway lines were built. [26] Their routes led through the Carpathian Mountains to the Dunaietz River from where the wines were transported by water along the Vistula to Danzig and then by boat to Scandinavia and Russia.

In making the dry grape wine Aszú, a certain consistency in the proportion of the dry berries and the must poured onto them began to be established by the end of the seventeenth century. That was a buyers' requirement, for the consumers insisted on a similar or identical quality. In 1701 on a farm in the Tokay area, one barrel of wine was poured upon one barrel of dry berries Aszú, producing three *átalags* or one and a half barrels of fine dry grape wine Aszú. This is identical with the Tokay Aszú of four tubs according to the standard of today. However, as a general rule weaker-quality wines were produced, and the quality of the wine could only be defined by the merchant by means of tasting.

However, standardisation was only possible by using identical measuring instruments for the whole territory. In the sixteenth and seventeenth centuries and even later, measurements varied in Hungary not only from region to region but in many cases from town to town, and from one important village to another. All the same, commercial needs dictated a movement towards standardisation, even in relation to the barrel sizes.

Outside the grape producing area, to the north, there is a small town, *Gönc*, which was invaded by a German population in the Middle Ages. It had always been famous for its coopers whose barrels were famous also in distant lands. The first record of the *Gönci barrel* that I have found dates back to 1577; the half-barrel was called the *Gönci half* or, in other words, *átalag*. At that time these barrels were equivalent in capacity to 480 Buda *icces*, the equivalent of 407.2 litres (one *icce* = 100.88 litre) [27]

In 1611 the Polish Diet defined precisely in what barrels the Hungarian, and primarily the Tokay wines, were to be transported. Since the Hungarian merchants failed to meet this regulation, they were severely punished. They turned to the king who intervened with the Polish king, but received the following answer to his letter: 'Even the king has no right to change the law' [28] . The fact that kings could deal with the question of the size of the barrels of Tokay demonstrates the economic significance of the wine produced here.

In the seventeenth century the barrels became smaller and smaller in the Tokay District. This, apart from the requirements of commerce, had a practical reason. There was less pressure on the walls of the smaller barrels, and so less danger of the wooden hoops being snapped off, especially in transport. As for the barrels of larger volume, only one could be transported

5. Inside a wine producer's premises at Tokay, about 1900. C19107.

6. A seventeenth-century wine-cellar at Sárospatak. Photo: I. Balassa. 53/50/66.

on one cart, as is proved by the carvings handed down to us from the sixteenth century. On the other hand, three or four of the smaller barrels could be placed by the carrier on the extended carts without sides. He put in the front an *átalag* (vascula) in which he guarded the most valuable wine, usually Aszú. In this way, he could generally transport even more wine (490-630 litres) more easily and safely.

From the early eighteenth century, attempts to standardise the *Gönci barrel* became increasingly positive. A well-known economic historian believes that it was standardised at 180 *icces*, i.e. 152.7 litres. A source of the 1720s states: 'The wine is poured into new barrels of precisely 180 *icces*. Here these are not fumigated with sulphur or nutmeg beforehand; they are not prepared, but only washed with clean, hot water, at times with boiling must or grape leaves. The dry (Aszú) berries are taken off the stalk and put into tubs. Into one ninety *icce átalag* 1, 2, 3 or even more tubs of dry grape juice are poured, depending on how strong the wine is intended to be. The content of the tub is poured into the cask'. [29]   By that period the proportions used today had also been essentially established.

This process, however, had not been definitively established, because both smaller and larger barrels were still made in this region, a fact which gave rise to a great number of abuses. That is why in 1745 the county officials ordered that those not storing their wine in barrels of the pre-scribed size were to have them smashed to pieces.

Although the Diet had made a decision on this question already in 1729, the following system became general only by the end of the eighteenth cen-tury: 1 *Gönci barrel* = 180 *icces* = 2 *átalags* (vasculae) = 2 x 90 *icces* = 4 *tubs* = 4 x 45 *icces*. This system remains valid but is now in litres: 1 *Gönci barrel* = 140 litres = 2 *átalags* = 2 x 70 litres = 4 *tubs* = 4 x 35 litres. The system was described as follows in 1867:

> It is, therefore, evident that Tokay wines may be made possessing very differ-ent quantities of saccharin matter, according as a greater or lesser quantity of dry grapes is employed in addition to a fixed quantity of must.
> The measures used for such a mixture are the tub for the dry grapes and the cask (containing 180 Halbe) for the must.
> If it is desired to have very sweet Aszú, then 5 tubs of dry grapes are taken to one cask of must; but should a wine of less sweetness be required then only 4, 3, 2, or 1 tub is taken, according to the degree of sweetness required. Hence it is that the Tokay Aszú is said to be of one, two, three, four or five tubs. [30].

The eighteenth century was the period when Aszú dry grapes spread not only in the Tokay area but in other wine-growing districts as well. They were grown in the seventeenth century in Sopron, a little north of the western end of the Hungarian language territory, in Szentgyörgy, in present-day Slovakia. At this time Aszú grapes were also written about in Eger, and they were filtered in the famous wine-producing areas of Transylvania as well. In the south in the vicinity of Arad, Aszú was and still is made today from red grapes on the Ménesi Hill.

It was in the eighteenth century that interest grew significantly in Tokay Aszú, especially north of Hungary where grapes cannot be grown any more. The Czar Peter the Great was a great lover of Tokay Aszú, of which Prince Ferenc Rákóczi II sent him large quantities on several occasions in the first decades of the eighteenth century. Later, he had his men purchase Tokay Aszú frequently, and he had an excellent knowledge of the prices. In one record he wrote:

> The price of one *antal* (= two tubs) of Aszú berries is identical with the price of a barrel of good Hungarian wine; the price of a barrel of good wine is 20-25 roubles, and if it is vintage wine, the price is double.

He regularly sent merchants to Tokay to provide his court with the quality of wine he required. His offspring had a separate Wine Purchasing Committee in Tokay between 1733 and 1798; they also had vineyards there, and had a church built which is still standing. They paid a priest and a cantor in it, and maintained soldiers as well. They took vine plants and experts on viniculture to the Ukraine and the Crimea, but the grapes of Tokay failed to produce the same quality as in Hungary under the different conditions of soil and climate. [31]

The greatest amount of Tokay Aszú was undoubtedly transported to Poland in the eighteenth century. Significant quantities were forwarded by Polish merchants to Scandinavia too. Investigation of this question is a task for the future; so also is the introduction of Scottish merchants to Poland, who fled from religious persecution first to Prussia and then to Poland in the second half of the sixteenth century. Here they became excellent merchant families, a significant proportion of whom traded in Tokay wine and frequently visited the Hegyalja District to buy wine in large quantities. [32]

The rarest type of wine associated with the Aszú dry grapes, today hardly known any more, is the *Essence*:

> The dry grapes which are obtained in this manner are next put into tubs, the bottoms of which are full of holes, provided with spigots, in order that the juice which is squeezed out by the weight of the grapes themselves may run into a vessel placed underneath.
> This liquid is the TOKAY ESSENCE, which, abounding in Saccharin mat-

ter, and as sweet as Syrup, becomes after a series of years, a drinkable wine, and has then acquired such an astonishing richness of bouquet and flavour, that the drinker is seized with wonder that Nature is capable of producing a fruit, whose juice possesses so high a degree of generous flavour.

It is to be remarked that the Essence, which in its developed state, possesses surprising sweetness, is considered rather as a rarity than as a usual beverage. [33]

We first meet it in 1706, in connection with Csar Peter the Great, to whom the Essence was sent by Ferenc Rákóczi II. The Hungarian ambassador reported that: 'The Csar received the *Essence* of the wine kindly, he mentioned it twice, and once even in Warsaw'. The Csar liked it so much that he wrote later: 'The *Essence* which flows from the Aszú dry berries themselves cannot be purchased for money, it may only be obtained from aristocratic, rich people—for friendship'. [34]

However, the Essence reduced the Aszú dry grape wine itself, as well as the table wine, in quality. An expert wrote in 1736 that a single barrel of Essence was identical in value with 30 barrels of Aszú dry grape wine. Consequently, its production caused great harm to the quality of the main wine and the table wine (ordinarium). It was believed that these were then more difficult to sell. [35]

A great many abuses were committed in the making of Essence, the most frequent trick being that instead of allowing it to drip by its own weight, it was pressed or even trodden upon by foot. Others poured must onto it, which increased its quantity but greatly lessened its quality. As a result, the County of Zemplén ordered in 1791 that 'Essence may not be sold so that people could not cheat by soaking the Aszú dry berries'. It seems, however, that trading in the Essence kept on growing, for ten years later an even more severe prohibition was made: 'The Essence must not be taken off the Aszú dry grapes and have must poured over it since it not only leads to the wine getting leaner but causes great harm to the buyer as well'. Should anyone persist, the Essence would be confiscated and he would be fined if he was a nobleman, and caned if he was a commoner.

In spite of that, the Essence was still made. Two ways of preparing it were generally adopted. One was used when it was an independent drink and constituted the highest level of the Tokay wines. However, because of its very high sugar content, it took years for it to ferment. If that happened and all went well, the recommendation was that it should be filtered into bottles because, if properly corked and sealed, it could be stored for decades and, some believe, even for a hundred years. The other use, highly encouraged by the authorities also, was to pour the Essence onto the Aszú dry grapes, and in certain cases onto the main wine Szamorodni or even onto the ordinarium, by which means the quality could be significantly enhanced [36]

It is not every year that Aszú dry berries grow in the Tokay wine-growing area. It generally happens once every five to ten years that there is a really good 'Aszú year', and only once every half-century is there an excellent crop of Aszú grapes that is remembered for a long time. Consequently, the Tokay Szamorodni, Aszú and Essence cannot be made every year, or at least are not of the same quality every year. The Essence too has existed up to the present day as a special kind of wine, a real rarity, and if there is a crop suitable for making it, even today a certain amount of it is made in Tarcal (in the neighbourhood of Tokay), for one of the European royal courts.

The above sketch is of interest also because it seems certain that the introduction and spread of the types of wine based on the dry Aszú grapes in the vicinity of Tokay occurred during the period of the Renaissance. It took place in Hungary later than in other parts of Europe, and the late Renaissance extended even to the seventeenth century, especially in Transylvania. These types of wine go back to the Greek and especially the Roman examples, via the medieval Italian traditions. Since they were the ones which affected viniculture in this region to the greatest extent, significant changes occurred in the types, forms of cultivation and the method of processing. It is remarkable that such a definitely Mediterranean technique of grape processing managed to invade the northernmost regions of grape growing in Europe, reaching the borderline of viniculture in the North-Eastern corner of Hungary.

NOTES

1. J. Kossuth, *Szölömüvelés és gyümölcstermelés* (Viniculture and fruit production), Budapest 1905, 192.
2. F.B. Szikszai, *Nomenclatvra Dictionarium Latino-vngaricum*, Debrecen 1570/1590, 54.
3. L. Makkai, *I. Rákóczi György birtokainak gazdasági iratai* (The economic documents of the estates of György Rákóczi I), Budapest 1954, 237.
4. J. Nagyváti, *A szorgalmatos mezei gazda* (The industrious farmer), 1-2 (Pest 1791), *passim*.
5. A. Szirmay, *Notitia historica, politica, oeconomica montium et locorum viniferorum comitatus Zempleniensis*, Kassa 1798, *passim*.
6. *J. Fábián, Columella Lucius Moderatus XII. könyve a mezei gazdaságról* . . . (The 12th book of Columella Lucius Moderatus on agriculture . . .).
7. P. Crescentius, *Opus ruralium commandorum libri XII*, Florence 1478, *passim*.
8. L. Hadrovics, *Jövevényszó vizsgálatok* (The investigation of loanwords), Budapest 1985, 106-108.
9. F.B. Szikszai, *op. cit.*, 54.

10. *Adalékok Zemplén vármegye történetéhez* (Contributions to the history of the County of Zemplén), 5 (1900), 42.

11. *Adalékok Zemplén . . . op. cit.*, 23 (1926), 149.

12. *A magyar nyelv történeti-etimológiai szótára* (Tesz) (The historical-etymological Dictionary of the Hungarian Language), I (Budapest 1967-1976), 990-91.

13. J. Bocatius, *Hungaridos libri poematum V* Bártfa 1599.

14. I. Balassa, A szölömüvelés és borkezelés változása a XVI-XVII. században Tokaj-Hegyalján (The changes in viniculture and viticulture in the 16-17th centuries in Tokay-Hegyalja). In *Agrártörténeti Szemle* (Review of Agricultur al History) (1973), 5-6.

15. A. Szirmay, *Notitia historica comitatus Zempleniensis*, Buda 1804, *passim*.

16. P. Keler, *Beschreibung des vornehmsten Weinburges in Ungarn*, III (Thoruni 1726), 252.

17. F.B. Szikszai, *op. cit.*, 54.

18. T.A. Szabó, *Erdélyi magyar szótörténeti tár IV* (Repository of the history of Transylvanian Hungarian words IV), IV (Bucarest 1984), 353-54.

19. I. Balassa, A tokaj-hegyaljai borféleségek terminológiája (The terminology of the wines of the Tokay-Hegyalja District). In *Magyar Nyelv* (Hungarian Language) (1975), 7-9.

20. *Album of the Tokay-Hegyalja*, Pest 1867, 75-77.

21. B. Radvánszky, *A magyar családi élet és háztartás a XVI. és XVII. században* (Hungarian family life and household in the 16-17th centuries), I (Budapest 1896), 45.

22. L. Makkai, *op. cit.*, 241, 246.

23. S. Szilágyi, *A két Rákóczi György családi levelezése* (The family correspond ence of the two György Rákóczis), Budapest 1875, 64.

24. *Adalékok Zemplén . . . op. cit.*, (1915), 339.

25. *Album of the Tokay-Hegyalja, op. cit.*, 73.

26. I. Orosz, A hegyaljai mezövárosok társadalma a XVII. században (különös tekintettel a szölöbirtok hatásaira) (The society of the agricultural towns in the Hegyalja District (with special regard to the impact of the vineyards)). In *Agrártörténeti Tanulmányok* (Studies in Agricultural History), Budapest 1960, *passim*.

27. B. Iványi, *Gönc szabadalmas mezöváros története* (The history of Gönc, a free agricultural town), Karcag 1926, *passim*.

28. *Magyar Gazdaságtörténeti Szemle* (Review of Hungarian Economic History), 6 (1899), 89.

29. I. Wellmann, *Magyarország népeinek élete 1730 táján* (The life of the peoples of Hungary around 1730), Budapest 1984, 409.

30. *Album of the Tokay-Hegyalja, op. cit.*, 73.

31. L. Tardy, *A tokaji Orosz Borvásárló Bizottság története (1733-1798)* (The history of the Russian Wine Purchasing Committee in Tokay (1733-1798)), Sárospatak 1963, *passim*.

32. Gy. Komoróczy, *Borkivitelünk észak felé* (Our wine exports to the north), Kassa 1944, *passim*.
33. *Album of the Tokay-Hegyalja, op. cit.*, 71-73.
34. L. Tardy, *op. cit.*, 6, 12.
35. Gy. Komoróczy, *op. cit.*, 19.
36. I. Balassa, A tokay-hegyaljai aszúbor és esszencia 1790-1810 között (The dry grape Aszú and the Essence of the Tokay-Hegyalja District between 1790-1810). In *Magyar Mezögazdasági Múzeum Közleményei* (Publications of the Hungarian Agricultural Museum) (1984), 136.

THE SILVER TRAVELLING CANTEEN OF PRINCE CHARLES EDWARD STUART

George Dalgleish

The travelling Canteen which belonged to Prince Charles Edward Stuart was lost by him at the battle of Culloden on 16 April 1746 and came into the possession of the family of the Earls of Albemarle. It is an example of an item produced for the luxury market, whose existence owes more to the demands of personal prestige, taste, symbolism and power than to functionalism. Coupled with this it has had the guise of an historical 'relic' thrust upon it, being connected indisputably, or so I hope to prove, with one of the most romantic figures of Scottish history. These parameters ensure that the evidence relating to its history, use and associations is of a different nature to that employed in the study of other, more functional, food containers. As there are so few other eighteenth-century canteens in existence with which to make comparisons, the more usual empirical methods of investigation do not necessarily apply. Any evidence relating to the Canteen, and indeed to any individual item supposedly connected with an historical figure has, because of the very nature of the existence of the 'cult of relics', to be subjected to a rigorously strict investigation. Jacobitism in particular, with that peculiar attraction of all 'lost causes', has produced a vast array of 'relics' and mementoes, most of which have little if any connection with the period, let alone with the principal figures involved. Perhaps, however, we have become over-cautious and have in fact swung too far the other way. Few scholars now seem prepared to believe that any existing material evidence for the central figure of the 1745-6 attempt to put the Stuarts back on the British throne is capable of proof. It is hoped that this essay will establish that, while one must be wary of taking an uncritical view of Jacobite 'relics' in general, Prince Charles Edward did have several personal possessions whose existence today can be demonstrated. It will also look beyond the luxury, prestige or symbolic nature of the canteen to the fact that it had a functional purpose which links it with its more humble brethren, the drinking cups and cutlery which were beginning to achieve a wider currency in the eighteenth century.

The Canteen is in effect an elaborate, although still functional, 'picnic set' for two people contained within a silver flask-shaped outer case with a domed, hinged lid. When closed it is 18cm high and at most 11cm wide(Fig.

1. The flask-shaped outer case of the Canteen.M/1115/A.

2. The Canteen, showing the two tumblers, the cutlery packed into the block, and the two-handled cup.M/1116/C.

1). This is heavily chased and embossed, in the prevailing rococo fashion, with flowers, fruit, leaves, swags, trophies of arms, cartouches and bands of linked thistles. All these decorative elements are set on a matted background and surround shaped panels of plain, undecorated silver. Immediately inside the outer case fit two plain oval tumblers with gilt interiors which also fit one inside the other, the inner having a simple everted rim which overlaps the outer. In turn the tumblers contain a green velvet-covered wooden block which is pierced to house the items of cutlery. These comprise: two knives, two forks and two tablespoons all with detachable cannon-shaped handles which in turn have removable end-caps and are capable of fitting inside one another (although there are spaces in the block for all six handles); a cylindrical cruet set; a mace-shaped combined nutmeg grater and corkscrew; and a combined teaspoon and marrow scoop (Fig. 2). All the cutlery is silver gilt and, although unmarked, is very similar in style to pieces made for several other travelling canteens in the first half of the eighteenth century (see below). The final piece of the set is a small two-handled cup which is secured inside the lid of the outer case by means of a screw finial. The inside of this cup is also gilded and is mounted with an English coin of James II. Although it is not a quaich, the

3. The Canteen showing all the items of cutlery.M/1114.

handles are decorated in a manner reminiscent of the engraving which was found on silver and silver-mounted wooden quaichs up to the middle of the eighteenth century. It has been suggested that this cup was not an original part of the set, and certainly the screw finial pierces the St Andrew's Cross on the cover in a rather ugly way, possibly pointing to a later addition. If this is the case, however, the cup must have been made and incorporated only a very few years after the manufacture of the Canteen, as the use of the design on its handles and the manner of the engraving largely fell out of use in the second half of the eighteenth century. [1] Altogether the Canteen is made up of 31 separate pieces (Fig. 3).

The bases of the outer case and the two beakers are all stamped with the following marks: 'EO' for the maker, Ebenezer Oliphant; a 'castle', the Edinburgh town mark; 'GED' for Dougal Ged, the assay master; 'L' (script) the date letter for September 1740 to September 1741.

The maker, Ebenezer Oliphant, was the fifteenth child and eighth and youngest son of James Oliphant, fifth Laird of Gask in Perthshire and Janet Murray of Woodend. [2] He was born at the house of Gask on 7th March 1713 and on 13th September 1727, at the age of 15, was booked apprentice to James Mitchelson, a goldsmith in Edinburgh. [3] (The sending of younger sons of Scots lairds into commerce and the professions was a common and necessary practice in the mid-eighteenth century. The sons of the fifth Laird of Gask illustrate this well: James, third son, became a merchant in Perth; William, fifth son, was apprenticed to a surgeon in Perth, but eventually sailed to Jamaica where he died; Patrick was also apprenticed to a surgeon in Kirkcaldy and was later sent to Leyden to continue his medical studies, before joining the East India Company; he died in Baghdad.)

Ebenezer was admitted as a master of the Incorporation of Goldsmiths of Edinburgh on 26th August 1737, after completing his seven-year apprenticeship with Mitchelson and the obligatory three years as a journeyman, presumably also with Mitchelson. He was given as his essay, or test of skill, 'a diamond ring and plain gold ring' which he made in his old master's shop, with William Ayton and Edward Lothian as his assay masters. He paid 200 merks as his admission fee and William Drummond, bookseller, burgess of Edinburgh, acted as his cautioner. [4] He was admitted as a Burgess and Guildbrother of Edinburgh on 26th October 1737 [5] and set up his own shop in Parliament Close. A member of a staunchly Jacobite family (his brother Laurence, sixth Laird, and his nephew, also Laurence, were 'out' with Prince Charles Edward during the '45), Ebenezer became a well-known and successful goldsmith and maintained his adherence to the Jacobite cause until his death in 1798. [6] From the evidence of the numerous extant examples of his work he was obviously an accomplished craftsman and seems to have prospered. So much so that in 1753 he was the only member of his family who could put up sufficient cash to buy back the forfeited estate of Gask from the Government. [7]

It would be difficult to suggest a goldsmith with a better pedigree to produce a piece of silver supposedly intended for Prince Charles Edward. This impression is further strengthened by the strong family tradition that he was responsible for a very fine gold and enamel Jacobite commemorative ring. The ring, which comprises two narrow entwined bands, joined to an oblong bezel by a thistle and a rose, depicts the initials of the Earls of Kilmarnock and Derwentwater, Lords Balmerino and Lovat, and 17 other Jacobites who were executed for their part in the Rising. [8]

A further point of interest arising from the hallmarks on the Canteen is that Dougal Ged, whose mark appears alongside Oliphant's, was not, strictly speaking, the assay master. During the period 1740 to 1744, there was a dispute between the Incorporation and Archibald Ure about his tenure of the office of assay master. This was only resolved when Hugh Gordon was appointed to the position in Ure's place. While the dispute continued, silver was supposed to be stamped by the eldest and youngest master, who in turn temporarily took over the assayer's duties. [9] Matters are further complicated by the fact that Ebenezer Oliphant and Dougal Ged are recorded as having been partners at this time. [10]

Oliphant's decoration of the Canteen's outer case is, as we have noted, deeply chased and embossed in the prevailing rococo manner of the day (Fig. 1). This is especially interesting within the context of the development of decoration on Scottish silver, for although it certainly exists, Scottish silverware with all-over rococo-style ornamentation is very rare. It has in fact been suggested that the decoration of the Canteen owes more to the revival of rococo taste in the first quarter of the nineteenth century than to the work of Ebenezer Oliphant and therefore in its present shape would have been unrecognisable to Prince Charles. [11] While it is undoubtedly true that this all-over type of ornamentation is unusual in Scotland in the mid-eighteenth century, with most craftsmen preferring to use rococo motifs in restrained, flat-chased narrow bands round the edges and rims of objects, there is a sufficient corpus of existing material of unarguable pedigree to show that some goldsmiths were capable of producing this more elaborate style of work. There are several such pieces in the collections of the National Museums, including in particular a small mug dated 1744-5 (now gilded) by Laurence Oliphant (possibly a kinsman of Ebenezer) which, although slightly less accomplished, displays many of the decorative elements used on the Canteen, including the background matting and the clusters of fruit and flowers. An ovoid tea urn, of slightly later date (1759), by Alexander Gairdner, also makes use of these techniques, with swirling cartouches and shaped blank panels surrounded with ribbon-tied bunches of fruit and flowers. Other collections also have comparable pieces, including a very fine tea kettle by Ker and Dempster, 1755-6, now in Huntly House Museum, Edinburgh. Even that 'Prince of teapot makers', James Ker, [12] so renowned for his plain elegant wares with sparse, flat-chased decoration, also made at least one excursion into the use of this more elaborate chasing technique, as shown on the magnificent gold teapot he made as the Royal Race Prize at Leith races in 1737, now in the possession of the Earl of Rosebery, Dalmeny House. (The chasing on this, however, is confined to a narrow band around the rim.) In a less quantifiable way, the 'feel' of the Canteen also suggests a mid-eighteenth century date, the work being executed in a softer and more restrained way than was the case with the hard, well-defined, almost mechanical, precision of the rococo revival of the 1820s and '30s.

This heavy chasing technique was therefore certainly in use in Edinburgh by the 1740s, and it is significant that one of the earliest references in Scottish goldsmiths' accounts to chasing as a separate item is in a bill dated March 1741 from James Mitchelson, Oliphant's old master.[13] He is also noted as having been the 'one man in Town [Edinburgh] that can do chased work and he has a great deal of business of the same kind on hand'. [14] This undoubtedly refers to the type of chasing which occurs on the Canteen. Although it was common for craftsmen to exaggerate their particular skills by claiming the exclusive ability to perform certain tasks, nevertheless the references to Mitchelson prove beyond doubt that this particular style of decoration was unusual enough at the time to merit special mention. Mitchelson certainly passed on his skill to his erstwhile apprentice Oliphant, for in bills and accounts from him he is noted for the use of chasing.

This recent research, coupled with the fact that we know of no other eighteenth-century Scottish travelling canteens, confirms that the Canteen is an outstandingly important piece of mid-eighteenth century Scottish silver in its own right, over and above its historical associations. Although it is unique in a Scottish context, it does, however, fit into a wider tradition of using travelling cutlery and canteens, and comparisons with several English examples may be instructive. All the pieces of cutlery in the Oliphant Canteen are unmarked and it seems unlikely that they were made by Oliphant himself (Fig. 4). The cannon-shaped handles of the knives, forks and spoons are also rather old-fashioned for 1740, and one would

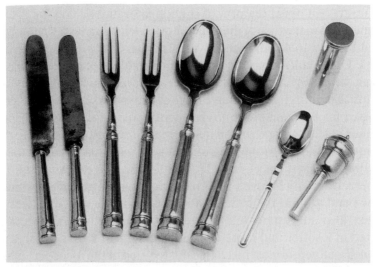

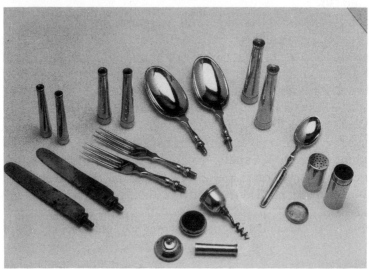

4. (a) The cutlery, cruet and nutmeg grater, dismantled.M/1116/A.
(b) The cruet, nutmeg grater and items of cutlery, showing the cannon handles.M/
1116/G.

perhaps expect pistol-grip style handles by this time. All this is consistent
with Oliphant having 'bought in' the cutlery, then making the tumblers and
case to suit. This is also suggested by the fact that the cutlery, particularly
the bowls of the spoons and the heads of the forks, is very reminiscent of
pieces in canteens made by several London goldsmiths. One such com-

prises a knife, fork and spoon, a cruet, a marrow scoop, an acorn or mace-shaped nutmeg grater and a plain beaker marked by Benjamin Pyne in 1722, [15] while another, with two sets of cutlery and two beakers which are again the only marked pieces, is this time by James Smith I, of London c. 1725. [16] Another single set now in a private collection in Scotland, with a tumbler marked by Aymé Videau, London, 1750-1, again has cutlery of a similar style to that discussed above. It also has a very fine mace- or acorn-shaped combined nutmeg grater and corkscrew, almost identical to the ones in the other two London canteens and also to that in Oliphant's Canteen. This time, however, the nutmeg grater bears the mark 'DF' (in script). Elizabeth Miles [17] has listed several examples both marked and unmarked by the same maker, and although the maker has not yet been identified, he made several other items, including a caster and muffineer in the 1740s. [18] It seems likely, therefore, that 'DF' made the nutmeg grater, if not the rest of the cutlery, for the Oliphant Canteen. It has been suggested, incidentally, that the mace-like shape of these nutmeg graters/corkscrews is a play on the name of the bright red outer covering of the nutmeg which was also used as a spice. The use of grated nutmeg and other spices to flavour wine and spirits was common throughout the eighteenth century and continued into the nineteenth. The Scots were particularly renowned for their fondness for both spiced claret and rum and whisky punches. There are many contemporary references to Prince Charles Edward drinking such beverages during his stay in Scotland. Therefore the implement in this Canteen had a dual purpose, to open and flavour wine. [19]

Having dealt with the Canteen's importance as a piece of silver, we now have to deal with its historical associations—the connections with Prince Charles Edward Stuart—which make it uniquely important as a part of Scotland's heritage. In fact, it is almost unfortunate that it is the Canteen's association with the 'Bonnie Prince' which has excited so much public interest, as this has tended to obscure its intrinsic importance as a piece of silver. There is no doubt, however, that the tradition that it was a personal possession of Prince Charles Edward has much more to validate it than is the case with so many Jacobite 'relics'.

The story of its link with the Prince and how it came into the possession of the Earls of Albemarle was first published in a book entitled *Fifty Years of My Life* by George, sixth Earl of Albemarle, [20] and is later repeated in his will dated 17 May 1888. [21] The Earl recounts that 'a punch bowl' was found in the tent of Prince Charles Edward at Culloden, and was then given by the Duke of Cumberland to his friend and aide-de-camp George Keppel, Lord Bury, son of the second Earl of Albemarle. The sixth Earl's description of the Canteen as a punch bowl is a slight mystery, although it is quite probable that an old man (he was 77 when his *Life* was published) could easily mistake the use of something which he had not seen properly for many years. In fact by the time he drew up his will in 1888 he had changed the description again to the more accurate 'silver bowl and cover and travelling case of Prince Charles Stuart the Pretender'. [22]   The remainder of the 'tradition' about it being found by Cumberland and given to Lord Bury remains constant, and a senior representative of the family today has commented 'that it has never for us been a question only of "family tradition" but a matter inviting no question or doubt'. [23]   Although the first part of the tradition that it was found in his *tent* is mistaken, since Prince Charles Edward was billeted at Culloden House immediately prior to the battle, and on the night before was involved in the abortive march to Nairn, there seems no reason to doubt that it was part of the victors' spoils, nor that the Albemarles would have acquired such a thing except as a trophy. This tradition seems to be confirmed in a remarkable contemporary account printed in *The Lyon in Mourning*, taken from a conversation between Robert Forbes, the Jacobite Bishop of Ross and Caithness, who compiled the *Lyon* and James Gib, 'who served the Prince in station of Master-Household and provisor for the Prince's own Table', recorded on Monday, June 27th, 1748. It runs as follows: ' . . . [bed and table linen] were taken by the enemy after the battle of Culloden . . . [along with other things in] . . . a covered waggon which he [Mr Gib] was forced to leave behind him in the open air near the field. . . . in the same hamper . . . were likewise contained a large silver soup spoon, two silver ragout spoons, a large silver lamp for keeping a dish warm upon the table, and the Prince's hunting equipage in a shagreen case, consisting of six silver goblets, doubly gilt, going into one another, two knives, two forks, and two spoons, all silver and doubly gilt. Mr Gib regrets the loss of the hunting equipage more than that of all the rest, for he says it was one of the most curious things he had ever seen in any place. The Prince brought it with him from France. Mr Gib told me he had heard it rumoured that the Princes's hunting equipage should have fallen into the Duke of Cumberland's hands, and that he had dispatched it from Inverness to London as a great curiosity . . . ' [24]   There is little doubt that the 'Prince's hunting equipage' and the present Canteen are one and the same. The description fits remarkably well, except for the number of 'goblets'. Gib probably misunderstood the nature of the outer case and thought it to comprise extra drinking cups. It would seem strange to have cutlery for two people and cups for six in what is obviously intended to be a single compact item. In every other travelling canteen I have seen, the number of cutlery settings is matched by the number of tumblers.

It has been suggested that another possible source of Mr Gib's inaccuracy over the number of tumblers is that he may have confused the number of detachable handles with the tumblers. There are six handles which all fit ingeniously into one another. The shagreen case, which was a normal part of travelling canteens, has presumably been lost. Mr Gib's remarks about it being 'one of the most curious things' he had ever seen also points to something that was unusually decorated rather than a series of plain cups and pieces of cutlery in a simple shagreen case. The fact that he says it was brought from France is also interesting. This suggests that it had been sent from Scotland, after having been made by Ebenezer Oliphant in 1740-1, possibly as a 21st birthday present for the Prince (20/31 December 1741). A Jacobite Association had been set up by this time in Scotland to promote an armed invasion, and there were frequent comings and goings between Scotland and the exiled Court in Rome. James, Duke of Perth, for example, sent Charles and his brother Prince Henry two sets of Highland dress, complete with a silver-mounted sword and targe decorated in the rococo style, now in the National Museum. Recent work on the Stuart Papers at Windsor has confirmed these as having been commissioned in London by Perth and then sent to Rome in 1740. A 'Hunting equipage' rather than a military camp canteen would have been a singularly appropriate present for a Prince who was a keen sportsman. We have numerous references to him shooting game in Northern Italy in 1740 and 1742, and he continued with this pastime throughout his campaign in Scotland and England during 1745-6.

Mr Gib's account obviously corresponds remarkably well with the Albermarle family 'tradition' that it was given by Cumberland to his ADC, Viscount Bury, later third Earl of Albemarle. Bury was dispatched on the evening of the battle (16 April) from Inverness to London, with a letter from Cumberland to his father George II. He arrived in London on 24 April where he was given a hero's welcome, the news of the victory having preceded him, and a gift of £1,000 from the King. He was so exhausted by the rigours of the campaign and journey that he immediately retired to bed with a fever which required heavy 'bleeding'! [25] It is also quite possible that the 'Prince's tent' mentioned in the Albermarle account was in fact an inaccurate description of the covered wagon which Gib said held the Prince's personal belongings.

The Government Commander at Culloden, William, Duke of Cumberland, also attested to the extent of the Jacobite baggage captured by his troops when writing to the Duke of Newcastle: ' . . . All their Artillery and Ammunition . . . is taken, as was the Pretender's and all their Baggage, which was in general plundered'. [26] It was probably during the 'mopping-up' operations after the battle that the Duke first laid eyes, and hands, on the Canteen.

Further corroborative documentary evidence that Charles lost silver plate, both at the battle and during his wanderings, is provided in an account by Ewan MacPherson of Cluny of the Locharkaig treasure (money sent from France, too late to prop up the rebellion, and buried for safety on the shores of Locharkaig), given to Charles Edward and his father when Cluny was called to France in the spring of 1755. Cluny declares: ' . . . I never saw or could hear of the casket of valuable things H.R.H. says was among his Plate'. [27]   He goes on to say that he saved some of the Prince's plate and personal dress on the night of the battle when he found a baggage wagon 'on the high road deserted by every person'. [28]   Obviously the Hanoverian army had not been as thorough as Cumberland thought!

5. The Canteen outer case, showing the engraved Badge of the Prince of Wales and the bands of linked thistles.M/1115/F.

Further evidence for the Canteen's association with Prince Charles Edward derives from the decorative scheme itself. Firstly, the frontal cartouche is engraved with the three-feathered Badge of the Prince of Wales (Fig. 5). It has been suggested that this could be a later addition, especially as the plumes terminate in 'sticks' rather than in the more usual short sections of plume. [29] The balance of evidence points, however, to the Badge being contemporary with the rest of the Canteen. The engraving is both skilful and interesting, although, from a heraldic point of view, slightly inaccurate. The ermine circlet should not appear below an open crown without the velvet cap as it does here. Interestingly, however, this inaccuracy is perpetuated in a contemporary work called *The British Compendium or Rudiments of Honour* (Vol III of this work deals with Scottish heraldry), [30] while by the time the reprinted edition of A. Nisbet's *System of Heraldry* was published in 1816, [31] crowns are shown correctly without the ermine circlet. Nisbet and the *Compendium* . . . also both show the plumes ending in 'sticks'.

Charles Edward, like his father, was created Prince of Wales immediately on his birth (20/31 December 1720). We have evidence for this and also for the fact that the Jacobites considered him as such. In a letter to the Emperor of Austria, dated 1st January 1721, James VIII states: ' . . . the Queen, your cousin, has borne me a Prince of Wales', [32] while shortly after the birth Norbert Roettier, engraver to the exiled court, produced a medal commemorating the event. On the reverse of this medal, the dies of which are in the British Museum, is the legend CAR.WALL.PR.NATUS.DIE. ULT.A.1720. [33] As the first-born son and heir of the king, Charles had the legal right to bear the Stuart Royal *Arms* (marshalled for Scotland or England depending upon which country they were being displayed in) with overall a label of three points argent, while as Prince of Wales he was entitled to use the personal *Badge* of the Prince of Wales. It would seem appropriate that the slightly less formal Badge, rather than the full Royal Arms, would be used on a piece such as the Canteen, especially if it is, as would seem likely, a hunting canteen. Several contemporary portraits of the Prince show him accompanied by the Prince of Wales Feathers. One, possibly by Antonio David, painted when the Prince was about seven years old, depicts him standing holding out his right hand toward a table, on which rests an open crown with three plumes emerging from it and the motto ICH DIEN on a label below it. [34]

There is absolutely no doubt that throughout his life Charles was recognised by his supporters as, and considered himself to be, the Prince of Wales. In the warrants appointing his Governors and Priest issued in 1727 he is referred to as the Prince of Wales, as he is in the commissions of Regency issued in 1743, 1750 and 1757. [35] Throughout the campaign of 1745-6, which of course was a British campaign, not a purely Scottish one, he was referred to as Prince of Wales. He issued commissions to officers in his army using this title (for example the commission to Captain Hamilton, tried at York, 20th August 1746). [36] This is an extremely important concept, for it emphasises that the whole Jacobite movement was seen, by the Stuarts at least, in British, not Scottish, terms. The '45 was an attempt to gain the crown of Great Britain, a point that has often in the past been misunderstood by English historians who have attempted to interpret the affair as an English-Scottish conflict. It should be remembered, for example, that the Duke of Cumberland's army included a significant number of Scots. This British dimension is well illustrated by the medal which was issued in anticipation of the arrival of Prince Charles Edward in Britain in 1745. This shows (obv) a bust of Charles with the legend CAROLUS WALLIA PRINCEPS/1745, while the reverse shows the figure Britannia awaiting the arrival of a fleet. [37]   There is no question, therefore, that it is entirely consistent with known historical fact that Charles used the Badge of the Prince of Wales.

Secondly, one of the major decorative elements of the Canteen is a band of leaved thistle heads, linked by C- and S-shaped scrolls around the join of the lid and body. This is undoubtedly a representation of the Collar of the Most Ancient and Most Noble Order of the Thistle (Fig. 5). James VII, James VIII and Charles in turn, all considered themselves to be the lawful sovereigns of Great Britain and were so recognised by their followers. James VIII, during the period under discussion, therefore considered that it was completely consistent with his Royal dignity to grant peerages, honours and knighthoods, both of the Thistle and of the Garter. The warrants for many of these creations still exist in the Stuart Papers at Windsor. It should be remembered, when considering the validity of these grants, that James was recognised as lawful sovereign by several Continental powers (particularly the Papacy and France), that his ambassadors were received, and that the titles he conferred were recognised by them. One should also bear in mind that the Order of the Thistle in particular was considered by the Stuarts to be *their* Order, as it was James VII who reconstituted and regularised it as an order of chivalry. (It does of course have a much more ancient history, [38]   but no statutes existed for it until James VII set these out in 1687.) In this way, James can be seen as the founder of the order as it exists at present. [39]   The natural concomitant of this is that the Stuarts saw the granting of Thistles by the Hanoverians as yet another example of usurpation of their Royal dignity, and considered such grants, along with other British and Scottish honours, illegal. In practice, however, what seems to have happened is that two parallel series of grants of Orders existed, the 'Official' Hanoverian grants and the Jacobite grants. This point is perfectly illustrated in the person of James, fifth Duke of Hamilton, whose support in the political manoeuvring leading finally to the '45 Rebellion was sought by both the Government and the Jacobites. He was given both the Thistle and the Garter by James VIII on July 30th 1723 (although the grant of the Thistle does not seem to have been acted upon, as a fresh warrant was issued to him on 27th July 1740), while George II also granted him the Thistle. [40]

Charles Edward was without doubt given both the Thistle and the Garter by his father, although the exact dates of these grants are unknown. Ruvigny notes that he had both orders by 1742, [41] but it is likely that these honours were conferred on him at birth or in his infancy, as was the case with his father. There are numerous well-authenticated contemporary portraits which show Charles wearing the St Andrew Badge of the Thistle. These include one by Antonio David, signed and dated 1732, when Charles was 12, [42] one by Louis Gabriel Blanchet, signed and dated 1739 (in the collection of Her Majesty the Queen), and one by Domenico Dupra, also dated 1739. To be completely accurate, in all of these paintings Charles is *not* shown wearing the *Badge* of the Order, which normally shows St Andrew set on a rayed background and is always worn with the Collar of Thistles (cf. Portrait of John Earl of Mar, by Sir G. Kneller, at Alloa House), but rather the *medallion*, sometimes referred to as the 'Jewel', of the Order. This depicts St Andrew bearing his cross set within an oval cordon bearing the motto of the Order, NEMO ME IMPUNE LACESSET, and was worn suspended from a ribbon. In this way, the oval medallion which is an integral part of the decoration of the lid on the canteen is an accurate representation of what Charles was portrayed as wearing (Fig. 6). The band of linked thistles is, on the other hand, a rather

6. The lid of the Canteen showing the St Andrew medallion. Note the pierced hole for the screw finial to hold the cup.M/1115/K.

stiff and formal representation of the actual gold and enamel Collar of the Order of the Thistle.

Comparisons with several contemporary heraldic works also suggest this to be the case. The same formalised thistles and plain linkages appear in the first edition of Alexander Nisbet's *System of Heraldry*, published in 1720 (for example see Royal Arms on the frontispiece). [43] This is of course heraldically wrong as the thistles are supposed to be, and in some early and most later collars are, linked by intertwined sprigs of rue. The C and S links, however, were in common use in the first half of the eighteenth century and their design would have been available to the maker from many sources, such as Sir George MacKenzie's *Scotland's Herauldrie* (Edinburgh, 1680) and set of playing cards produced by the Edinburgh goldsmith, Walter Scott, in 1691.

It has been suggested that these C- and S-shaped links refer to the initials of Charles Stuart's name, [44] but it does not seem consistent with the Royal dignity assumed by Charles that he would ever have used his surname.

In summation, therefore, the decoration of the Canteen accurately depicts the insignia and devices that Prince Charles Edward Stuart was legitimately, in the eyes of the Jacobites, entitled to display. It is also significant to note that the *de facto* Prince of Wales of the time, Frederick Louis, son of George II, was not a Knight of the Thistle.

The Canteen remained a prized possession of the Albermarle family until 1963, having been displayed publicly on only four occasions. [45] It was then sold by Christie's, London for the then Viscount Bury to a Scottish collector, [46] but its adventures did not end there. In 1984 a dealer, who had since acquired it, applied for an Export Licence to sell it in America. The granting of this was delayed by the Minister for the Arts to allow time for the National Museum of Antiquities of Scotland to mount a public campaign to raise the purchase price. This campaign was wonderfully successful, and generous contributions by both commercial interests and private individuals alike, including a last-minute underwriting of a deficit by the Glenmorangie Distillery Company, enabled the Canteen to be saved from export. [47] The Canteen is now one of the treasures of the Scottish National Collections.

Acknowledgements
I would like to thank Mr Stuart Maxwell, Mr Henry Stuart Fotheringham and Mr Godfrey Evans for making available information included in this essay. The staff of the Royal Museum of Scotland Library, Queen Street have, throughout the prolonged period of research on

this and related topics, been unfailingly helpful and resourceful. The Hon. W.A.C. Keppel very kindly gave me access to previously unpublished material from the Albemarle family papers. Finally, I wish to record my thanks to Mr Ian Larner and Ms Doreen Moyes of the National Museums of Scotland's Photographic Department for the photographs which illustrate this essay.

NOTES

1. S. Maxwell, Quaichs. In D.V. Clarke and A. O'Connor, eds. *From The Stone Age to the '45, studies presented to R.B.K. Stevenson* (Edinburgh 1983).
2. E. Maxton Grahame, *The Oliphants of Gask* (London 1910), 106.
3. *Ibid.* 171; C.B.B. Watson, ed., *Edinburgh Apprentices Register* (Scottish Record Society), Edinburgh 1929, Vol. II.
4. *Minute Book of the Incorporation of Goldsmiths of Edinburgh* (Scottish Record Office, GD1/482/2), Vol. 2, 109.
5. C.B.B. Watson, ed., *Edinburgh Burgesses and Guild Brethren* (Scottish Record Society), Edinburgh 1930, Vol. II.
6. E.M. Grahame, *op. cit.*, 173.
7. A. Smith, *Jacobite Estates of the '45* (Edinburgh 1982), 12; T.L. Kington Oliphant, *The Jacobite Lairds of Gask* (London 1870), 282.
8. A. Sharp, Notes on Stuart Jewellery. In *Proceedings of the Society of Antiquaries of Scotland*, 57 (1923), 232-3; R.B.K. Stevenson, Jacobite Rings. In *Proceedings of the Society of Antiquaries of Scotland*, 80 (1945), 129.
9. Sir Charles Jackson, *English Goldsmiths and their Marks* (London 1920), 497.
10. *Edinburgh Evening Courant*, August 15, 1745. An advertisement states that as Ged and Oliphant 'intend to give over working in company, it is necessary towards clearing their affairs that their Customers and Debtors pay up their Accompts'. They seem to have commenced business together by 1738.
11. *The Antique Collector*, March 1986, Correspondence, 102.
12. I. Finlay, *Scottish Gold and Silver Work* (Edinburgh 1956), 126-8; G. Dalgleish and S. Maxwell, *The Lovable Craft* (Edinburgh 1987), 14-15, No. 52.
13. Bill from James Mitchelson to Mr William Hall, Advocate, March 10, 1741.
14. Letter from William Grosse, Edinburgh, to Prof George Ross, University of Glasgow, August 5, 1746.
15. *Christie's*, London, 11 July, 1984, Lot 384.
16. *Sotheby's*, London, 22 November, 1984, Lot 65.
17. Elizabeth Miles, *The English Silver pocket nutmeg grater—a Collection of fifty examples from 1693-1816* (Cleveland, Ohio 1966).
18. A. Grimwade, *London Goldsmiths 1697-1837* (2nd ed., London 1982), 251.

G

19. *The English Silver pocket nutmeg grater*, 34.
20. George Keppel, sixth Earl of Albemarle, *Fifty Years of My Life* (London 1876), 101.
21. Will of George, sixth Earl of Albemarle, 17th May 1888. In Albemarle Family Papers, Hampshire.
22. Ibid.
23. Personal communication from Hon. W.A.C. Keppel, DSC, 16 September 1984.
24. *The Lyon in Mourning* (Scottish History Society) Edinburgh 1895, II, 164-5.
25. *Scots Magazine*, April-May, 1746; P. Cunningham, ed., *Letters of Horace Walpole* (London 1891), Vol. II, No. 213.
26. Historical Manuscripts Commission, 10th Report, *Weston Papers*, 442.
27. *Miscellany* (Scottish History Society) VII, 158, taken from the Stuart Papers at Windsor, Vol. 358, No. 28
28. *Ibid.*
29. *The Antique Collector*, March, 1986, Correspondence, 102.
30. Anon., *The British Compendium or Rudiments of Honour* (London 1741).
31. Alexander Nisbet, *A System of Heraldry* (new edn., Edinburgh 1816), Vol. I.
32. M. Hailes, *James Frances Edward, The Old Chevalier* (London 1907).
33. *Medallic Illustrations of Great Britain*, Vol. II, Geo I, No. 61.
34. Scottish National Portrait Gallery, S.Ph. IV 92-5/1.
35. Marquis of Ruvigny and Rainval, *The Jacobite Peerage* (Edinburgh 1904), 249.
36. *Scots Magazine*, October 1746, 483.
37. *Medallic Illustrations*, Vol. II, Geo II, No. 251.
38. *Journal of Heraldry Society of Scotland*, 5 (1983), 39.
39. C.J. Burnett and H. Bennett, *The Green Mantle* (Edinburgh 1987), 7.
40. *Jacobite Peerage*, 193-4; R.E. Bell, ed., *Memorials of John Murray of Broughton* (Scottish History Society) (Edinburgh 1898), xii.
41. *Jacobite Peerage*, 193-4.
42. Scottish National Portrait Gallery, No. 887.
43. Alexander Nisbet, *A System of Heraldry* (first pub. Edinburgh 1720), Vol. I.
44. *Christie's* London, 20 March 1963, Lot 111.
45. *Loan Exhibition of Scottish Art* (London 1931), No. 112; *Exhibition of Scottish Art*, Royal Academy (London 1939), No. 1071; *Royal Stuart Exhibition* (Edinburgh 1949), No. 53; *Royal Gifts*, Christie's, London, No. 198.
46. *Christie's*, London, 20 March, 1963, Lot 111.
47. A complete list of all those who contributed to the appeal is available on request from the Royal Museum of Scotland, Queen Street, Edinburgh. A copy was published in the *National Museum of Antiquities of Scotland Annual Report 1984-85*, 16-20.

THE *NÉCESSAIRE DE VOYAGE* OF THE PRINCESS PAULINE BORGHESE: A STUDY IN THE DEVELOPMENT OF THE TRAVELLING SERVICE

Godfrey Evans

In 1986 the National Museums of Scotland were able to purchase an outstanding travelling service: the *nécessaire de voyage* of the Princess Pauline Borghese, the favourite sister of the Emperor Napoleon I.[1]

To fully appreciate the importance of this major *nécessaire*, it is essential to see it in the context of the development of the aristocratic travelling service. Accordingly, the first part of this essay is devoted to a review of earlier services. The Borghese *nécessaire* itself is examined in some detail in the second half.

The Development of the Travelling Service

The origins of the Borghese *nécessaire* can be traced back to the magnificent silver-gilt toilet services made during the reign of the 'Sun King', Louis XIV (1643-1715). Sadly, all the French royal services have been melted down, but four Parisian services survive more or less intact.[2] They demonstrate that such services were assembled as matching (or nearly matching) sets and were supplied in large, impressive chests, which enabled them to be transported from one residence to another.[3] All four surviving services contain a large mirror, salvers, boxes, bottles for powders or sweet-smelling waters and a pair of candlesticks to illuminate the dressing table. In addition, three services also include a ewer and basin. A large brush and a small brush are also represented together twice, as are a snuffers and tray.

However, not all services in use at the French court were limited to articles for the *toilette*. One service recorded in the *Inventaire Générale des Meubles de la Couronne sous Louis XIV* in 1673 comprised:

> *un bassin, une esguière, quatre petits plats, quatre assiètes, une escuelle couverte, deux cuilliers, deux fourchettes, deux couteaux, deux petites tasses à une oreille, deux ferrières avec leurs couvercles, deux petites tasses à deux*

oreilles, une tasse en ovalle avec une oreille, deux chandeliers, deux goblets couverts, un sucrier, une cassolette, une petite tasse couverte, deux petites bouteilles de verre avec leurs bouchons d'argent, une petite salière platte, une petite cuillier, un miroir, une paire de cizeaux, des mouchettes, une brosse, une peigne, un ancrier, un poudrier, deux boestes à mouches, un agenda, un canif, une percelette, un cousteau pour couper du papier, une règle et un plissoir.[4]

It is intriguing to see that this service and the one listed immediately before it are described as *'toilettes d'argent vermeil doré d'Allemagne'*. The simplest and most obvious interpretation of this is that they were made either in Germany or by a German goldsmith working in France, but 'd'Allemagne' is somewhat cryptic and could have meant 'like a German service' or might have referred to the style or standard of the silver.

Whilst it is not possible to determine exactly where these two services were made, it is abundantly clear that Augsburg, in South Germany, was the principal centre for the production of combined toilet and tableware services from the late seventeenth century to the end of the third quarter of the eighteenth century.[5] Fortunately, it is not necessary to embark upon an exhaustive (and exhausting) survey of all the travelling services made in Augsburg over the course of a century, many of which have survived.[6] All that is required is for us to have a reasonably clear basic understanding of the contents and arrangement of the more important mid-eighteenth century Augsburg travelling services.

The first point to note about such services is that they generally contain between about fifty and sixty items (as opposed to the fifteen to twenty-two pieces in the four surviving French seventeenth-century toilet services). The selection of toilet articles is not radically different from those in the earlier French toilet services, as the following comparison shows:

Lennoxlove Toilet Service, assembled in Paris about 1677 (National Museums of Scotland, Edinburgh)	Travelling Service by Johann Martin Satzger and others, assembled in Augsburg, early 1770s (Wallace Collection, London)[7]
Large table mirror	Large table mirror
—	Small table mirror
Pair of large rectangular boxes	Four pairs of boxes of different sizes
Pair of large circular boxes	—
Pair of small circular boxes	—

Jewel box with pincushion in the lid	Pincushion
Pair of bottles for powders or sweet-smelling waters	Pair of glass bottles with silver-gilt screw-tops
Circular footed salver	Footed salver
Pair of shaped footed salvers	Two pairs of trays or salvers[8]
Large clothes brush	Clothes brush
Small clothes brush	Clothes whisk
Pair of candlesticks	Pair of candlesticks
—	Small covered bowl
—	Oval basin
—	Small knife (probably for preparing make-up)

The essential difference lies in the inclusion of tableware. For example, the service in the Wallace Collection also contains: a coffee pot, teapot, milk jug, spirit lamp, pair of caddies, pairs of cups and trembleuse containers, covered dish, plate, spice box, two covered glasses, knife, fork and spoon, six teaspoons and a marrow scoop. Also included is a writing set consisting of a tray with candlestick, bell, inkwell, sand box and receptacle for wafers. An important feature to note about these large Augsburg services is that they generally contain porcelain and glass.[9] As we have just seen, the service in the Wallace Collection contains a pair of glass bottles for the *toilette* and two covered glasses. There are also two porcelain cups. Some services include more ceramic, particularly more porcelain. A good example of this is the service formerly owned by Lady Abdy, now in the Thyssen-Bornemisza Collection, which contains 13 pieces of Meissen porcelain—a slop bowl, five cups, five saucers and two chocolate cups—as well as 53 articles of silver-gilt.[10]

All the items were stored in a large fitted chest. Generally, these chests follow a fairly standard pattern, with the lid hinged at the back and the front formed by two doors mounted on hinges. The large mirror is normally accommodated on its side in the lid, with the top pointing to the left-hand side, while the remaining articles are divided between a fixed tray in the top of the chest and a sliding lower tray. To gain access to the items in the lower tray, one simply opens the doors and pulls the tray out.

Examination of these mid-eighteenth century Augsburg travelling services shows that they are far from ideal travelling services (at least as we understand them). They are much too large and heavy. This stems from the fact that they were not really intended for travelling. For most of the time they would probably have been kept in bedrooms to impress visitors. They only 'travelled' when their owner moved to court or to an important residence for any length of time, and then they were *transported*, along with other possessions. To all intents and purposes, they are formed of standard articles of silver-gilt, porcelain and glass. True, some items are slightly smaller and lighter than their normal counterparts, but the differences are really quite minor and do not greatly reduce the overall size and weight of the selection. A corollary of a bulky, heavy selection of items is, of course, that it necessitates a big, cumbersome chest. The chest in the Wallace Collection measures 40 x 103.5 x 73.5cms: much larger than the chest containing the Lennoxlove toilet service (which is only 36.5 x 81 x 47.5cms).

It seems that it was only in the 1780s that any real effort began to be made to produce a combined toilet-tableware service which would be suitable for use on journeys. Ideally, such a service should be as comprehensive as possible, consisting of small, light articles of simple design which can be stored easily, and contained in a small chest of minimum dimensions. The resulting services are among the less obvious products of the Enlightenment or the Age of Improvement. They may have been inspired, to some degree, by the development of the officers' canteen-trunk. Certainly their production was greatly assisted by the preference in the Neo-classical period for simpler, more austere design. Two interesting examples of a more functional treatment are the travelling tea and chocolate service and the travelling dinner service of the 4th Duke of Bedford and his wife, made in London by John Scofield in 1786-87 (Woburn Abbey).[11]

It is much less easy to trace the development of French travelling services than their German equivalents. Nevertheless, it is clear that they did not suddenly change from rococo, Augsburg-type services[12] into *nécessaires* like that of the Princess Pauline Borghese. In between came an unknown number of *nécessaires* supplied for the use of Queen Marie-Antoinette and other ladies connected with the French court. They are a significant advance upon the Augsburg-type services and served as prototypes for the Borghese *nécessaire* and other related services.

The most important of these *nécessaires* is the one made for Marie-Antoinette, now in the Musée du Louvre.[13] It contains silver-gilt by Jean-Pierre Charpenat (master 1782, d. 1806), which is struck with wardens' (date-letter) marks for 1787-88. The most obvious difference between the rococo-style travelling services and this *nécessaire* is the reduction in sheer physical size. Whereas the chest in the Wallace Collection measures 40 x 103.5 x 73.5cms, the severely rectangular, mahogany chest in the Louvre is almost a quarter of the size, at 21 x 56 x 44cms.

The selection of items in the Marie-Antoinette *nécessaire* is much larger and more diverse than that found in the Augsburg services. The silver-gilt items for the *toilette* include a ewer and basin, a few boxes, a small funnel (for filling bottles, etc) and an eyebath. Among the silver-gilt articles for meals are an *écuelle* (a covered bowl), two plates, a beaker, a 'chocolate pot' (a cylindrical container with a handle and a removable lid with a hole in the top through which an implement can be inserted to stir chocolate), another cylindrical container with a handle and a removable lid, and two spirit burners. Also included are a large bedwarming pan (whose presence goes a long way towards explaining the omission of other items), a silver-gilt mortar and pestle and a tray of sheet metal. Three points strike one's attention. The first is the reduction in the number of articles of silver-gilt and the corresponding increase in the quantity of ceramic. In addition to 31 glass bottles of different sizes (most of which were intended for the *toilette*), there are two glasses, a glass inkwell, a glass pounce pot and eight items of porcelain: a teapot, spittoon, three cups, two pomade pots and a sugar box. Secondly, there is a large number and variety of articles made of ivory, wood and other non-precious materials. These include a small knife for the *toilette* (which has equivalents in earlier services), six *étuis* (small containers) made of ivory and ebony, two ivory measures, a large ivory needle, a pair of scissors, two penknives, an ivory paperknife and two pairs of compasses. The third feature is less obvious: it is the fact that many of the items have been specially designed and made for inclusion in a travelling service. They are of smaller size and simpler design than their normal counterparts. Whereas Augsburg travelling services contain many oval items, the Marie-Antoinette *nécessaire* includes many pieces of cylindrical section, which take up less storage space. Another point to notice is that the eating equipment can be used for a wide variety of meals and liquids. In this context, it is significant that both the 'chocolate pot' and the other cylindrical container with a handle can be used for preparing any hot liquids and can even be used for cooking, if necessary.

At this point we may begin to concentrate our attention upon the *nécessaire de voyage* of the Princess Pauline Borghese (1780-1825).

The *Nécessaire de Voyage* of the Princess Pauline Borghese

This wonderful *nécessaire* (Fig. 1) was supplied by the famous Martin-Guillaume Biennais (1764-1843). It is important to appreciate that he was not the actual maker of the service. Indeed, he was not even a trained goldsmith.

The appearance of a non-goldsmith as a supplier marked a definite break with the past, but was also the inevitable consequence of long-term historical developments. Up until now, regulations had restricted the making and selling of plate to goldsmiths and jewellers. However, there was no real reason (besides self-interest) for allowing these restrictions to continue. A first-rate assay system, involving the use of makers' or sponsors' marks and adequate checks on outlets, would soon lead to the discovery and punishment of retailers selling sub-standard silverware. A further point to note is that leading goldsmiths no longer actually made the plate which bore their mark. As their businesses developed, they ceased to make items and became managers of increasingly large workshops, striving to organise the production and delivery of huge quantities of diverse items. This sort of management could obviously be undertaken by non-goldsmiths. Indeed, entrepreneurs might make better managers and organisers of goldsmiths' workshops than men trained in the actual craft. Moreover, certain activities presented relatively few technical problems to the non-goldsmiths. Assembling travelling services was probably the most obvious of these.

The need for a specialist assembler of travelling services had been growing since the seventeenth century. The three marked French toilet services referred to at the beginning of this essay and in note (1) all include items by more than one goldsmith, thus necessitating some degree of coordination if not cooperation. By the mid-eighteenth century, Augsburg travelling services frequently include silver-gilt by two, three or even more goldsmiths, along with porcelain and glass obtained from other sources. The *nécessaire de voyage* of Queen Marie-Antoinette, assembled in the late 1780s, is even larger and more diverse, requiring even greater coordination. In its turn, the Borghese *nécessaire* contains an even more diverse selection of articles: it virtually demands the attention and expertise of a specialist assembler-supplier.

Assembling a travelling service required a talent for management and administration, without the need for any personal skill with hammers, spikes and other goldsmiths' tools. Above all, it involved careful, time-consuming planning and attention to detail. A shop had to be opened at a prestigious central location and staffed for sales and the receipt of orders.

1. The *Nécessaire de voyage* of the Princess Pauline Borghese, supplied by Martin-Guillaume Biennais. Neg. 7588.

Letters had to be written and ledgers kept. Stock had to be assembled. Additional items had to be ordered to meet special commissions, and complex arrangements made, day after day, week after week, with a large number of goldsmiths' workshops, other specialist makers, decorators and suppliers. To produce the Borghese *nécessaire*, the assembler had to gather together a very wide range of silver-gilt, gold, porcelain, glass and various other small articles made of ivory, wood, mother of pearl, tortoiseshell, steel and other non-precious materials from many different sources. Some items may have had to be made specially. Certainly an engraver had to be organised to cut the initial 'P' (for Pauline) on many of the articles. Last, but by no means least, a cabinet-maker and other craftsmen had to be commissioned to make a chest which would accommodate all the selected items and also incorporate certain agreed features. Such a complex exercise in logistics could have been organised from within a major goldsmith's workshop, but was really a separate undertaking. Provided there was sufficient demand, assembling and supplying travelling services was best 'hived off' and run as a separate operation by an independent entrepreneur.

Biennais was particularly well placed to undertake this sort of work. In 1789 he had opened a shop in the rue Saint Honoré, in Paris, as a *tabletier* (a person who makes or sells small items of wood, ivory and tortoiseshell). 1789 was not, of course, the ideal year to open a shop selling luxury items, but the location could hardly have been bettered. Before the Revolution, Biennais would have been prevented from selling plate; however, the Revolution swept aside this restriction. In 1791 it led to the dissolution of the Paris guild of goldsmiths. Almost overnight, the hitherto closed, highly regulated world of the Parisian goldsmiths was thrown open to outsiders. Biennais seized the opportunity and began to acquire silver from goldsmiths to sell alongside his existing lines.

At first he specialised in travelling services. These were both a continuation of his activities as a *tabletier* and the first steps in his ascent to the top: to the position of principal supplier of plate and other related luxury articles in Paris during the Napoleonic period. Besides being practical, these travelling services were also excellent status symbols. They appealed to the French officer class (which was frequently on the move during the French Revolutionary and Napoleonic Wars) and to a wider potential clientèle: the new, nouveau riche, governing elite.

Patronised by Napoleon at least as early as 1796, Biennais went on to become official goldsmith to the First Consul and, subsequently, the Emperor. Among his later commissions were the imperial insignia for Napoleon's coronation in 1804, the insignia for the coronation of the King of Bavaria in 1806, and plate for the marriage of Napoleon and the Archduchess Marie-Louise of Austria in 1810. Biennais was also responsible for supplying large quantities of plate to the courts of France, Austria, Russia, Würtemberg, Baden, Westphalia and Tuscany. Demand was so high that, at one stage, Biennais is reported to have employed six hundred workers in various materials. Biennais' rise was closely interwoven with the fortunes of Napoleon. Although he survived the Emperor's downfall and the return of the Bourbons, it was obvious that he could not continue as the principal supplier of plate to the French court. Retiring in 1819, he sold his business to Jean-Charles Cahier, who later became goldsmith to Charles X.

Although no documentation has so far been located which sheds light upon either the commission or the delivery of the *nécessaire de voyage* of the Princess Pauline Borghese, it is nevertheless possible to establish an approximate date for the service and to link it, albeit tentatively, with a particular event. An inscription engraved on the brass along the front of the chest describes Biennais as '*Orfèvre du Premier Consul.*' This would mean that the service was finished after February 1800, when Napoleon was elected First Consul. The *terminus ante quem* for the completion of the service is less clear. Napoleon became an hereditary emperor on 18 May 1804 and crowned himself on 2 December of the same year. It seems likely that Biennais would have stopped referring to himself as 'goldsmith to the First Consul' sometime after 18 May 1804, but the exact date of the changeover to 'goldsmith to the Emperor' is not known.

Whilst it is possible that the service could have been assembled at the very beginning of the Consulate, comparison with other services coupled with Pauline's life-history[14] suggests that this is unlikely. It is also improbable that the *nécessaire* was commissioned and supplied between 14 December 1801 and 1 January 1803. Between these two dates Pauline Bonaparte was abroad, accompanying her first husband, General Leclerc, on his ill-fated expedition to suppress the revolution on San Domingo, in the West Indies. Sometime in 1803 or 1804 would therefore seem to be indicated. Two letter 'B's engraved on the lid suggest that the *nécessaire* was commissioned in connection with the marriage of Pauline to the Prince Camillo Borghese, the head of the famous Italian family. Married in secret on 28 August 1803, they were united in a civil ceremony two months later, on 6 November. In this connection, it is perhaps relevant to note that there was a tradition, stretching back to at least the seventeenth century, of brides receiving toilet services around the time of their marriages. Normally these were presented by the future partner or husband. However, such a tradition does not rule out the possibility that Pauline could have received the *nécessaire* from Napoleon or another member of the Bonaparte family.

We come now to the examination of the contents of the Borghese *nécessaire*.[15] Comparing the items with those in the Augsburg services and the Marie-Antoinette *nécessaire*, one finds many 'old faithfuls', albeit in a more modern style. Beginning with the toilet articles, we have: a large mirror, a small (hand) mirror, a silver-gilt ewer and basin and two candlesticks, which are standard components in Augsburg-type travelling services. The nine glass bottles, jars and flasks with silver-gilt mounts for cosmetics, and the silver-gilt funnel and eyebath, have direct parallels in the Marie-Antoinette *nécessaire*.[16]

So far as toilet articles are concerned, the main difference between the Borghese *nécessaire* and the earlier services is the presence of such a large number of small toilet items in the later service. This may be distorted by losses from the Marie-Antoinette *nécessaire*. However, there appear to be the following 'new' items in the Borghese *nécessaire*: two silver-gilt tooth brushes with spare heads, a tongue scraper, a nail scissors, a set of manicure tools with mother of pearl handles, a pair of tweezers and three tortoiseshell combs. In addition, there is also an impressive range of sewing items. They comprise: two pairs of scissors for cutting fabric, sewing and styling hair, a gold *étui* for needles, a bodkin, a thimble, a very small pincushion, a hook, an ivory folding rule and two cylindrical ivory *étuis*, one containing a wooden spool for five varieties of thread. Not all of the sewing items are 'new'. Some have closely related counterparts surviving in the Marie-Antoinette *nécessaire*, as, for example, the ivory rule and ivory *étuis*.

Most of the tableware in the Borghese *nécessaire* is also represented in the earlier services. Thus the 'old' silver-gilt items include: an *écuelle*, a coffee pot, a teapot (with a small strainer which would have been suspended from the spout on a wire), a cylindrical 'chocolate pot' with separate stand and spirit burner, a cream jug, a tea caddy, containers for coffee, chocolate and sugar and a spice box. The 'chocolate pot' is closely related to the 'chocolate pot' in the Marie-Antoinette *nécessaire*.

Perhaps the most interesting development in the selection of tableware is the inclusion of more plates and cutlery than are contained in the services discussed previously. It will be recalled that the Augsburg service in the Wallace Collection only contains sufficient plate for one person to be served a complete meal (although a second cup and a second glass enabled the owner to offer refreshment to one other person). For its part, the Marie-Antoinette *nécessaire* only permitted two people to eat together. The Borghese *nécessaire* is much more generously equipped. In addition to the two silver-gilt cups, it contains six silver-gilt plates and four complete sets of dinner knives, dessert knives, forks and dessert spoons.

Comparison of the Borghese *nécessaire* with the earlier travelling services also highlights another 'new' feature: the provision, within the chest, of writing surfaces and storage space for stationery, correspondence and money, which goes well beyond anything encountered earlier.

Indeed, the chest containing the Borghese service merits very careful examination and deserves to be regarded as a work of art in its own right. The wooden interior is in the form of a removable tray (Fig. 2). Most of the large articles are stored in the top, in beautifully turned, deep resting places. A section of the front has been cut out to enable flat and small items to be stacked in layers. The six silver-gilt plates, along with the forks and spoons, go in the bottom. Over them is placed a shaped wooden tray containing the knives, the two cups, four of the canisters and the spice box. The silver-gilt basin rests above the knives. Into it is lowered an oval wooden container enclosing the *écuelle*. Hinged 'wings' close over the *écuelle*. Small individual rests have been cut out of the tops of both wings to accommodate the three pairs of scissors, two toothbrushes, the gold *étui*, small toilet articles, bodkin, tweezers and hook.

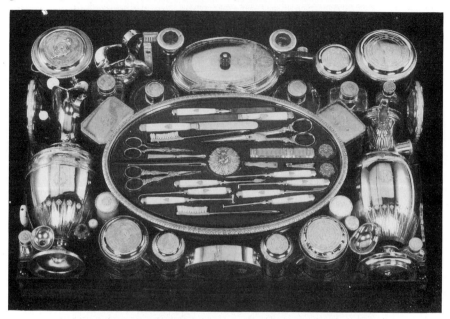

2. Removable tray from the Borghese *nécessaire* with the items stored. Neg. 7587.

The large mirror clips into a shaped recess in the lid. It can be removed by pressing a button and is either supported on its own stand or hung from a ring at the top. Three tortoiseshell combs are stored in individual hollowed-out slots in the back of the mirror (Fig. 3). The 'lid' is, in reality, the underside of a writing surface, which can be lowered by sliding a bolt. Red leather wallets for stationery are mounted on the back of the real lid (Fig. 4).

Moving round to the right-hand side of the chest, it is possible to unlock and pull out a removable writing board, equipped with a silver-gilt inkwell and pounce pot, separated by a pen tray. The writing surface can be unlocked and raised on hinges to reveal a secure place for correspondence and documents. This writing board does not extend the entire length of the chest. Behind it, underneath all the stored items on the left-hand side of the chest, is a secret money tray for coins. It will therefore come as no surprise to learn that the chest is fitted with internal screws and strong locks which enable the *nécessaire* to be screwed down to a carriage or the floor of a building.

Careful examination of the Borghese *nécessaire* reveals a great deal

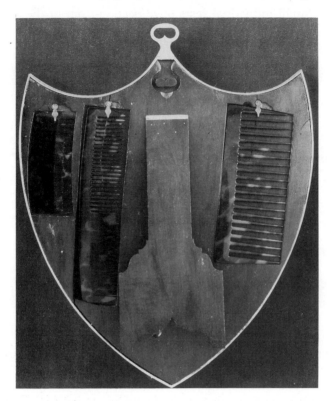

3. Back of the large mirror from the *nécessaire*, with the three tortoiseshell combs in their hollowed-out compartments. Neg. 10111.

about the way in which Biennais assembled the material for his travelling services and, indeed, his other commissions. Here we will confine the discussion to the silver-gilt. Most of the principal items in the *nécessaire* were made by Marie-Joseph-Gabriel Genu (master 1788, still working 1806, d.1811 or before), reflecting the fact that Biennais was neither a goldsmith nor the actual maker. Genu was responsible for: the ewer and basin, two candlesticks, coffee pot, teapot, oval tea caddy, milk jug, 'chocolate pot', stand and spirit burner, all six canisters, five of the six plates, the two cups, spice box, chamber candlestick and the pounce pot. The inkwell cannot be removed and inspected, but is probably also by him. Setting aside this last item, all Genu's pieces are struck with the head of Apollo and the number '1', which is believed to be the unofficial assay mark in use between 1794 and 1797. This suggests that they may have been in stock for some time before being incorporated into the Borghese *nécessaire*. They were all subsequently struck with assay marks for the period 1798-1809. Some were also punched with Biennais' own

4. Borghese chest with the inner lid lowered to reveal the writing surface and the leather wallet for stationery. Neg. 6812.

maker's or sponsor's mark: the distinctive seated monkey above the letter 'B' (for Biennais) in a lozenge-shaped shield.

With two exceptions, all the remaining pieces of silver-gilt are impressed with assay marks for 1798-1809. (The two exceptions are a pair of beakers, marked for 1809-19, which were added to the service later.) Some of these items (for example the *écuelle*, one of the plates and the four dessert knives) bear Biennais' own mark. It is not clear whether they were made in a workshop under his direct control or were bought in from an independent goldsmith's establishment. The maker's mark simply records that Biennais was their official sponsor, declaring them to be up to the necessary standard of silver.

The four forks, four spoons and two teaspoons were obtained from the workshop of Pierre-Benoît Lorillon (master 1788, still working 1836). He was a specialist maker of flatware who was closely associated with Biennais, supplying him with cutlery for many of his services. The work of three more goldsmiths is also represented in the *nécessaire*. The gold *étui* is imperfectly punched with a maker's mark consisting of three initials. In all probability, it is by a maker who specialised in such items. The sugar tongs also bears another indecipherable three-letter maker's mark, while two of the lids of the rectangular cut-glass jars are struck with the goldsmith's mark

$$J \quad \begin{matrix} M \\ \\ D \end{matrix} \quad F$$

It is obvious from our survey of earlier services that Biennais did not invent or create a wholly new type of travelling service. In essence what he did was to develop, and also to popularise, the *nécessaire de voyage* of Queen Marie-Antoinette. It is worth analysing exactly what this involved.

Biennais' first main aim was clearly to assemble a service that was more comprehensive, diverse and useful than the Marie-Antoinette *nécessaire*. His decision to omit an equivalent of the large bedwarming pan in the latter service freed a large volume of space and enabled him to include the mix of 'old' and 'new' items we have been examining. As a *tabletier* (or former *tabletier*), he naturally included a large number of small articles made of ivory, mother of pearl, tortoiseshell and other non-precious materials. In addition, he made a concerted effort to ensure that the traveller would be more self-sufficient than previously. As well as the improved selection of toilet and eating utensils, he included a large number of sewing items, two multi-purpose tools, a penknife, a pair of compasses, a chamber candlestick and a corkscrew! (It should perhaps be mentioned in passing that the penknife and pair of compasses have closely related counterparts in the Marie-Antionette *nécessaire*.) Biennais' concern to make the traveller self-sufficient is also evident in his selection of eating utensils which can be used for a wide variety of meals and foodstuffs. The 'chocolate pot' and canisters are particularly good examples of 'adaptable' utensils, for they can be used to heat liquids and even to cook food, if necessary. This 'adaptability' was evident in the Marie-Antoinette *nécessaire* and has been developed in the Borghese service.

Biennais took care in the selection of types of items. He also took great trouble choosing specific objects. Here his principal concern was to keep sizes and weights as low as possible. It is clear from a careful examination of the service that many of the items have been specially designed and made for inclusion in a *nécessaire*. The 'chocolate pot' and canisters are obvious examples. At first sight, the teapot and caddy may not appear to have been specially designed and made for inclusion in a travelling service, but they were. The entire top comes off the teapot so that the plain oval caddy, with its folding recessed ring-handle, can be placed inside for storage, swallowed like Jonah in the whale's stomach! The pair of candlesticks can be unscrewed to form two sticks and two bases. Removing a nut underneath the base of the chamber candlestick allows the handle to be pulled free. Although the handle of the teapot is fixed, the handles of the coffee pot, 'chocolate pot', spirit burner stand and hand mirror all unscrew to facilitate storage. Very sensibly, Biennais reduced the number of items of breakable porcelain and glass which are found in the Marie-Antoinette *nécessaire* and included, in their place, silver-gilt equivalents (for example the teapot, cups and canisters). The medium-sized items which were selected are roughly rectangular or cylindrical in section, which ensured that they could be packed in tight, neat formations. So far as the small items are concerned, Biennais definitely thought small was beautiful.

Lastly, Biennais' experience as a *tabletier* is reflected in the chest, in the brilliant utilisation of potential storage space and in the features we have discussed: the false writing lid, the layout of the interior, the sophisticated stacking system and the removable writing and money trays. The final result is a chest which is slightly smaller than the chest of the Marie-Antoinette *nécessaire*, whilst at the same time including a more diverse selection of items and the features mentioned above. While the Marie-Antoinette chest measures 21 x 56 x 44cms, the Borghese chest is shaved down to 18.8 x 57.3 x 40cms.

Biennais must be applauded for developing the *nécessaire* of Queen Marie-Antoinette and producing the Borghese service. Our last thoughts, however, should concentrate on the continuity exhibited in the two services. In normal circumstances we would expect to find marked similarities in the actual selection of items, and in the style of these pieces, in two services separated by less than twenty years. It is nevertheless quite astonishing to encounter almost linear development during these two decades: it seems that the enormous upheaval of the French Revolution made almost no impact upon the production of the Borghese *nécessaire*. Typological and stylistic continuity leads on to the continuity in taste between the *ancien régime* and the Consulate (and thereafter the Empire). Ignoring all the rhetoric, it is clear that Napoleon and his circle wanted essentially the same types of trappings and toys as Louis XVI and his courtiers. The new hierarchy obviously thought it entirely fitting that Napoleon's favourite sister should own an up-to-date version of the *nécessaire de voyage* of the last, executed Queen of France.

A few years later, Biennais would assemble an even more magnificent *nécessaire* for Napoleon's second wife, the Empress Marie-Louise (Residenz, Munich).[17] Her importance as the daughter of the former

Holy Roman Emperor and the wife of the colossus of the age would be reflected in elaborate decoration of the chest and the inclusion of fifteen
gold items.

NOTES

1. The service was acquired with the assistance of the National Heritage Memori-
   al Fund and the National Art-Collections Fund. Bequeathed by the Princess
   Pauline to Alexander, 10th Duke of Hamilton (1767-1852), the *nécessaire* was
   one of a small group of important Napoleonic items assembled by the Duke. For
   further information about the Duke's acquisitions of French furniture and
   Napoleonic items, see G.H.Evans, *French Connections: Scotland and the Arts of
   France* (Edinburgh 1985), 71-93. The Napoleonic material is also discussed by
   the same author in 'French Splendour in Edinburgh'. In *National Art-Collections Fund Review 1987* (London 1987), 102-109.

2. The most important of these toilet services is the stupendous service of
   twenty-two pieces by Pierre Prévost, now at Chatsworth. Made in Paris in
   1670-71, it was owned by the Princess Mary, later Mary II, the wife of
   William of Orange. (For illustrations, see Faith Dennis, *Three Centuries of
   French Domestic Silver* (New York 1960), I, 190-195, 231-232.) Next in
   importance is the Lennoxlove toilet service owned by the National Museums
   of Scotland. It comprises fifteen pieces bearing the mark of a Parisian
   goldsmith using the initials PF separated by a flame (? Pierre Flamand or
   Flament), together with two candlesticks by Pierre Masse. The latter are
   marked for 1661-63, while the other articles were made between 1666-67 and
   1677. Discovered at Lennoxlove in East Lothian around 1900, this service is
   believed to have been owned by Frances Teresa Stuart, Duchess of
   Richmond and Lennox (1647-1702). (For colour illustrations and discussions
   of this service, see Evans, *French Connections*, 48-54 and 144-145, and the
   article cited in note 1.) A closely related but unmarked service of fifteen
   pieces, formerly in the Chatsworth and Stonor Collections, has recently been
   acquired by Toledo Museum of Art, Ohio. (Arthur Grimwade has discussed
   and illustrated this service in 'Mr Francis Stonor's Collection of Silver-gilt—
   II: The Toilet Service from Chatsworth'. In *Connoisseur*, June 1961, 36-41.)
   The last of the services is a composite service of eighteen pieces, made in
   Paris between 1658 and 1676. It was owned by the Princess Hedvig Sofia of
   Sweden, who married the Duke of Holstein-Gottorp, and has been at
   Rosenborg Castle, Copenhagen, since 1867. (Gudmund Boesen has examined
   this service in 'Le Service de Toilette Français de Hedvig Sofia'. In *Opuscula
   in Honorem C. Hernmarck* (Stockholm 1966), 22-38.) Illustrations of three of
   the services, together with a photograph of three of the items in the
   Lennoxlove service, are published in Carl Hernmarck, *The Art of the
   European Silversmith 1430-1830* (London 1977), II, 262-264. All four
   services appear to owe their survival to the fact that they were exported from

France shortly after completion, and therefore did not fall victim to the edicts of 1689 and 1709 which required owners to surrender their plate so that it could be turned into coin.

3. The chest containing the Lennoxlove service has survived. Its sturdy carcass is veneered in walnut and decorated with imposing gilt mounts. Toilet services belonging to the French royal family and other important nobles would have been stored in even more magnificent chests.

4. J. Guiffrey, *Inventaire Générale des Meubles de la Couronne sous Louis XIV* (Paris 1885), 30ff.

5. Augsburg had a long history of producing high-quality plate. By the late seventeenth century it was a major centre for the production of travelling sets of eating utensils. These generally consisted of no more than a knife, fork and spoon in a case, but larger sets were available, or were becoming available. Various items, including a teaspoon, a beaker, an egg cup, a spice box and a writing case, could be combined with a knife, fork and spoon. As Augsburg goldsmiths began to produce toilet services it would have been very natural for them to have included examples of the tableware they were already making. On Augsburg silver generally, see Helmut Seling, *Die Kunst der Augsburger Goldschmiede 1529-1868* (Munich 1980), 3 vols. Seling illustrates some small travelling sets in Vol. II, pls. 520-527. A more elaborate set, including an *écuelle*, footed salver, egg cup and spice box made by Gottlieb Menzel, Augsburg, 1717-18, is illustrated in the catalogue of Sotheby's sale of *Important Silver*, held in New York, 7 April, 1987, lot 37.

6. Most of the important Augsburg travelling services are listed by Bernhard Heitmann in his doctoral dissertation, *Die deutschen sogenannten Reise-Service und die Toiletten-Garnituren von 1680 bis zum Ende des Rokoko und ihre kulturgeschichtliche Bedeutung* (Repro-Lüdke, Hamburg 1979). For illustrations of some of the principal services, see Seling, *op.cit.*, II, pls. 942-958, and Hernmarck, *op.cit.*, II, 270-271. The service by Gottlieb Satzger and Johann Georg Kloss, made in Augsburg between 1755 and 1757, now in the Württembergisches Landesmuseum, Stuttgart, is illustrated in colour in Alain Gruber, *Silverware* (New York 1982), 263.

7. For illustrations and a discussion of this service, see A.V.B. Norman, 'An Augsburg Travelling-service'. In *Apollo*, June 1965, 444-448.

8. These trays could also be used in conjunction with the tea and coffee equipment.

9. Glass and porcelain had other advantages besides being cheaper than silver-gilt. They did not conduct heat to the same extent and added colour and variety to the service. Glass could be decorated using various techniques: engraving, gilding, enamelling and sandwiching and sealing gold and silver foil between two layers of glass (*zwischengoldglas*). Early Augsburg services sometimes contain Chinese or Japanese porcelain. Later, European porcelain was included. Most of this came from the Meissen factory, near Dresden, and some of it was decorated in Augsburg.

10. Sotheby Parke Bernet Monaco SA, *Orfèvrerie, Objets d'Art et bel Ameublement*, Monte Carlo, 23-24 June, 1976, lot 210 (illus.). The service is reproduced in Vanessa Bell, *The Sotheby's Directory of Silver 1600-1940* (London 1986), 88, no. 206. It is catalogued and illustrated in detail in Hannelore Müller, *European Silver in the Thyssen-Bornemisza Collection* (London 1986), no. 77, 240-261.

11. The tea and chocolate service is illustrated in Arthur Grimwade, Family Silver of Three Centuries. In *Apollo*, December 1965, 501.

12. A partly dismembered service made in Strasbourg about 1749-51 is examined by Otto Wittmann in A Great Lady's *Nécessaire de Voyage*. In *Apollo*, August, 1971, 145-149. Most of the articles are now in Toledo Museum of Art, Ohio.

13. For the *nécessaire de voyage* of Queen Marie-Antoinette, see Musées Nationaux Departement des Objets d'Art, Musée du Louvre et Musée de Cluny, *Catalogue de l'Orfèvrerie du XVIIe, du XVIIIe et du XIXe siècle* (Paris 1958), cat. no. 66, 46-53, pls. LV-LVIII. The service is also illustrated in *Les Grands Orfèvres de Louis XIII à Charles X* (Collection Connaissance des Arts 'Grands Artisans d'Autrefois', Paris 1965), 244-245.

14. For information about Pauline Bonaparte, later the Princess Pauline Borghese, see W.N.C. Carlton, *Pauline, Favorite Sister of Napoleon* (New York and London 1930) and Pierson Dixon, *Pauline, Napoleon's Favourite Sister* (New York 1966).

15. A full list of the items giving the measurements and details about the marks is published in Evans, *French Connections*, 147-152.

16. One of the small glass flasks is a replacement.

17. For the *nécessaire de voyage* of the Empress Marie-Louise, see Herbert Brunner (ed.), *Schatzkammer der Residenz München Katalog* (3rd edition, Munich 1970), cat. nos. 939-1061, pp. 311-316, pl. 73.